East Elevation

This Plate is Dedicated
to the Warden & Fellows
of Wadham College by
their special permission:
also to Joseph Wells M.A.
Fellow & Tutor, and to
Percy C. W. Laws, M.A.
(both of this College)
through whose generosity
this Drawing has been
made and Engraved.

Edmund Hort New A.D. 1909-10

❋ OXFORD ❋ An Dōmi 1910
Wadham & Dorothy his Wife

WADHAM COLLEGE

1610–2010

EDITED BY
CLIFF DAVIES AND JANE GARNETT

WADHAM COLLEGE
1610–2010

EDITED BY
CLIFF DAVIES AND JANE GARNETT

THIRD MILLENNIUM
PUBLISHING, LONDON

Wadham College: 1610–2010

© Wadham College and Third Millennium Publishing Limited

First published in the UK in 1994 by Anness Publishing
This edition published in 2009 by Third Millennium Publishing Limited, a subsidiary of Third Millennium Information Limited.

2–5 Benjamin Street
London
United Kingdom EC1M 5QL
www.tmiltd.com

ISBN 978 1 906507 00 8

British Library Cataloguing in Publication Data
A CIP catalogue record for this book is available from the British Library.

Cliff Davies and Jane Garnett (eds)

1994 edition:
Edited by Penelope Cream
Designed by Bill Mason

2009 edition:
Production by Bonnie Murray
Reprographics by Studio Fasoli
Printed in Slovenia by Gorenjski-tisk

Contents

The College Archive before 2000.

Preface to 1994 Edition

The contributors hope that this book will interest past and present members of Wadham; perhaps, too, some of that increasing number of people who visit it, or who stay in the College for a conference or summer school, and who often express an interest in the buildings and gardens, and maybe wonder a little about the institution in which they find themselves. It is not a substitute for a full-scale modern academic history of the College, which is badly needed. Arguably such a history is best written by outsiders; it would certainly need to include a good deal in the way of detailed analysis and statistics which would be out of place here. All the contributors are members of the College, and we have tried to keep the tone reasonably light. But we have endeavoured to avoid the pitfalls common to in-house publications of this sort. We have aimed to be critical and detached, rather than complacent or self-congratulatory. We have tried to convey the flavour of College life over the centuries, and to say something about the origins and the career patterns of students, rather than retailing anecdotes about the 'great' figures of College history or boasting about famous old members. We have tried, too, to do justice to the less spectacular, more humdrum, periods in the College's history. This has not been easy. The College archives are packed with material on estate administration, but have little on personal or even academic matters; student letters home are rarely preserved, academic exercises, essays, notebooks and so on even less so; and few sports clubs chronicle their activities with the assiduity of the Boat Club. When and if a full-scale College history is available, it will be easier to produce a popular version. This book is very much an interim report.

The editors are grateful to a host of friends and colleagues. The original idea for the book was Ralph Johnson's. Ralph's overflowing energy led him even while active as the University's Director of Postgraduate Medical Education (1987–93) to throw himself into the life of the college of which he was a professorial fellow, and to direct, with enormous success, the Development Appeal. He was impatient of academic procrastination and incredulous that a simple project should take so long. He died suddenly of a cruel accident in July 1993, before he could see the result of his suggestion. Keith Barnes, Ian Crombie, Mark Curthoys, Ben Lenthall, Jake Polonsky, Shaun Pye, Gervase Rosser and Bob Williams all made valuable contributions, if not always, due to our editorial indecision, quite the contributions they thought they were making. The contributors themselves (especially those who got their contributions in on time) have been extraordinarily patient. We are grateful to John Freeman for taking many of the photographs. Penelope Cream, our editor, has been literally invaluable; she has shown us how much more there is to book production than the writing.

C.S.L. Davies
Jane Garnett

Preface to 2010 Edition

In revisiting a book produced fifteen years ago, the editors have applied a light touch to the contributions made at the time, adding in some new information and references, but essentially leaving the structure of the chapters intact. In order to bring the history up to date, they have added a new chapter surveying the period since 1970. As with the other historical chapters, this has been necessarily selective in its focus. Care has been taken to deal sensitively with the recent past. It has particularly benefited from the responses of old members to a questionnaire sent out in the summer of 2008, and we are very grateful to those who took the trouble to fill it in, and to reflect so thoughtfully and often vividly on their time at Wadham. All the responses will be stored in the archive for future generations, and we would encourage others reading this to send in their reminiscences. A larger-scale academic history of the College will be able to draw on more of this material. We would also refer readers to our collection of essays, *Tutorial Teaching at Wadham College* (2008), which had space to go further into discussion of developments in individual subject-areas and the roles played by particular tutors. The opportunity of the new edition has also enabled us to include many more illustrations, and we are indebted to Bi Scott, Caroline Mawson, Francesca Heaney, Cornelia Carson and Amanda Rowe for their help in gathering the images, which bring the College to life. Our thanks also go to Matt Wilson of TMI Ltd for his work on the design of the book.

CHAPTER ONE

Nicholas and Dorothy Wadham and the Foundation of the College

Robin Robbins

In the first decade of the seventeenth century, Nicholas Wadham, a childless West Country landowner, 'was wont to say', according to Anthony Wood 'that "he had a good estate, and had no children to leave it to, and his kindred to whom he thought to leave his estate did not care for him"'.[1] He conceived the wish, as his widow Dorothy later put it in her preface to the statutes, 'to found, erect and establish a certain perpetual college of poor and needy scholars in the University of Oxford, to the praise, glory and honour of Almighty God, the increase of sound letters, and the common utility of this kingdom, and of times while he was among the living, and especially a little before his death, declared to me that intention of his mind, and vehemently asked me to further it myself if God should grant a longer life to me than to him'. His inherited estates in Somerset, Devon and Dorset had by law to pass to the right heirs, through his sisters, of his father, but Nicholas Wadham had already out of his income gained a reputation for generosity, and saved enough to found almshouses locally at Ilton in Somerset. Now, perhaps sharing the reforming enthusiasm which swept Oxford with a tide of expansion from 1560 to 1630, he determined by fathering a new college to benefit the nation at large.[2]

Dorothy Petre, whom Nicholas Wadham had married in 1555, came of a family noted in the sixteenth and seventeenth centuries for adhering to Roman Catholicism, and Anthony Wood later reported a story that the Wadhams had first intended to found a college in Venice for English Roman Catholics.[3] The anecdote may have been suggested not only by the known religious preference of Dorothy's family, but more cogently by the fact that she was charged with recusancy soon after the founding of the College (she submitted, and was pardoned in 1615). However, her father, Sir William Petre,[4] a Devonshire man who had enriched himself by taking an energetic part in the Dissolution of the Monasteries under Henry VIII, had, on his retirement from public affairs some thirty years later in 1566, practically refounded his old Oxford college, Exeter, by endowing eight Fellowships.[5] It is conceivable, given this paternal precedent, that Dorothy helped form her husband's idea, which at first was to settle his endowment, as her father had done, on an existing Oxford society, either Gloucester Hall (later Worcester College), or Jesus College, still cripplingly underendowed.[6] Whatever the Wadhams' private beliefs, their Oxford foundation was inevitably firmly within the Church of England.

When Nicholas Wadham died in 1609, Dorothy was already 75, but it was on her as executrix of his will that the burden fell of carrying out his wish to found a college. This

Above and left: Nicholas and Dorothy Wadham (now in Hall, one of several pairs). The portrait of Nicholas was painted in 1595 when he was 63, and apparently repainted with the skull after his death in 1609. The portrait of Dorothy was allegedly painted in 1611, when she was 77, but is probably an adaptation of the portrait of 1595, done when she was 60.

did not just involve employing the property he left specifically for the purpose: four days before his death he expressed the hope that 'out of her benevolence … she would impart a portion … unto his College during her life' of her lands in Essex. As much a mother to the College as Nicholas had been its father, Dorothy pursued this trust with vigour and devotion, protesting to the Lord Treasurer against a detractor, Sir John Davis of Pangbourne, who was accusing her of delay if not embezzlement, that she would 'rather leave a poor and mean estate to myself than anything shall be wanting for the well effecting thereof'. Her family, in the person of her brother John, Lord Petre,

supported the execution of Nicholas's intentions, but he cautioned her in a letter against submerging her own contribution anonymously in her husband's: 'How much more convenient were it for you first to spend that which is specially appointed; and what you shall find necessary to add, to do it of yourself, so as the works of your husband's and your own may be distinguished, and so may leave to posterity a commendable remembrance of your name.' His sister's devotion to duty remained unshaken: she replied that 'if such things to be sold do not come to a sufficient sum for the the defraying of that charge, I must then be driven to give a supply out of mine own private

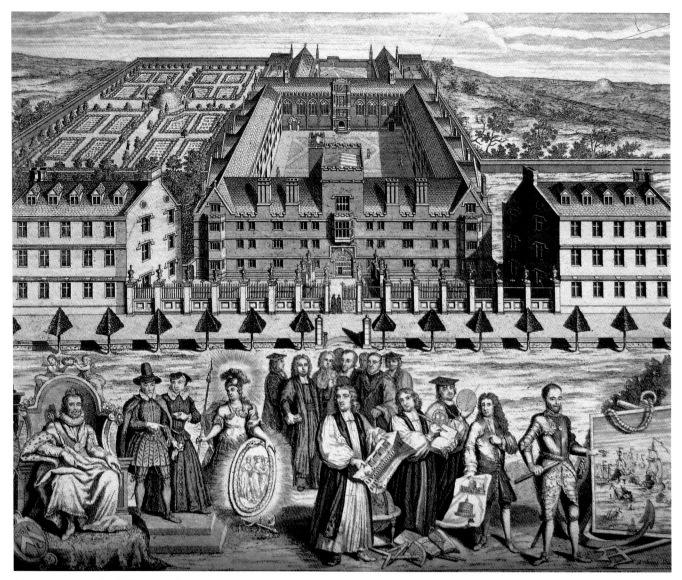

Above: *An engraving by Vertue for the University Almanack of 1738. On the left is James I, with Nicholas and Dorothy between him and Learning. At the back are Hody, Bisse, Goodridge, Smyth, Godolphin and other benefactors. In front are Wilkins, with drawings of Wadham and Gresham Colleges; Sprat with his* History of the Royal Society; *Seth Ward; Christopher Wren, with views of St Paul's and the Sheldonian; and Admiral Blake with a picture of his naval victories.*

store, being to that effect willed in secret by my deceased husband, and tied in conscience not to violate his trust'.[7] Given the example set by her father with Exeter College, however, we may see in her energetic commitment something more than devotion to a dead husband's wishes, hinted at by a habit of referring to the foundation in her statutes and letters as 'my' college.[8]

Such a public work could not be achieved by private benevolence alone: in the sixteenth century the monarchy had brought the universities firmly under central control. Like his predecessor, Queen Elizabeth, in 1566 and 1592, King James, with his own pretensions to learning, had shown his personal interest in Oxford by a state visit in 1605.[9] It was necessary to secure Royal sanction for any new

Right: *Sir John Davis, Dorothy Wadham's rival at Nicholas's deathbed.*

collegiate foundation and, if possible, active patronage. In practice, this entailed first gaining support among high officials in Church and State. Such men were not to be persuaded merely by the merits of a case, so, according to his great-nephew, Sir John Davis, Nicholas Wadham instructed him to take three sums of £50 each out of his estate to provide presents for the Earls of Salisbury, Northampton, and Suffolk (Lord Treasurer, Lord Privy Seal, and Lord Chamberlain respectively). He was also to present to Henry Frederick, Prince of Wales, 'a white and pied nag which he much esteemed, and in like manner to entreat His Highness's favour'. Gifts were certainly made to the Lord Treasurer and the Bishop of Bath and Wells.

Though he had avoided the showering of inflated honours by James I, Nicholas Wadham displayed himself in this a successful courtier: one of the overseers of his will, Sir Edward Hext, was able to write to another, Lord Petre, in March 1610, that 'Our dread sovereign hath seen the plot [i.e. plan] and doth so greatly approve of it as he hath most graciously promised to give it all furtherance. So hath my lords the Archbishop, the Lord Chancellor, and Lord Treasurer, who like it all so well as they have promised the like.'[10]

This patronage was immediately useful. Dorothy Wadham's father, Sir William Petre, had been enabled to re-endow Exeter College with proceeds of the Dissolution of the Monasteries. Other sixteenth-century foundations such as Christ Church, Trinity and St John's Colleges, and Gloucester Hall, had all arisen, despite their essentially Roman Catholic origins, on the re-assigned sites and incomes of dissolved religious houses. To the backers of the Wadham project, the ideal site seemed to be that of the dissolved Austin Friars. Outside the medieval City wall, just to the north of Smith Gate, this House had, at the time of its dissolution, long been a part of university life, since 'Disputations in Austins' were a statutory requirement for the BA. They were held in the friary church (said to be about half as long again as the present cathedral). Since the Dissolution, the disputations had kept their name but been relocated in St Mary's, the University Church, while the quickly cleared site of the Austin Friars passed from owner to owner, ending up in the hands of the City.

The City councillors were intent on driving a hard bargain: the land had already been partly rebuilt on, with a pub (the Lion, roughly where Staircase 11 now is), and a few houses and shops in front of its groves, orchards, and gardens, so on 23 February 1610, they resolved to demand £1,000. But Sir Edward Hext, in the letter quoted above, claimed formidable support: 'My Lord Bishop[11] hath been

Above: *Late sixteenth-century buildings on the site of the Austin Friary, fronting on to what is now Parks Road. The Lion pub is on the right.*

thoroughly satisfied that the Friary is the only meet place to build this College in, which he having certified unto His Majesty, His Majesty hath promised him his earnest letters unto the Mayor and Aldermen of Oxford to depart with it for a valuable consideration. The like letters hath the Lord Archbishop and the Lord Chancellor, who is Steward of the town, promised to write, all which letters my Lord Bishop hath assured me I shall have within these two days.' In case of failure, Wadham's promoters had secured an offer of an alternative site of eight acres from the Warden of Merton.[12]

But after only a week, the King's letter had persuaded the City Council to accept the Wadham agents' offer of £600, although, according to the Council's minute, 'every man thought it too little'. Hext could now report to Lord Petre: 'Having been at Oxford with His Majesty's most gracious letters, my Lord of Canterbury's and my Lord

Above: *Robert Wright (1566–1643), briefly first Warden. Portrayed when he was Bishop of Coventry and Lichfield in 1632.*

Chancellor's, to the Mayor and Aldermen of the City of Oxford, for the obtaining of the site of the late dissolved Friary of St Augustine's, the same letters have so much prevailed with them as we have compounded for £860' (the difference presumably reflecting the value of houses already on the site).[13] The City was granted its request to nominate a Fellow and two Scholars.

Of the old friary nothing now identifiable remained: even at the Dissolution its buildings were reportedly about to collapse. From the great church there survived only the monument to Walter Curson and his wife, transferred at the Dissolution to its present place in the church of Waterperry. The College's sole memento of the friars' tenure is Edward IV's charter of 1474, which granted the right to hold a fair in the grounds annually on 6 May (a prime factor in the City's purchase of the site in 1587). Thomas Hearne recorded on 9 May 1706: 'Some time since an old Brass Piece was found under one of the Buildings belonging to Wadham College, on one side of which 3 flower de luces and Ave Maria Gracia Dei, on the other a Cross Flore.' In the nineteenth century two skeletons were dug up near the lime tree on the back quad lawn, in what had presumably been the friary's cloister garth. Some fragments of medieval tiles and painted glass have been found, and in the early 1970s some probably fifteenth-century window masonry was identified in the old eastern wall, demolished to make way for the New Library.[14]

Despite litigation with relatives who wanted more of Nicholas Wadham's estates, including Dorothy's jointure, for themselves, and the slanderous campaign against her by Sir John Davis, all parties moved swiftly to bring the new college into being. On 9 April 1610, 29 workmen were engaged. Two days later, John Floyd wrote from Oxford to the diplomat William Trumbull in Brussels: 'A College is to be built here shortly, … and the land whereon it is to be built is already purchased. The King hath passed his approbation, and wishes his statue to be over the gate.' (It eventually appeared above those of the founders over the entrance to the Hall.)[15] The deed of sale by the City, expressly including 'the Augustine Fair within the said site yearly to be holden with all rights thereunto belonging', was dated 29 May 1610. A trust for 'the erection and

Above: *Statues of the founders, restored copies of the originals carved by John Blackshaw, who was paid £11 for the work.*

endowment of Wadham College in Oxon.' was formally set up in July. On the last day of that month, the foundation stone was laid on the site of the Chapel, in the presence of the Vice-Chancellor, Doctors, Proctors and others, with the mayor and corporation, and the accompaniment of choristers, three barrels of beer, wine, cakes, biscuit, and 'prince bread'.[16] A Latin account of the ceremony heads the Admission Book in which new Wardens and Fellows still write their subscription to the statutes. In December, King James granted Dorothy Wadham a Royal Charter. She promulgated the College statutes in 1612. The first Warden, Fellows and Scholars were admitted to the College on 20 April 1613, and on 29 April the Chapel (dedicated to St Nicholas), Cloister, and Cemetery were consecrated by the Bishop of Oxford and celebrated with an extravagant feast.

Meanwhile, the foundress had chosen a Warden, not an entirely straightforward proceeding. In November 1610, her brother John reproached her in a letter for going back on a promise to appoint one Dr Osborne to the Wardenship, in favour of Robert Wright.[17] She pleaded ignorance of her promise, and an irrevocable pledge given to the King.[18] Her choice was probably regretted, since, after only three months since the College had opened in 1613 and already on bad terms with her, Wright left in order to get married. He

eventually made his way up the church hierarchy to become Bishop successively of Bristol and of Coventry and Lichfield, a prominent associate of Archbishop Laud, and one of the twelve bishops sent briefly to the Tower by Parliament in 1641.

THE FIRST THIRTY YEARS

For its first five years, the College was dominated from afar in the West Country by the foundress. She reserved to herself the right of nomination to all the positions named in her statutes, from the Warden to the Cook.[19] Her continuing active interest in College affairs is recorded in letters concerning appointments, and emphasizing religious discipline: 'I would have prayers and fasting-days duly observed in the House, not allowing any in their chambers to break it, or elsewhere in the College'; 'hoping that your whole company will behave themselves religiously towards God, obediently to myself, and lovingly one towards another, which will be an especial comfort to me'. Her concern for harmony was reiterated: 'And above all things I would have you avoid contentions among yourselves, for without true charity there cannot be a true Society.'

None the less, Dorothy Wadham intervened to enable as well as to direct, providing special help with Library

Left: *Charles I and Henrietta Maria, grisaille and enamel on glass, now in the Buttery passage, originally in the Hall oriel window. These likenesses were probably done in commemoration of the royal visit of 1629, although the Queen's image looks as if it might have suffered nineteenth-century restoration.*

expenses, and a substantial sum for the College's first Christmas feast. Early in 1614, in view of the College's insufficient endowment, she made over to it more than half the revenue of her lands in Essex, most of which it possesses to this day. In doing so she ignored the urging by her nephew, William, Lord Petre, to 'be your own paymaster, and so retain it always in yourself either to enlarge your heart or straiten it towards them according to their deserts, which, no doubt, will… keep them best in obedience and respect'.[20] In 1615, she further increased the College's share, after losses caused by an untrustworthy agent (but blamed on tenants). Thus she fulfilled to the utmost her late husband's wishes, and when she died at the age of 84 on 16 May 1618, she could feel that in her last decade she had admirably acquitted herself of her promise to him and her vows for the public good. It is not surprising that the memorial service in College was far more lavish than the decent funeral she had requested.

Despite the role of King James as patron, the College soon found itself called upon to maintain its legal integrity when in 1618, on the day after the execution of Sir Walter Ralegh, the King himself ordered it, 'notwithstanding anything in your statutes to the contrary', to admit one Walter Durham of St Andrew's to a Fellowship. He was not a legitimate candidate, not being a Scholar, nor was there a vacancy. The Fellows, under the third Warden, William Smyth, declined to breach the statutes which they had sworn on the Bible to uphold: though they 'feared the King, they feared Almighty God still more'. According to the official Latin narrative, Durham left no stone unturned in trying to secure a favourable vote, canvassing Fellows even in their bedrooms.[21] They remained unmoved, and implicitly administered a further snub to the King in the following year, when they admitted Sir Walter Ralegh's son, Carew (born in the Tower of London), who had been dismissed from Court by James as looking like his father's ghost. In the Register of Admissions, his father was, exceptionally, styled 'most courageous and learned', the latter, presumably, for his *History of the World* of 1614.[22] Relations with Charles I were less eventful. In 1629 he and Queen Henrietta Maria came to view Wadham before going on to the Bodleian and a banquet at Merton. The painted-glass portrait-roundels of the couple of *c.*1633, now in the east window of the Buttery passage, perhaps commemorate this visit.

COMPOSITION OF THE COLLEGE

The statutes substantially follow long-established convention and prejudice (the Warden, apart from being of blameless life, should not be a foreigner; Fellows were to be elected from among the graduate Scholars, who, though they had to be poor – that is, with an income of less than £8 a year – should have been born in wedlock). Yet Nicholas Wadham had some fresh ideas. One of these was that fellowships should not be held for life: wishing the fruits of his benefaction to be widely spread, 'his intent being chiefly to nourish and train up men unto learning', he reportedly desired the Fellows 'after they were Masters of Arts of a competent number of years to depart the College, and not live there all their time like idle drones, but put themselves into the world, whereby others might grow up under them'.[23] However, his intention that they should stay for only 12 years after graduating MA was modified by Dorothy under pressure from the Visitor, the Bishop of Bath and Wells, to allow 20. Another sign of Nicholas Wadham's relative progressiveness was his intention that Fellows should not be tied 'to any profession, as either Divinity, Law, or Physic, but … every man free to profess what he liked, as it should please God to direct him'. He also desired that the Warden should be allowed to hold a doctorate in any of the faculties of Divinity, Law or Medicine, but this again was denied by the eventual statutes, at the request, it is said, of the College itself: until 1878 the Warden had to become a Doctor of Divinity. Less liberally, Nicholas Wadham directed that the Warden as well as the Fellows should remain unmarried – the cause given for the resignation of the first Warden within months of his installation.[24]

Above: 'Dorothy Wadham's shift': a woman's linen smock embroidered with pink silk, and edged in bobbin lace, c.1605–15. Given to the College in 1913 by Revd W.E. Lush of Auckland, NZ. It had been in his mother's family for generations, and the (unsubstantiated) tradition was that it had belonged to Dorothy.

There were many fewer members of College then, and for centuries to come – in fact, only so many as could be lodged within the original quadrangle.[25] The statutes decreed that as well as 15 Fellows there should be as many Scholars, 2 Chaplains with 2 Clerks to assist them, and a domestic staff of a Manciple, 2 Cooks, 2 Butlers, and a Porter, presumably with various subordinates. The Scholars and Clerks were outnumbered by students not on the foundation, including Fellow-Commoners, who paid more than Commoners, and sat with the Fellows in Hall; Commoners, who paid entirely for themselves; and Battellars, who reduced their charges by looking after themselves, for example, by fetching their own food from the kitchen. In its first year the College admitted 11 Fellow-Commoners, 18 Commoners, 9 Battellars, and 11 more pupils of undetermined status, making, including the 2 Clerks, whose chapel-duties subsidised their studies, 66 junior members in all.

Thereafter during the first 30 years the College probably maintained roughly constant numbers, admitting usually between 19 and 34 new members per year, with an average of 27.

Nine of the 15 founding Fellows chosen by Dorothy Wadham came from Somerset, Devon, or Dorset, where lay her husband's principal hereditary estates. Regional and family links made it appropriate that three of Wadham's founding Fellows should be West Country graduates of Exeter College. Out of three locally born Fellows, a fourth Exeter graduate, Thomas Harris,[26] had been nominated by the City Council under the terms of their sale of the site, being the son of the mayor who attended the laying of Wadham's foundation stone. Exeter College was laid under further contribution by Dorothy Wadham. Despite the statutory requirement that the Warden should be elected from among past or current Fellows, she ordained that if Robert Wright should resign within five years he should be succeeded by John Fleming, Fellow of Exeter and son of a Cornish gentleman. Like Wright, Fleming was able to proceed quickly to a DD, and became Chaplain to the King, whereas there was no founding Fellow of Wadham of comparable status.

While the statutes reserved six scholarships on the foundation for applicants from the founders' home counties of Somerset and Essex, the other nine scholarships were to be open to men from anywhere in Britain.[27] Dorothy Wadham rejected a proposal from Alexander Gill, the High Master of St Paul's School in London (whose son nevertheless came up to Wadham at its inception as a Clerk) for more closed scholarships. In a letter to her brother John, Lord Petre, in April 1611, she wrote: 'I have no liking to hearken unto any of those projects, minding to be at liberty, and not tied to one place, for if I had any opinion to such a course, there is greater reason to cull out some scholars of schools in this country where Mr Wadham was born and ever lived … who hath left many of his kindred … that will desire to be preferred before strangers.'[28] She in fact implemented this preference after the foundation in a supplementary statute providing for three of the Fellows and three of the Scholars to be elected from among those who could establish that they were 'founder's kin'. This privilege was later abolished in the Parliamentary reform of 1855.

Predictably, despite the provision of scholarships open to people from all parts of Britain, most students came during this period from the South West – in the case of the founding Scholars, at least 9 out of 15, with 3 from Oxford, and 2 of unrecorded origin. Of 788 admissions from 1613 to 1642, the Registers note the geographical origins of four-fifths. Of these, 97 per cent came from southwest of a line drawn from Chester to Harwich, none at all from anywhere north of Yorkshire (including Scotland, which had eminent universities of its own), or from Norfolk (East Anglians usually preferred Cambridge). Somerset, Devon, and Dorset provided 52 per cent, with 5 per cent from Cornwall (whence Nicholas Wadham's mother derived), and 4 per cent from Essex, Dorothy Wadham's county of birth. A further 40 per cent comprised substantial contingents from the southern counties, the West Midlands, Home Counties, South Midlands, and London.

The founding Fellows in 1613 were all (except a nephew of the benefactor of the Library, Dr Bisse) graduates of other Oxford colleges. Seven of them had been recorded at matriculation as of plebeian origin, four

as gentle-born, two as sons of knights, and two unspecified. Among the Scholars were two kinsmen of Dorothy Wadham's steward, John Arnold, and one of an overseer of Nicholas Wadham's will, Sir Edward Hext, while the Fellow-Commoners included two grandsons of another overseer, Dorothy's brother, Lord Petre.

The social origins recorded in the Registers for 75 per cent of entrants in this period are usual for the universities at the time: in round numbers, the fathers of 12 per cent were titled (mostly knights), while those of a further 44 per cent bore heraldic arms or were of the gentleman class; the fathers of 13 per cent possessed academic doctorates or were, more often, clergymen, and those of 32 per cent were set down as 'plebeians'.

On entering the College, students would find themselves reclassified according to partly academic, partly economic, and partly social criteria. In an average year, there would be one Scholar, 4 Fellow-Commoners, 11 Commoners, 5 Battellars, and 6 of other or now indeterminable status. This last category, on relatively rare occasions, included entrants either well below the usual age,[29] or for some other reason needing tuition before matriculating for the BA course. At the other end of the age-scale, up to the age of 22, students might transfer from another college to complete their BA or go on to study for a higher degree. However, the statutes prescribed that Scholars should be from 14 to 19 years of age on election, and the ages of 9 out of 10 entrants, whether on scholarships or not, were in this range, two-thirds being from 16 to 18 years old, with 17 the commonest age.

LIFE IN COLLEGE

The feel of life in Wadham in its early years differed in many ways from the twenty-first-century experience.[30] Such innovations as there were in the statutes only slightly modified traditional ends and means. This is visually expressed in the buildings, which materially embody the usual medieval functions of chapel, library, accommodation, kitchen, cloister, and cemetery, ranged in compact order round a quadrangle, with the Warden lodged over the main gate, as William of Wykeham had

decreed for New College, so as to keep an eye on everyone's behaviour.[31] Some notion of the ideals aimed at are set out in the largely traditional prescriptions of the statutes. For the most part, they follow those of previous colleges, keeping close in content and even wording to the forms established by William of Wykeham 230 years earlier, and repeated for more recent foundations such as Nicholas Wadham's probable college, Corpus Christi, founded by Richard Fox in 1517. How far these prescriptions were kept or enforced is of course problematic.

Hierarchical distinctions within College were to be rigidly maintained: no MA was to be too intimate with a BA, nor the latter with a Scholar, who for his part was allowed no informality at all with a Master. A Bachelor should doff his cap to a Master, while a Commoner or Battellar should remain always uncovered in his presence. A Scholar might don his cap in College only with express permission. The distinctions were physically figured in the dining arrangements in Hall: Fellows, Scholars, and Commoners dined at separate tables; High Table was for the Warden and Doctors only, with MA Fellows by invitation. Strict orderliness was prescribed in other respects: if talking were to be allowed in dinner, it should be in Latin or some other useful language, not English. Fellows and Scholars should always wear black or dark clothes with cap and gown whether in or out of College, except in their own rooms. No Scholar below the degree of Master might go about alone, except on his way to a lecture, or by permission, but should always be accompanied by some Scholar, Commoner, Battellar, or College Servant 'as a witness of his honest and upright conversation'. Statutory provision was made for a barber to shave and trim the Fellows and Scholars, 'for I do not permit any poor student in my college to grow his beard, or let his hair fall on his shoulders, nor to crop it too close'. Noisy behaviour, as a threat to people's work, was to be severely punished.

To preserve social harmony, the statutes prescribed a Latin oath for the Scholars that they would not 'disturb the peace of the College by detractions, evil speakings, or abusive language, nor make odious comparisons of family, country, or learning against any member of the College'. Commoners and Battellars had to swear not to show themselves 'any ways untractable to the good orders and discipline of this College'. They were further enjoined to avoid, in their compulsory weekly declamations in Hall, any bad-tempered, angry or spiteful speeches. If quarrels or disputes did arise they should be settled within the College, not by going to law.

Above: *The cellarer's door.*

Left: *Spiral staircase to the Old SCR.*

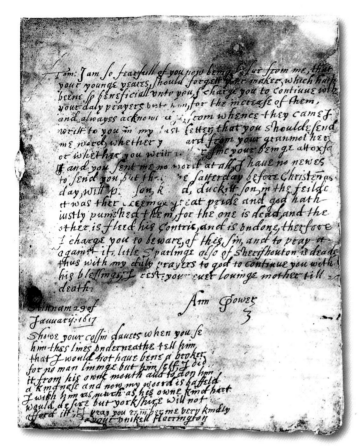

Left: *A letter from Lady Ann Gower to her undergraduate son Thomas in 1618 (see note 33), expressing her concern for his welfare.*

Despite all the detailed provisions of her statutes, however, Dorothy Wadham recognized that 'Human nature is so prone and inclined to evil, … that it is not in my power to frame laws and statutes which an astute and shifty man may not violate … though tied by Hercules himself'. Consequently, she appointed the Bishop of Bath and Wells as Visitor, with power to decide the meaning of statutes and enforce their observance. He could, for example, remove the Warden for gross offences, intolerable negligence, frequent drunkenness, or absenteeism. It was presumably up to the Visitor to define what was gross, intolerable or frequent.

Various other threats to order were specifically dealt with. Gambling was forbidden, except at Christmas-time and on two other feast-days, for small stakes at a suitable time. Hunting and hawking were seen (notoriously in the person of King James himself) as damaging distractions from serious business; no one was to use guns or crossbows, to wear arms except when travelling, or to keep dogs, rabbits, ferrets, hares, or any kind of bird.

Another threat of subversion also arose from nature, and was dealt with statutorily with regard to the highest and the lowest: the Warden and Fellows were to remain unmarried throughout their tenure (the first Warden left after only three months to get married). To safeguard the virtue of members of College, all its servants were to be male except for the Laundress, and she, as well as being of such age, condition, and reputation that there should be no chance of any evil suspicion lighting upon her, should be allowed no further than the outside gate (beyond the Lodge, at the edge of the road), and then only on fixed days. Thus the Warden himself could vet all her transactions from his oriel window over the main gate, which was to be locked at nine o'clock or a quarter past nine every night and the key taken up to him in his chamber. No Fellow or other member was to sleep outside College without leave, or to climb in over the walls. No Scholar might be absent for more than 30 days in a year, no Fellow for more than 40. The ideal envisioned in the statutes was thus almost total immersion in the life of godliness and good learning.

Godliness was hotly controversial: during the reign of James I, the dominance of Calvinist doctrines in the Church of England was challenged by a movement to restore some pre-Reformation liturgical practices.[32] These were personified in Oxford and the nation at large by William Laud, Fellow of St John's from 1593 and its President from 1611, Visitor of Wadham as Bishop of Bath and Wells from 1626 to 1628, and Chancellor of the University in 1629, as well as Archbishop of Canterbury from 1633. The enforcement of religious orthodoxy was as prominent a concern in Dorothy Wadham's statutes as in those of previous Oxford foundations. All Bachelors and junior members were to attend Chapel twice daily, from five to six o'clock in the morning, and from eight to nine o'clock in

available to students, which they were expected to study closely, a central academic activity in both College and University was the lecture. The knowledge and understanding thus gained from the written and the spoken word was exercised in formal disputation, routinely with contemporaries, and, for examination purposes, against certain Bachelors and Masters. In these exercises, a student would be given a prepared question on which to respond. At the early stages of the Trivium or Grammar, Rhetoric and Logic, it might be an appropriately trivial topic, such as whether ale was superior to beer. Further regular exercise of skills was required in 'declamations', which were formal, prepared speeches.

Within College, Bachelors and Masters, for example, had to dispute twice weekly in term, Theology disputations taking place in Chapel, the rest in Hall, while Commoners and Battellars had to declaim weekly. There were lectures by a Praelector of Philosophy, and a Praelector of Humanity expounded Greek and Latin authors. The study of these was replaced in the long vacation by Arithmetic, Geometry, and Geography. These could be particularly exciting subjects, presenting many new developments such as the invention of logarithms by Napier (1614), William Gilbert's revelations about magnetism and the mariner's compass (1600), and the ever-extending discoveries in East and West. The lectures, disputations and other exercises ordained by the College amounted to 24 hours a week, over and above those required by the University. 'In all matters of education', begins the foundress's statute on disputations, 'nothing is better than practice'. The tiny attendance of University lectures in Mathematics, for instance, illustrates how far these regulations represented ideal rather than reality.

Even in the Laudian Statutes of 1636, which tended to collect and codify previous decrees, the official curriculum was largely that of the medieval university, and some areas, such as Music, though formally prescribed, had fallen into neglect. In the 1540s the establishment of the Regius Professorships in Theology, Greek, Hebrew, Civil Law, and Medicine had promoted the new humanist interest in languages as well as reinforcing medieval subjects. Similarly, despite the fossilized course-structure, the founding

the evening, while the Warden, Fellows, and other Scholars should attend on Sundays and festivals (of which there were up to 33 in a year). The Sub-Warden was to assist the Warden in presiding over disputations in divinity, while a catechist was to be appointed to give fortnightly religious instruction to all undergraduate Scholars during term. Dinner in Hall was to be preceded and followed by a grace in which all should join. During dinner, a Clerk or Scholar should read aloud from the Bible, and any breach of silence would be punished by the loss of free food.

Good learning, then as now, entailed long hours of work for students. For a Bachelor's degree, a student was allocated, under the Elizabethan statutes of the University, two terms on Grammar, four on Rhetoric, five on Logic, three on Arithmetic, and two on Music, amounting to four years (in those days the academic year from October to July was divided into four terms). For a Master's degree, he spent three further years on Geometry, Astronomy, Natural Philosophy (what we now call 'science'), Moral Philosophy, and Metaphysics. Despite the arrival of printed textbooks between 1618 and 1627 of University Lecturerships in Natural Philosophy, Moral Philosophy, Anatomy, Geometry and Astronomy, History, and Music (William Heather's chair, now attached to a fellowship at Wadham), infused new vigour into the University's teaching, particularly for those reading for the MA and higher degrees. For undergraduates, the college's provision was more far-ranging and important, often extending beyond the traditional, Greek- and Latin-centred syllabus of the University into modern authors and new discoveries.[33]

THE FIRST ALUMNI

Wadham in its first 30 years produced a number of men of distinction, in varying spheres of life. Perhaps the most surprising was Robert Blake (1617), son of a Bridgwater merchant, Member of Parliament for his native town, a soldier on the Parliamentary side in the Civil War,

Opposite top left: *The Chapel.*

Above: *Coat of arms of Bishop Montagu (d. 1618, first Visitor of the College) in the Cloister passage.*

subsequently one of England's greatest admirals, with exploits in the West Indies and Mediterranean as well as against the Dutch in home waters. Buried in Westminster Abbey, he was disinterred at the Restoration. Another prominent anti-Royalist was the lawyer Nicholas Love (1625), son of the Headmaster of Winchester: he was one of the judges at the trial of Charles I and, although he avoided signing the King's death warrant, had to flee to Switzerland in 1660. Another Wadhamite, John Cook, as solicitor-general presented the case against the King. He was executed in 1660. Philip Hunton (1623) wrote an influential *Treatise of Monarchy* (1642), arguing that sovereignty was shared between King, Lords, and Commons. Cromwell made him head of his new (and short-lived) university at Durham. The College produced several eminent Dissenters, ranging from Cornelius Burges (1613), Presbyterian member of the Westminster Assembly in the 1640s, to Francis Bampfield (1631), a Seventh-Day Baptist, who argued for observance of the Jewish Sabbath and the derivation of all knowledge from the Bible. There were probably an equal number of Royalists, including John Gauden (1630) who was made a Restoration bishop for ghost-writing the highly successful record of Charles I's sufferings, *Eikon Basilike*; and Nicholas Monk (1628), a clergyman who acted as a go-between for his brother George, the Cromwellian general who restored the monarchy in 1660. Indeed, the College's reputation before 1648 was distinctly Royalist and 'high church'. William Smyth, Warden 1617–35, acted as Archbishop Laud's willing collaborator and Vice-Chancellor.

More entertaining, perhaps, is Shackerley Marmion (1616), mercenary soldier, poet and playwright, who lived a riotous life as a follower of Ben Jonson.[34] Alexander Gill, 1613, was in deep trouble for drinking the health of the Duke of Buckingham's assassin in 1628, published fulsome praise of Charles I and Laud when he was pardoned, and went on to succeed his father as High Master of St Paul's, only to be dismissed for inflicting beatings too savage even for that age. The founders would have disapproved of almost all of these except, perhaps, Gauden; but certainly the College was fulfilling their intention of contributing to religion, learning, and the utility of the kingdom.

CHAPTER TWO

John Wilkins and the Experimental Philosophy in Wadham

Allan Chapman

The 1640s seemed to offer little encouragement or hope to Wadham. College revenues were depleted, stipends reduced, and undergraduate entrants down to four, five, and even none per year, as in 1645.[1] The Civil War, which broke out in 1642, was the cause, for Oxford became the Royalist stronghold and seat of the besieged court, and academic activity was almost suspended. Wadham, along with other colleges, even lost its table plate in what was tantamount to a forced loan to the empty Royalist coffers, although it did retain the communion chalice and paten which still survive.[2]

When the triumphant Parliamentary Commission visited the University in the spring of 1648, they evicted Wadham's fifth Warden, Dr John Pitt, and nine of the 13 Fellows on the grounds that they refused to take an oath acknowledging Parliament's authority, independent of the now imprisoned King, to re-order the University.[3]

THE NEW WARDEN

Considering this conspicuously political eviction, the enforcement of a hard-line Puritan Warden upon the college might have been expected. It must therefore have been of considerable relief to the College when the new incumbent, John Wilkins, proved to be a man whose learning, toleration, and gift for friendship turned Wadham into what was perhaps the most enlightened college in the University.

In an age dominated by sectarian intolerance on both sides, Wilkins, at only 34 years of age, emerged as a unique figure, not only among Oxford Heads of House, but also in the wider realm of public life. The son of an Oxford goldsmith, and grandson of a famous Puritan preacher, John Dodd, he had come up to Magdalen Hall (which stood adjacent to Magdalen College) in 1627 at the age of 13, and took his MA in 1634. Here he filled his 'spare hours' in a novel manner by reading books on machinery and invention, while at the same time preparing for Holy Orders and sounding out potential patrons. Being an ambitious man, Wilkins soon learned how to combine his wider intellectual interests in science and invention with the practical business of ascending the Caroline, and later Parliamentary, ladders of preferment.[4]

Opposite: *John Wilkins (1614–72), Warden 1648–59. In addition to his intellectual distinction he was a shrewd politician.*
He married Cromwell's sister, yet still became Bishop of Chester in 1668.
He is here depicted as Bishop by Mary Beale (1633–99).

At a time of life when most young clergymen were lucky even to be curates, Wilkins procured the living of Fawsley, near Daventry – through family interests in that area – and then became Chaplain to Lord Saye of Broughton Castle, Banbury, who was a leading anti-Stuart activist. This was followed by further chaplaincies to Lord Berkeley in 1641 and to the exiled Elector Palatine in 1644, in addition to influential preaching appointments at Gray's Inn and the Savoy. From these marks of patronage, culminating as they did in his Parliamentary induction into Wadham, one might well have expected Wilkins to be a revolutionary in politics and a Puritan in churchmanship, but he was neither. Instead he walked the Aristotelian 'middle way': for by temperament he was a man who detested extremes, was willing to serve any balanced *de facto* government, and saw God as a reasonable creator of nature rather than the upholder of sacred kings or popular covenants.

Christopher Wren (1632–1723), Fellow-Commoner 1650. Although best known as an architect, Wren's reputation up to the age of 40 was in mathematics, astronomy and physiology.

One signal component of Wilkins's extraordinary success was his personality. Intellectually honest without being austere, sincerely religious without being sectarian, and possessing a charm which enabled him to maintain friends in disparate camps, Wilkins was a healing force in lacerated times. The impact of his qualities upon Wadham was both immediate and sustained. By 1650, freshmen had risen from the wartime three or four per year to 57. But even discounting this post-war bulge, freshman numbers levelled out at around 40 per year compared to the 30 or so prior to 1642.[5]

His moderation and dislike of Puritan extremism were clearly well known, as witnessed by the types of parents who entrusted their sons to his care. Christopher Wren, who came up in 1650 at the age of 17, was the son of the deposed Dean of Windsor and nephew to the imprisoned Bishop of Ely. Thomas Sprat, a future Stuart bishop, came up in 1651, while those literary rakes of the Restoration, John Wilmot, Earl of Rochester, and Sir Charles Sedley, began their education at Wadham in this period. Indeed the leaning of the College from 1648 onwards seems to have been officially Parliamentarian, but more anti-Puritan than anti-monarchy, so that it formed a natural milieu for youths from Royalist backgrounds. On the other hand, while Wilkins could nurture a sincere friendship with the Revolution-hating John Evelyn, he could still relate himself to the Protectorate by marrying Cromwell's sister, Robina, in 1656, taking advantage of the 1652 change of statute that permitted the Warden to marry.[6] His persuasiveness must also have been behind Wadham's restored capacity, in 1651, to elect its own Fellows and Scholars, which began the process of devolving the Commission's power of making appointments back to the colleges.[7] Even so, the Commission laid down detailed rules for the conduct of academic and spiritual affairs, such as the regulation that the Tutors had to find time to pray with their pupils between 7 and 10 o'clock each evening.[8] However, what tells us so much about Wilkins's persuasiveness was not that he could accommodate himself to such a diversity of demands, but that he could do so with dignity and success.

Right: *Arms of Thomas Sprat (1635–1713), Fellow 1657. Author of the first* History of the Royal Society *(1667) and a Wilkins protégé. He became Bishop of Rochester in 1684.*

Far right: *John Wilmot, Earl of Rochester (1647–80), who came up briefly in 1660. Rochester's career represented a different type of distinction: he was the most famous wit, debauchee, poet and deathbed convert of the Restoration.*

THE NEW SCIENCE

If John Wilkins brought stability and moderation to Wadham in the 1650s, he also brought an unprecedented intellectual energy. The range of his learning and the richness of his conversation formed the bedrock upon which the other achievements rested. This is especially important when considering the issues that were of most interest to Wilkins, for in the university world of 1650, most of those interests would have been considered as fringe at best and downright eccentric at worst. Any man who could accompany his induction into the politically sensitive Wardenship of Wadham with the publication of a book dealing with projected designs for submarines, flying machines, and perpetual motion devices, as he did with *Mathematical Magick* (1648), lacked neither courage nor confidence.

Nor had his career thus far been formed by composing the right books to please the right people. His first publication, when he was 24 years old, argued in favour of the feasibility of a voyage to the moon and a defence of Copernican astronomy, while his other published works dealt with secret codes, applied mechanics, and universal language. One looks in vain for cautiously crafted panegyrics that conformed to party lines and followed traditional career paths.

It is probably true to say that during the dozen years of Wilkins's Wardenship, Wadham became one of the scientific foci of Europe. Certainly the College became the regular meeting place for the nucleus of experimenters who after 1660 became the Royal Society. Though none of this scientific activity possessed any curricular status within the College or the University, the informal 'Philosophical Club' of astronomers, anatomists, and chemists which regularly met at the Lodgings as friends of the Warden became England's first real body to pursue systematic experimental research.[9]

Their ideas, as well as those of the Warden, were original and deeply challenging to the traditional philosophy of 'the Schools' of ancient learning. While all of these men – such as Seth Ward, Thomas Willis, Robert Boyle, and others – had been classically educated and deeply respected the ancient intellectual ideals, they were none the less aware of the weaknesses of traditional Aristotelian science in the wake of recent discoveries.

Seth Ward, who had been intruded by the Commissioners into the Savilian Chair of Astronomy in 1649, came to reside in Wadham at the invitation of Wilkins. Ironically, Ward had already left Cambridge because of his sympathy with episcopacy, while his fellow Cantabrigian, John Wallis, another friend of Wilkins, moved in to the vacated Savilian Professorship of Geometry.[10] Like Wilkins, these two mathematicians were leading exponents of the new science who realized that Galileo's telescopic discoveries after 1610 had seriously challenged the classical earth-centred cosmology. At the same time, at Christ Church, Thomas Willis, the expelled Royalist physician, acknowledged that William Harvey's circulatory physiology of 1628 did the same for Galenic medicine. Robert Boyle, though not a matriculated member of the University originally, came to Oxford at the personal invitation of Wilkins, and from his lodgings in the High came to assemble a corpus of experimental evidence that overthrew the ancient doctrine of the four elements, advanced an atomic theory of matter, and discovered the laws of gas pressure which still bear his name.[11]

Boyle came to employ as an assistant the young Robert Hooke, an ex-sizar, or poor scholar, of Christ Church, whom he introduced to the informal 'Philosophical Club' at Wadham and who later recorded having experimented with flying machines in the Warden's garden. At this time, the young John Locke was involved in chemical projects in Wadham and elsewhere upon which he was spending considerable sums of money at one stage, while men from Brasenose, Trinity, and other colleges attended Club meetings to discuss current investigations and compare ideas.[12]

Perhaps the most precocious of their number was Christopher Wren who, prior to winning his enduring fame as the architect of post-Fire London, had distinguished himself as an astronomer and physicist. Leaving Wadham to become a Fellow of All Souls in 1653, he continued to attend the Wadham meetings as a good friend of the Warden. During the 1660s, when he was establishing himself as an architect, he occupied the chair of Astronomy at Oxford, and from 1663 he rented a room at Wadham.[13] When Wren designed the Royal Observatory at Greenwich in 1675, he provided a unique example of a professional astronomer being called upon professionally to draw up the plans for a new observatory.

Wilkins's influence as an inspirer of scientific ideas even extended to the College staff. The College Manciple, Christopher Brooke[s], was a skilled instrument-maker and the inventor of a new quadrant. Wilkins also recruited a former chef to the Prince of Wales as cook, allegedly for his expertise in botany.[14]

The 'Philosophical Club' shared several ideals that singled out its members in the world of learning at that time. Their disavowal of official Aristotelianism came not from a disrespect for that philosopher, but from a recognition of his limitations and the intellectual sterility of many of his disciples, who argued that all knowledge could be encompassed within his logical categories. Aristotle underpinned the University Laudian Statutes of 1636, which still largely defined the undergraduate curriculum of the Wilkins era, and it was for this reason that the 'New Philosophy' of experimentation had to be a private activity for senior members and their friends. As John Aubrey records, in the universities of 1649 ''twas held a strange presumption for a Man to attempt an Innovation in Learning'.[15]

The New Dynamism

One subject that would have made the Wilkins circle conspicuously avant-garde in its day was its collective view concerning academic authority. Not only were its members sharply critical of the official Aristotelian philosophy, but they would have vigorously rejected the implied assumption that no fundamental new discoveries could be made beyond the traditional classical categories.

University, or 'School', Aristotelianism comprised a rigid body of ideas that attempted to define the powers, sequences, and boundaries of human thought. There was no place in it for ideas of intellectual freedom, not through any bigoted intolerance, but from the simple fact that knowledge was limited to what God had made it possible for man to know, and Aristotle's categories had delineated its limits. True knowledge was seen as existing

Above: *Frontispiece, Wilkins's* Discourse concerning a new world *(1640). This book popularised the new sun-centred cosmology in England. Galileo with his telescope is debating astronomy with Copernicus (left).*

assumption that discrete parcels of human knowledge existed to human view and, while we could not change them or discover their inner workings, we could use our divine gift of reason to order and arrange them into meaningful sequences.

But the scientific revolution had come to challenge this view, largely on the grounds of new evidence that presented itself through sensory or experimental avenues. The geographical discoveries of the Renaissance most exemplified the power of experience against tradition, and in his *Discovery of a new world … in the moon* (1638, 1640) Wilkins drew attention to the discoveries of Columbus as a symbol of the new knowledge. The whole tenor of Wilkins's thought was rooted in the recognition of the fact that man's senses, when employed within controlled enquiry, as suggested by Francis Bacon (1561–1626), could break the bounds of the old learning and open up fresh prospects. This 'experimental philosophy' was part of the new dynamism and sense of intellectual adventure that brought Wilkins to Wadham. Moreover the new knowledge which resulted should form the foundation for yet further enquiries, to produce chains of experimentally derived discoveries that would grow exponentially.

In addition to Bacon, John Wilkins had been influenced by Galileo, whose telescopic discoveries and application of mathematical analysis to problems in physics had struck a death blow to the static science of Aristotle. He had also been impressed by William Gilbert's *De Magnete* (1600), with its experimental demonstrations of a force in nature that provided more plausible explanations for the motions of planetary and terrestrial bodies than did the physics of Aristotle.

Both Galileo and Gilbert were Copernicans, who used the fruits of their investigations to argue against the ancient cosmology that placed the earth, rather than the sun, at the centre of the universe. Galileo's telescopic views of the moons of Jupiter and the phases of Venus argued in favour of a sun-centred cosmology, while his experiments on the motions of bodies under controlled 'laboratory' conditions indicated that mathematical laws operated with equal precision on the sinful earth as they did in the

only in the mind and attained by deductive reasoning. Observation of the external world of nature played a part – such as Aristotle's descriptions of animals and natural forces – but it was essentially passive and subservient to reason. One might say that it was the approach of the librarian or museum curator: it worked on the

perfect heavens. Similarly, Gilbert had demonstrated that magnetism had an experimental basis and could be understood in terms of physical relationships between bodies rather than as an occult force. Galileo's further realization that the moon, when viewed through a telescope, appeared as a world, complete with mountains, continents, and 'seas', was of fundamental importance to Wilkins's intellectual development. John Wilkins's first book, the *Discovery*, published when he was only 24, seized upon these possibilities.

'Proposition XIV'

In his *Discovery*, Wilkins marshalled evidence to demonstrate that the earth was a planetary body, sharing features of topography and possible composition with the moon. He added a new 'Proposition XIV' to the third edition of the book in 1640, which stated that if the earth and moon were planets, then a journey between them should be feasible. Although Wilkins was by no means the first writer to speculate about a journey to the moon – he had, for instance, read Francis Godwin's *Man in the Moon* (1638) – he was the first to consider such a journey not as a fictional device but as an undertaking within the light of the best available scientific information. Wilkins's *Discovery* attempted to take into consideration all of the known scientific facts and to place emphasis on the foreseen mechanics of the journey. The rationale of 'Proposition XIV' hinged upon an ingenious theory of gravity that formed something of a half-way house between the vitalist dynamics of Aristotle, which argued that objects fell because they were heavy, and the mathematical gravitation of Isaac Newton. Developing an idea initiated by Johannes Kepler, Wilkins argued that gravity was analogous to magnetism and produced a 'sphere of magnetick Virtue' around the earth. All that one needed to fly was the ability to rise above that sphere, which Wilkins calculated extended upwards no more than twenty miles. Once above it, there was no reason why one should not be able to coast away towards the moon.

To perform the crucial twenty-mile ascent, Wilkins discussed four potential conveyances. These included the use of spirits, the harnessing of powerful birds, and wings. Eager to display both his literary erudition and experimental knowledge, he cited documented examples of previous attempts to fly using these several techniques, from the spirit-powered aeronautical antics of Simon Magus in the Acts of the Apostles, to the winged contraption of the Saxon monk, Elmirus of Malmesbury. Generally speaking, however, he regarded flying as a skill similar in character to tightrope walking or circus horse riding: difficult, but attainable by patience.[16]

The 'Flying Chariot'

His most favoured mode of celestial conveyance was the 'Flying Chariot'. We can assemble its essential characteristics from the *Discovery* and *Mathematical Magick*. Here Wilkins drew upon his impressive knowledge of contemporary technology and added to it a dimension of remarkable insight by positing what might yet be achieved in the right hands. He was familiar with all the 'machine book' writers of the previous hundred years, and took great delight in regaling his readers with accounts of their devices.

Springs and gears especially fascinated Wilkins, and it was by their powers that he hoped a man might rise above the earth. Nature, after all, was full of spring-like forces: ships and mills were propelled by the changing pressure of the wind, the tides fluxed and refluxed, and coiled steel springs could be used to power watches, automata, and 'engines'. Muscle tissue was a versatile and powerful spring material, for it made possible the flight of birds and the physical strength of living creatures. Nature contained an abundance of natural arrangements of bone-levers, muscle-springs, and wind-blown wings whereby tractive forces were multiplied and directed. Why, therefore, should not mankind use the 'artificial muscle' of powerful springs combined with gears and levers to achieve stupendous ratios of energy? *Mathematical Magick* is full of real and suggested devices that worked on these principles, including smoke-jacks, gear races and wind-cars. All that an inventor needed to succeed was to 'follow nature'.

The 'Flying Chariot' therefore emerges as a machine powered by springs working via gear and lever ratios to

Above: *The Land Ship from* Mathematical Magick. *Such 'ships' operated across the drained Dutch polders in the mid-seventeenth century.*

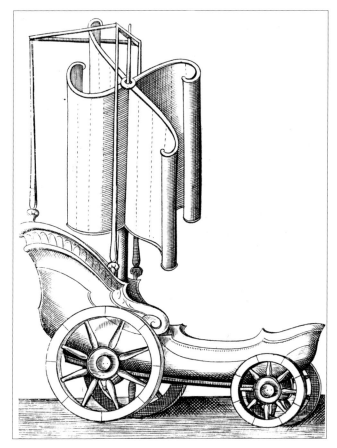

Above: *The Wind Car from* Mathematical Magick. *The rotary vanes connected to the back axle with a gear system like that of the modern motor car.*

operate wings. It would bear the traveller up beyond the twenty-mile 'sphere of magnetick Virtue', after which it would float effortlessly towards the moon. Re-entry would be achieved by simply rewinding the machinery for an easy descent.

Wilkins thus lived at the honeymoon period of Western science, when enough had already been discovered to reveal wonderful possibilities, but not yet enough to reveal such limitations as the law of inertia. Also, the argument that inter-planetary travel would be prevented by the cold and airlessness of space was countered by theological argument: cold and airlessness, such as found on mountain tops, was the result of original sin, which only applied to earth. Perhaps the most far-sighted use that Wilkins envisaged for his 'Flying Chariot' was as a vehicle for terrestrial travel. To travel across the globe, one only needed to ascend vertically for 20 miles, hang motionless for 6 or 12 hours until America or Cuba had turned beneath one, and then descend.

Rational Ingenuity

Flight symbolized the freedom of the scientific revolution, as antiquity became a springboard to pastures new rather than a prison. Most of all, it affirmed the power of the rational ingenuity of mankind to comprehend the Creation and acquire an even more awesome appreciation of its Creator than had been possible previously. This new appreciation was gained by means of machines or physical contrivances that combined the eternal principles of mathematics with the skills of handicraft for what Francis Bacon had called 'the relief of man's estate'. By combining these factors, Wilkins was able to emphasize his point about the creative importance of handicraft, for, unlike the classical philosophers who disdained manual knowledge, he elevated it to a virtual co-partnership with pure thought. Truth, craftsmanship, experiment, utility, and progress therefore formed the cornerstones of his physical world.

WILKINS THE TEACHER

In practical terms, Wilkins's specific ideas were less important than his organizing abilities and his capacity to make friends across political and religious party boundaries.

First and foremost, he was an educator of genius. What really captured his imagination was the communication of rational knowledge from pure researchers to potential users. He saw the inspirational force of knowledge, and possessed that elusive gift for setting minds ablaze. Wilkins could borrow from Galileo, Mersenne, or Godwin, and somehow give other men's discoveries a potency which even their initiators had not perceived. Thus he might be considered the first great popularizer of the new science; the first of a great tradition of scientist-popularizers, whose gift for elucidation of scientific ideas at times made a greater impact upon history than their own individual discoveries, not unlike T.H. Huxley and evolution in the nineteenth century, and Sir Arthur Eddington and relativity in the early twentieth.

One of Wilkins's most conspicuous acts was to abandon Latin as his language of published communication. His early scientific works were aimed primarily at an English readership, which in the 1660s indicated a non-university audience. The English style which he developed possessed a freshness that avoided pretence or condescension. Comparing the style of the *Discovery* or *Mathematical Magick* with their nearest vernacular technical equivalents – astrological almanacks or treatises intended for the land surveyor or navigator – one is pleasantly surprised by the lack of that self-conscious pedagogy so common in books intended to impart technical skills to artisans. For an English reader, brought up on a diet of preaching, warning, and being talked down to, Wilkins's books must have opened doors of delight into hitherto unimagined worlds.

Religion

The views held by Wilkins on education, religion, and science possess a common foundation that give a rounded coherence to his thought. In his scheme of things, God is a supreme, well-ordered, and temperate being, though

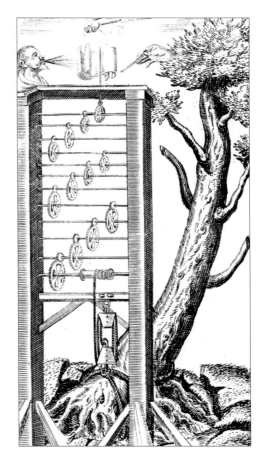

Above: *Before the laws of inertia and resistance were discovered, it was thought that a puff of breath could be geared up to uproot a tree.*

original sin was recognized as a fundamental and cosmological event that broke the ordered sequence of God's plan.[17] Christ had been sent to heal the damage and show the way out of the confusion. In many ways, however, Wilkins saw sin as a rejection of good reason and order, for God was a reasonable deity. The hallmark of man's unique relationship with God lay in his capacity to use his intellect. Therefore religion was to Wilkins an exploration of the relationship between a designer, God, and His intelligent, adoring Creation, whereby man can hope for forgiveness if he uses his divine gift more wisely in future. The new discoveries in geography, astronomy, and mechanics could be seen as signifiers of Redemption.

In many ways Wilkins's Christianity is free from angst, passion, and guilt, but it is more than a mere facile optimism. He could not ascribe illogicality, peevish vengeance, or ancestral cruelty to the Supreme Being, since His principal moral attributes were forgiveness and generosity of spirit. To assume, as some scholars do, that Wilkins's religious writings were sops offered by a 'rationalist' to a fanatical establishment is to misunderstand a mind of sincerity and sophistication.

Language and communication

If the hallmark of the divine in mankind was intelligence and ableness, the hallmark of the human was sociability and communication. Language lay at the heart of all that was human and also expressed the divine gift of reason. One of the consequences of original sin had been the confusion of tongues mentioned in Genesis 22. In *Mercury, or the Swift and Secret Messenger* (1641), the first of Wilkins's books on the problem of language, he explored various devices used for communication. In addition to the 'natural' languages spoken by men – the dissonance between which had originated at Babel – there were special languages such as mathematics that sometimes overrode traditional linguistic divides. The development of a universal system of notation for the expression of precise ideas was to occupy a substantial part of his thought for the rest of his life, culminating in the *Essay Towards a Real Character and Philosophical Language* (1668), regarded by Wilkins as his major achievement.[18]

Left: 'The allegorical foundation of the Royal Society', *Wenceslaus Hollar, 1667. Francis Bacon (seated, right) and others are depicted in a gallery of applied technological devices.*

Yet Wilkins was not attempting to invent another artificial language, but to isolate and define those mental processes common to all men, and to guide them out of the confusion of Babel to the discovery of their true spiritual and intellectual nature. Just as the Apostles at Pentecost had found that they could preach the Word to each man in his native tongue, so man's contemporary redemption would come with clear speech and thought. This linguistic quest worked closely with science and experiment, for the clarification of tongues and the exploration of nature were only aspects of the same enterprise.

THE FORMATION OF THE ROYAL SOCIETY

That group of men that met at the Warden's Lodgings during the 1650s shared similar views with Wilkins, and when they were constituted into the Royal Society in 1660, and met at Gresham College in London, they displayed a 'Latitudinarian' religious and intellectual policy in line with that found in Wilkins's writings. When Thomas Sprat, a former Wadham undergraduate and future Bishop of Rochester, wrote his *History of the Royal Society* in 1667, he argued that the origins of that body lay in the meetings held in the Warden's Lodgings and the stimulus that Wilkins gave to it. He also emphasized that its temperate and non-sectarian pursuits provided a haven of peace and intellectual curiosity in the midst of 'troubled times'.

Yet it was largely on the discoveries made by his Oxford friends and their continental associates that Wilkins's hopes for a possible lunar voyage foundered. The most decisive blow was struck by Robert Boyle when, in 1660, he published a set of ingenious experiments which showed that not only did a vacuum exist in nature (as Torricelli and von Guericke had previously indicated), but that it possessed precise physical characteristics. Boyle had also shown that living creatures died when atmospheric

33

pressure fell below a certain level in his airpump. This occasioned the penning of an anonymous satirical verse c.1663, when the astonished Danish Ambassador witnessed the asphyxiation of a cat in Boyle's air pump:

To the Danish Agent late was showne
That where noe Ayre is, there's noe breathe,
A glass this secret did make knowne
Where[in] a Catt was put to death.
Out of the glass the Ayre being screwed,
Pusse died and ne'er so much as mewed.[19]

If Pusse could die in a vacuum in the Royal Society's laboratory, then a lunar voyager was likely to do the same in space. Likewise, the twenty-mile-high 'sphere of magnetick Virtue' upon which the whole of Wilkins's theory of flight depended was shown to be non-existent by the 1660s. Yet there is no evidence to show that Wilkins in any way resented these new discoveries that undermined his own hopeful suggestions of a quarter of a century before. He had, after all, been one of the initiators of the experimental movement and was now *the* elder statesman of British science. Among his pupils, for example, John Mayow (1658) developed the pneumatic researches of Boyle and demonstrated experimentally that common 'air' contains a large 'inert' and a small 'vital' component. As this vital component sustained both respiration and combustion, Mayow was the first scientist to recognize the chemical relationship between the two main components of air.[20]

THE COLLEGE IN THE WILKINS ERA

During his Wardenship, the Lodgings must have contained a veritable treasure-trove of curiosities. When his friend John Evelyn visited Wadham in 1654, he was amazed at the contraptions which he saw, including a 'monstrous magnet', measuring devices, artificially coloured stones prepared by Christopher Wren, and Wilkins's famous 'transparent apiaries', which were glass beehives to make possible the study of the internal organization of the bee community, and to permit honey to be gathered without having to

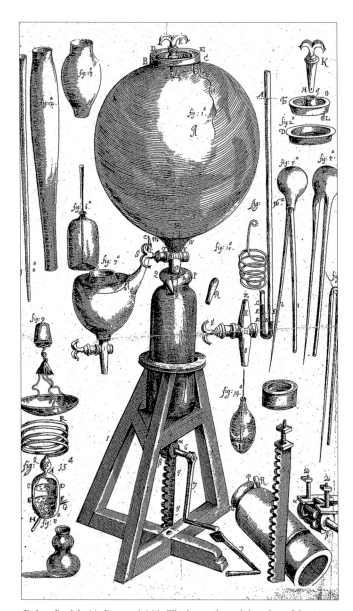

Robert Boyle's Air Pump, 1661. The large glass globe, about 38cm in diameter, could be evacuated of air so that experiments could be performed in the ensuing vacuum.

destroy the bees. Wilkins also had his celebrated 'brazen head' set up in the Gardens, through which he could speak by means of a concealed tube. Although this device clearly related to his ideas on speech projection, it also tells us something about the Warden's sense of humour.[21]

The College Gardens were probably the location of a physiological experiment attempted by Wilkins, Wren and Boyle in 1656, when they injected a dog with a mixture of sack wine and opium to test the speed of its action. So rapidly did the intravenous opium act on the dog, however, that the three men 'caused him to be whipped up and down a neighbouring Garden' to prevent the animal from falling into a fatal coma. This may have been the first scientifically conducted experiment using an intravenously administered drug.[22]

Robert Hooke, whose subsequent scientific career was strongly moulded by Wilkins, mentions several Wadham recollections in his writings. In February 1675, he records listening to a paper on avian anatomy delivered by Dr Croon to the Royal Society, to which he added comments on 'my way of flying by vanes [wings] tried at Wadham' some 20 years before.[23] Hooke's *Micrographia* (1665) used the newly invented microscope to study the wing structures of a variety of flying insects. Hooke's interests in muscle, spring and elasticity probably had their origins in the Wadham meetings, as when in 1678 he recalled for the Royal Society seeing 'in Wadham Colledge, in the Garden of the learned Dr. Wilkins … a Fountain so contrived as by the Spring of the excluded Air to throw up to a great height a large and lasting stream of water: which water was first forced into the Leaden Cistern thereof by two force Pumps which did alternately work, and so condense the Air included in a small room'.

During the Wilkins era, Wadham was also renowned for its learned conviviality. The celebrated violinist Baltzar performed as a guest of the Warden, when Anthony Wood of Merton was prevailed upon to accompany him in a duo. In Michaelmas 1656 alone, over £6 (more than a Fellow's quarterly stipend) was spent on 'wine for gaudies', while on 5 November the 'Bursars' Accounts' recorded annual expenditure of three shillings to buy faggots and shot to celebrate the overthrow of Guy Fawkes's 'Gunpowder Treason' in the gravelled quadrangle. The College also spent freely on the funeral of John Goodridge – a foundation Fellow and a very generous benefactor – expending £9 in all.[24]

It was no doubt Wilkins's marriage to Robina Cromwell that prompted her nephew Richard to appoint him as Master of Trinity, Cambridge, in 1659; from which he was expelled at the Restoration in 1660, to the regret of the Fellows. He received in compensation an excellent London living and other preferments, and became Bishop of Chester in 1668, helped no doubt by the new King's patronage of scientific learning.

John Wilkins's impact on Wadham had been enormous. The College had been a haven of sanity and good learning in difficult times, and had nurtured the beginnings of systematic experimental science within its walls during what was probably the most illustrious single decade in Wadham's history.

Illustrations from R. Hooke, Micrographia *(1665), copy in the College Library.*

Above: *Of Blue Mould, facing p. 125.*

Left: *White Featherwing'd Moth, facing p. 197.*

CHAPTER THREE

Decline and Revival: 1660–1900

Cliff Davies

Wadham, like Wilkins, accommodated itself fairly easily to the Restoration in 1660. Walter Blandford, who had succeeded Wilkins as Warden in 1659, had good Royalist connections, and soon became Chaplain to Charles II's chief minister, the Earl of Clarendon; not surprisingly he became Vice-Chancellor, then in 1665 Bishop of Oxford. His successor, Gilbert Ironside, was a Wilkins protégé, but also son of a bishop. Admissions in the 1660s averaged 32 per year; a good deal higher than at any time subsequently before the twentieth century. The cosmopolitan excitement of the Wilkins years was over; the College settled back into routine.

The context, until about 1800, was an unfavourable one. Historians now challenge the view that the University was sunk in utter degeneracy in the eighteenth century. Nevertheless it remains true that the total number of students declined dramatically; that it became much harder for poor students to attend; that the formal curriculum was anachronistic and the process of gaining a degree a matter of form. By the crude test of numbers Wadham held up better than the University as a whole before 1700 (University matriculations averaged 460 per annum in the 1660s and 310 in the 1690s, whereas Wadham averaged 32 and 24 per annum respectively); but then did much worse (University 200 per annum in the 1750s, Wadham 8).[1]

The root of the problem at Wadham lay in the Fellowship. Only Scholars of Wadham could become Fellows.[2] When a Fellowship became vacant, it went to the senior Scholar in residence, with little fuss about merit. A Scholar so determined could hang around for 12 years after taking his MA waiting for a vacancy, provided he was prepared to survive on a minimum stipend in the interim. Similarly a Fellowship could be held for 20 years, unless the Fellow acquired a livelihood worth £10 or more meanwhile.[3] By and large Fellows were in Holy Orders. They were comfortably off but not well paid; moreover they were not allowed to marry. Inevitably, those who could moved on as soon as possible to an attractive rectory or vicarage. So those who became Fellows in the first place, and those who stayed longest as Fellows, tended to be those who lacked the necessary connections to get themselves a better ecclesiastical niche. The Fellows were not obliged to teach, but to devote themselves to study; there was little evidence that this obligation was honoured.

Opposite: *Walter Blandford (1615–75), who came up to Oxford as a Servitor of Christ Church and transferred to Wadham as a Scholar. He had strong Royalist connections, but remained a Fellow under Wilkins, and was elected Warden in 1659. Portrayed here while Bishop of Worcester (1671–5).*

Doctor Blanford
Bishop of Worcester.

J.th Wardn of Wadh. Coll.
Adm.d Sept. 5. 1659.

Left: *Alice George, by George Sonmans, 1691. She may have been the College Laundress. There is a detailed description of her by John Locke in 1680, when she claimed to be already 108! Sonmans painted her at the same time as he painted William III for the College.*

Above: *Thomas Dunster (1657–1719). Designated 'son of a poor man', he came to Wadham as a Servitor in 1673, going on to be Scholar, Fellow and from 1689 Warden.*

Of course, there was a bevy of College offices to be occupied; as Sub-Warden, Bursars, Librarian, 'Moderators' in Humanities, Philosophy and so on. The custom seems to have been for Fellows to share these out amongst themselves each year and then leave Oxford to pursue their careers; as chaplains, private tutors, curates, even fully-fledged rectors and vicars. A couple of Fellows and, with luck, the Warden, remained in residence; the resident Fellows deputized for their colleagues, for a consideration. Of course, this is the situation at its worst. But when, in 1739, a crisis involving the Warden hit the College, there was only one Fellow available; the rest, including the Bursars, had to be summoned from London or the country.[4] Philip Speke, Librarian, ex-Sub-Warden, Chaplain in Whitehall, and

vicar of a parish in Somerset, had still not presented his accounts for the several years he had been Bursar, in spite of attempts to sequester his Fellowship in 1737. By 1746 the College was glad to accept £100 from him in settlement of a disputed debt of £213 owed since 1733.[5]

This plunge into the nadir of College history is premature. Up to about 1700 Wadham had a fairly high profile in the University. Warden Ironside was Vice-Chancellor 1687–89, and thus very much caught up in the politics of the 'Glorious Revolution'. He remonstrated with James II when James offended Anglican susceptibilities by trying to intrude his nominees, many of them Catholics, into Magdalen.[6] He collaborated with Lord Lovelace (Wadham 1655), one of the instigators of

Above: Humphrey Hody (1659–1707), Regius Professor of Greek, and major benefactor, founder of Exhibitions in Greek and Hebrew.

Above right: Edith Hody, née Daniel, died 1736. There is another portrait of her, rather younger (see p.136).

the Revolution against James and commander of the local Williamite forces.[7] Ironside steered a less-than-enthusiastic University into recognition of the new regime. In 1689 he was duly rewarded with a bishopric.

His successor as Warden, Thomas Dunster, was memorably described by the bilious Tory gossip Thomas Hearne as 'one of the Violentest Whiggs & most rascally Low-Church Men of the age … much given to luxury & like his crony Royce [Provost of Oriel] to spend all upon his Gutt'.[8] While Hearne's verdict is hardly impartial, there are signs of maladministration in Dunster's time, above all a failure to keep either records of Governing Body decisions or accounts. In 1698 some of the Fellows presented a comprehensive indictment to the Visitor, instancing the employment of female bedmakers (several of whom had enticed students into marriage, allegedly, while one had

killed herself while pregnant), easy access by townsmen and women into the College via the King's Arms, and embezzlement of College funds. The Visitor supported the complaints, but adopted the wrong remedy by producing a new set of statutes which Dunster managed to resist as unconstitutional.[9] Against these scandalous proceedings must be set Dunster's opposition to attempts to ban the reading of the work of John Locke in the University.[10] Humphrey Hody, Fellow, became Regius Professor of Greek in 1698 and founded Exhibitions in Greek and Hebrew which were to do a good deal for the College's reputation in the next two centuries. And Wadham can claim a fortuitous connection with the greatest of English classical scholars, Richard Bentley, who 'incorporated' from Cambridge in 1689 as private tutor to James Stillingfleet.

Dunster's death in 1719 was followed by a scandal which delighted the Oxford wits. The eight Fellows were evenly divided on the election to the Wardenship. The junior Fellow switched sides at the last moment to give the election to William Baker. Gossip had it that Baker had promised him a substantial reward but went back on his word; the victim took to his bed and had to be restrained in a strait-jacket.[11] Baker departed for the Bishopric of Bangor in 1724, to be succeeded by Robert Thistlethwayte. Thistlethwayte's career (he was Chaplain to George II and on his way to a bishopric) was brought to an untimely end in 1739 when he was accused of sexual assault on an undergraduate. Rather than face his accusers he fled to France, to Boulogne, where he died in 1744. One George Baker tried to widen the issue by printing scabrous evidence about Thistlethwayte's proclivities from the College Barber and Butler, and by

bringing accusations (which he was later compelled to withdraw) against a Fellow, John Swinton.[12] The Fellows turned to a respected elder statesman, an ex-Fellow, Samuel Lisle, Archdeacon of Canterbury, to be their new Warden. Shortly afterwards the College first took out fire insurance:

Well did the prudent sons of Wadham
Their house secure from fire and flame.
They knew their crime, the crime of Sodom,
And judged their punishment the same. [13]

Above: *An engraving of the College by W. Williams, 1727, dedicated to Thistlethwayte. This plate was included in Williams's* Oxonia Depicta *(1732).*

During the second half of the eighteenth century blatant scandal was avoided. Nevertheless the record was hardly distinguished. Admissions rose slightly (8 per year in the 1750s, 10 in the 1790s). Opportunities for the less well-off declined. In the 1690s Wadham admitted 152 sons of gentlemen, 38 sons of clergy, and 54 'plebeians'. In the 1790s, the figures were 76, 30, and 3 respectively.[14] To some extent this reflects the clerical profession's becoming more hereditary. Moreover to a degree the definition of 'gentleman' loosened, so that many who would have qualified as such in 1790 would not have done so earlier.[15] But it is also true that it was becoming much harder for the less well-off to attend. Only seven students were admitted as 'Servitors' or as 'Bible-Clerks' in the 1790s, compared to 42 in the 1690s – positions which provided a small stipend in return for work in Hall or Chapel.[16] Scholarships, remaining at the £10 laid down in the statutes, increasingly failed to cover the cost of undergraduate education.

So, theoretically, were the Fellows' stipends unchanged, at twice the Scholars' rates; but Fellows benefited in other ways, from perks, fees, windfalls from College estates, and the right to sub-let their over-lavish accommodation.[17] A Fellowship had evolved, in modern terms, from being a rather austere graduate studentship, into a comfortable style of bachelor life; the transformation was marked (some time between 1690 and 1724) by the introduction of a Senior Common Room. The picture, implicit in a host of memoirs, of dons sitting long over their port, dates from the eighteenth century. The minimum acceptable level of comfort rose for undergraduates as well as dons. Rooms were no longer shared; hence the conversion of the attics into rooms, in spite of reduced numbers of students. The cost of an Oxford education increased – £60 a year was quoted in 1715, about £100 in 1750, about £200–£300 by 1800 – over a period when the general price level roughly doubled.[18]

Essentially eighteenth-century Oxford allowed everybody, dons and undergraduates, to do much what they wanted; and a few took the opportunity to pursue scholarship. John Swinton, the Fellow libelled in 1739, was a considerable Semitic scholar, if also a figure of fun to Dr Johnson and his circle. Benjamin Kennicott, son of a Totnes baker, came up as a Servitor in 1744, and went on to do distinguished work on the text of the Old Testament. He became a Fellow of Exeter. It does look as if Wadham's restriction of its Fellowship to its own Scholars worked to its disadvantage; it could export talent, but not import it. Two distinguished Wadham Scholars, John Eveleigh and John Parsons, went on to be, respectively, Fellow then Provost of Oriel, and Fellow and Master of Balliol.

With Cyril Jackson, Dean of Christ Church, Eveleigh and Parsons were the instigators of the new examination statute of 1800. This recognized that the gaining of a degree had become a formality, and introduced examinations (largely oral), with the added incentive of honours for the best candidates. The new system had its deficiencies, but it did at least provide a positive incentive for serious study, and introduced competition between colleges to do well in the Schools. Large audiences turned up for the examination of fancied candidates, and outstanding performances were immortalized in the folk-memory, rather like sporting performances later.

Above: *The Old Senior Common Room, constructed out of the Bursary between 1690 and 1724.*

Above: *A watercolour of the Fellows' Garden by C. Wild, 1819.*

Wadham climbed back to respectability during those years. Wardens Wills (1783–1806) and Tournay (1806–31) were respected figures in the University. In Wills's time the Gardens were extended and re-ordered.[19] Improvements to the Hall and the extension of the back quad to take in the present Staircases 10 and 11 took place when Tournay was in office. Wills, reputedly 'very close and rigid' in money matters, was a substantial benefactor, founding, amongst much else, Fellowships and Exhibitions in Medicine and Law, and the 'Warden's Exhibition Fund' from which a great number of financially embarrassed undergraduates have benefited.[20] Tournay was distinguished, according to his epitaph, for 'playful fancy, refined taste, and peculiar powers of conversation'; also, in his last years, for never attending Chapel, in spite of being Prebendary of Peterborough and Canon of Westminster.[21]

The reason for Wadham's new reputation as a 'serious' college was probably due to accidents of personality among the Fellowship. The future Dean Church was sent to Wadham in the early 1830s 'because B.P. Symons and Thomas Griffiths and [Thomas] Vores, the tutors, were of evangelical principles, and it was a college where some men worked'.[22] Symons, indeed, is one of the important figures in the College history. He took Schools in 1805, before, in the words of Warden Wells, 'the examination was modified so as to be more adapted to human powers'. It involved both Lit. Hum. and Maths, with a requirement of distinction in both.[23] As Tutor he played the chief role in building up the College's new academic and religious reputation. Tournay is said to have resigned in 1831 to ensure that Symons would succeed him; otherwise Symons's Fellowship was due to expire under Dorothy Wadham's twenty-year rule. His election also gave Symons the opportunity to marry, the first Warden to do so – with the exception of Wilkins – under the terms of the Act of Parliament secured in 1806.[24]

It is worth pausing to look at the freshmen who came up in 1831: 3 of them were sons of the clergy, 2 of medical men, one of a colonel, 11 of 'esquires' and one of a mere 'mister'. Of the 19, 7 (a very respectable proportion) took honours; one got a first, 5 got thirds, one a fourth. All these were in Lit. Hum., but one of the thirds took Maths as well, the only other honour school available, getting a 'double' third. Seven more took pass degrees, and 5 disappeared without degrees at all. The 'first', Joseph Arnold, was briefly a Fellow, read for the Bar, and became a Supreme Court judge in Bengal. Nine of the 19 became clergymen.[25]

Generalization about student life is hazardous. Dean Church talks of 'a very clever set at Wadham' including two winners of the Ireland Scholarship. He himself 'shrank from the very pronounced evangelical men; my friends were mostly of no special colour, …. But all sets touched more or less; the quiet set had relations with the fast set and met occasionally at wine parties and breakfasts'.[26] Edward Boys Ellman, who came up in 1834, took a daily eight-mile walk (always to Sandford Lock), claimed to read 14 hours a day, and helped found the Debating Society, hoping the subjects debated would be useful for Schools. Ambitious to do well in Maths, he paid for private tuition (at 7am daily), got his first (along with a fourth in Lit. Hum.), and became a Sussex parson.[27] William Maclaine (1837), in letters home, claimed to attend 14 lectures a week, attended Chapel daily, and also joined the Debating Society (to go on its Nuneham outing). He claimed Wadham as the 'strictest college in Oxford' and also 'the most expensive'. He rowed, claimed to need £200 per annum (rather modest by most standards, but his father cut it to £150), took a pass degree, was called to the Bar, but settled down as a country gentleman. He relates a story of a shy man, E.N. Mangin, who, walking in the High 'suddenly appeared convulsed'; 'I can't bear this High St.; all these flash men look down at one so; they know I am a Wadham man'.[28]

Rowing was the first organized sport. Wadham Boat Club was founded before 1837, and in 1849 famously won both the Grand and the Ladies' Challenge Cups at Henley. Warden Symons disapproved, so the crew set off surreptitiously by coach daily, at 2pm, and arrived at Henley at 5pm. Sub-Warden Griffiths covered up on their late return. Symons may have been less hostile than he pretended to be. What seems to have been the first bump-supper, with the defeated (Second Trinity) Cambridge crew as guests, took place, the Warden stipulating only 'no hot lush'.[29]

Symons was a larger-than-life character, around whom anecdotes cluster, mostly uncomplimentary. He was autocratic, fiercely evangelical, but worldly, close about money, prejudiced, intolerant, and ready to use transparently dishonest arguments to get his own way. He was also genial enough when in good temper, shrewd, and not averse to teasing, himself as well as others. Known because of his size as 'Big Ben' or on horseback as the

MCV
May 1880

"Under-Grads"
Little Maggs (Wadham) 'I quite expected that you would have got a first-class –"
Hon'ble Spynks (Magdalen) 'Aw,' 'no, these Radical beggars all go first-class now, I prefer taking a gentlemanly third!'

Above: *Wadham's continued inferiority complex? Or a reputation for radicalism and hard work?*

Right: *A silhouette of Benjamin Symons (1785–1878), Scholar, Fellow and Warden 1831–71, by Augustin Edouart. Edouart began to take silhouettes in 1826. Since Symons is designated Sub-Warden, the image must have been taken between then and 1831.*

Left: *A cartoon of Warden Symons.*

Below: *Stereoview of the front quad: albumen photograph by Stephen Thompson, published 9 Feb 1860 by T. & G. Shrimpton, Broad Street, Oxford. Only five English views by this photographer have been recorded. Such images were designed to be viewed in a stereoscope, where through the operation of lenses and mirrors the two photographs combined to give a three-dimensional effect.*

'Elephant and Castle', he would embarrass the audience of his 'Articles' lecture with a double-take, stroking his leg and saying 'but for God's Providence, it might have been the leg of an elephant'.[30] A reputation as an evangelical college was useful when parents were reluctant to expose their sons to the modishly popish temptations of the Oxford Movement. Undergraduates believed that Sunday dinner was timed to stop them succumbing to the seductions of Newman's sermons at St Mary's.[31]

The Newmanites attempted to prevent Symons's nomination as Vice-Chancellor; R.W. Church, now Fellow of Oriel, interposed his veto as Proctor on Symons's proposal to condemn Newman's notoriously Romanizing 'Tract 90'. Symons must have felt vindicated when, a few months later, Newman seceded to Rome. Wadham was relatively unscathed by the Movement, although T.W. Allies, former Fellow, was deprived of common-room membership for a public attack on Symons. Allies followed Newman into the Roman Church; even the gentle Wells, writing in 1898, could still refer to him as a 'pervert to Rome'.[32]

The serious set at Wadham would stay up well into the small hours debating the University Sermon. But the result was not a nest of evangelicals, but of earnest, secular-minded reformers, hardly to Symons's taste, though no doubt preferable to Romanizers. Richard Congreve (Scholar 1836, Fellow 1844, a product of Arnold's Rugby) was an inspiring tutor, and also particularly influential with a set that was up around 1851: J.H. Bridges, E.S. Beesley, Frederic Harrison and George Thorley. Congreve gave up his Fellowship in 1854, met Auguste Comte, founder of 'Positivism' in 1855, and together with his pupils founded an English Positivist movement: an attempt to marry high ethical ideals to a rigorously scientific approach to philosophy. They went on variously to become prolific authors and social reformers; except Thorley, who remained at Wadham, eventually to become Warden.[33]

By the 1850s Symons was increasingly out of sympathy with the modern world. Harrison recalls a successful campaign by Congreve for Fellows to be chosen from the Scholars by merit rather than seniority.[34] Bigger changes were on the way with the great University reform commission (imposed by Parliament) of 1850–5, bitterly fought by Symons.[35] The main result for Wadham was the throwing open of Fellowships to general competition, rather than restricting them to Wadham Scholars; while also beginning the change in the concept of a Fellowship from, in modern terms, a rather extended research fellowship with little in the way of formal duties, basically a preparation for a career outside the University, into that of a professional scholar and tutor.[36] The first non-Wadham man to be elected was Patrick Henderson, from Balliol, in 1867; he was also the first Fellow allowed to marry, in 1870, and went on, having changed his name to Wright-Henderson, to become Warden in 1903.

Symons resigned in 1871, amid a good deal of acrimony. Aged 86, he had become increasingly unpopular with the Fellows, and, in spite of much protest, impotent to prevent

such changes as the abolition of religious tests for admission.[37] He was accused of cutting through proper procedures, especially about College property; there were dark suspicions that he had confused College and private property to his own advantage. The final straw was a Trollopian dispute about the Warden's Garden.[38]

The next 30 years were to be dominated by financial problems. The cause was the great agricultural depression, which set in in 1878, producing a dramatic fall of farm

Top right: John Griffiths (1807–85), Scholar, Fellow, and Warden 1871–81. From a drawing by Sam Cousins, after a painting by G.F. Watts, 1854.

Right, below and below right: Strip-cartoon of the Wadham 'Row' of 1879 by F.J. Tebbutt, Commoner of Hertford. 'Jam' refers to the incarceration of the Dean by 'jamming' his door.

rents. For many colleges there was compensation in a buoyant urban property market; but Wadham was peculiarly unfortunate in having next to no urban property, and most of its land was in Essex, one of the areas worst affected by the depression. External income fell from £7,300 to £2,000 from 1871 to 1903, while Brasenose's, for instance, rose from £7,400 to £10,300. Fellows' stipends were cut from £250 or £300 to £210, then to £130; in 1882 the Warden had to forego the last quarter of his salary. Wadham had been a reasonably well-endowed college, with, in the eighteenth century, an income comparable to Balliol and Brasenose. By 1903 it was the third poorest of the older men's colleges.[39]

Poverty prevented Wadham building on the high academic reputation it had won earlier in the century. Admissions in the University as a whole doubled. In Wadham they remained at about 25 a year. Part of the reason was Wadham's inability to provide extra accommodation. A scheme by Thomas Jackson to open up

Above: *George Thorley (1830–1904), Scholar, Fellow and Warden 1881–1903.*

Right: *Cartoon of Frederic Harrison by Spy, 1886. 'At Oxford he rowed, cricketed, and rode moderately … learnt as much as Oxford could teach … and became a Fellow and Tutor of Wadham.'*

the back quad rather like the Broad Street frontage of Trinity, could not be afforded.[40] Oddly, the College also blamed the relaxation of the University's residence statutes to allow undergraduates to live out of College. As Wright-Henderson explained, 'more popular or fashionable colleges' were able to scoop the pool of potential talent. Poorer students were attracted to the much more economical Keble or the new 'non-collegiate' society, the future St Catherine's, or indeed the new universities. Oxford expenses were less extravagant than they had been, but the number of young men wanting to come to Oxford, qualified to do so, and able to afford it was not enough to set up competitive pressures to get in.[41]

Not that the College's administration was unblemished. Symons's successor John Griffiths had been a formidable Tutor and University figure in the 1840s, before resigning his Fellowship under Dorothy Wadham's regulations. He was indeed a gifted man, a connoisseur, collector, friend of artists; he also put the College archives into order and began serious work on its history.[42] But relations with undergraduates were not, it seems, his forte, at least as Warden. The upshot was a crisis in 1879, which grew out of an attempt to tighten College discipline.[43] New regulations were issued (a spoof satirical set soon followed) and the College concert held in the week after Eights (a tradition going back at least to the 1850s) was cancelled. Windows were broken, and a 'detective', hired to guard the Bursary, was assaulted. It was alleged (and this is still sometimes repeated in print) that the entire College was sent down as a result. In fact about eight men were rusticated for the rest of term; only one was permanently sent down.[44]

Griffiths resigned in 1881, to be succeeded by George Thorley (as Sub-Warden a star performer at the concerts). Thorley, however, was increasingly deaf, ill, and remote. Something of the flavour of the period is indicated by the 1890 entry. They were 25 in all, from a variety of backgrounds, usually comfortably off, but none from the great public schools; Dover College and Radley rubbed shoulders with Boston Grammar School and Lord Weymouth's, Warminster. Most were still sons of gentlemen, clergymen, or medical doctors; but a chemist, a timber merchant, a mill-owner, and a music-master are to be found among the fathers; one was the twelfth son of a deceased Bishop of Tasmania. There was one local lad, J.S. Crisall, son of an Oxford boatbuilder. Eight of the 25 took honours; 4 in Lit. Hum. (one first, one second, 2 thirds), one each in Maths (a second), Theology (a third), Natural Sciences (a second), Law (a fourth), and History (a fourth – Crisall). Overall, compared to 1861, or even 1831, there had been little change, except for the broadening in the number of subjects, and perhaps (though status indicators are notoriously unreliable) in

Redress of grievances at Wad*h*m.

Undergraduate to Sub-Warden — "I wished to say, Sir, that my chimney smokes very badly."

S.W. to Undergrad: "Does it indeed! – It's a peculiar-ity in College chimneys. Mine smokes too. Good morning."
[Exit.

Right: Cartoon of the College at the time of the 1879 'Row'. The Sub-Warden is Thorley.

47

Above: *The Shakespeare Club, established (or possibly refounded) in 1866. It had 12 members and met weekly to read plays by Shakespeare and others, and fortnightly for a breakfast.*

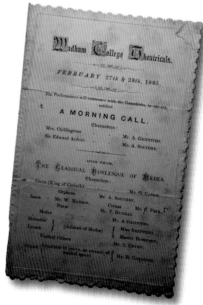

Left: *Wadham Theatricals, 1865.*

social origins, though it seems highly unlikely that 16 out of 25 would go into the Church, as their predecessors of 1861 had done.[45]

What had changed significantly in the second half of the century was the teaching system. As we have seen, early in the century undergraduates attended a large number of 'lectures' in College, 12 or 15 a week. In modern terms these were classes, going through the texts: 'like lessons at school, in which we were put on to construe in turn'. Honours students tried to get themselves excused, and hired private coaches. In 1857–8, his final year, Jackson went to his coach (not a member of the College) three times a week, and attended three College lectures on Aristotle's *Ethics* a week.[46] From about 1874

48

something like the present system of 'inter-collegiate' lectures evolved, more like lectures in the modern sense; Tutors had time for tutorials, making coaches redundant. By 1892 Wright-Henderson was voicing the modern complaint that Tutors had in effect turned themselves into coaches 'with perhaps unwise devotion' at the expense of scholarship or research.[47] The 1881 reforms reduced the number of fellowships to eight, six of them Tutorial Fellows – with the intention that they should be career academics on a professional salary, an aim somewhat stymied by the agricultural depression. Subjects not covered by Fellows could be dealt with by official College 'Lecturers'. Richard Abbay took a first in Maths in 1867, and went off to organize the new Physics Department at King's College London, to return as a Fellow in 1869 before departing in 1872 to be a clergyman in Ceylon.

There were regular Lecturers in Natural Science from 1868, and for the combined school of History and Law from 1867 (they split in 1874). By 1891 the pattern had settled down to three Tutorial Fellows in Classics, one (Dixey) in Physiology, with Lecturers in Law,

Above: *Sir Thomas Jackson, Bart (1831–1924), Scholar, Fellow, Honorary Fellow, architect of the Examination Schools (and much else). By Hugh Rivière, 1900.*

Left: *From 1886 to 1897 the College hired a barge. This one, left, was built for the College by R.A. Talboys in 1897. It was sold in 1973 as beyond economic repair, and, after an unsuccessful venture as a floating restaurant, was broken up.*

Above: *C.B. Fry in classic pose.*

Above: *A Max Beerbohm cartoon (1913): 'Wadham Wisdom: Sir John Simon and Mr F.E. Smith agreeing that the reason why Gentlemen of the Long Robe are so acceptable yonder is that so many don't know how not to look like hustlers.'*

Natural Science, History, Classics, Maths and Physics (together), and Hebrew. Of the other four Fellows one was the Professor of Experimental Philosophy (that is, Physics), and three the still-remaining old-style non-academic Fellows.[48]

Something recognizably like the modern College was emerging in the late nineteenth century. Sport, previously confined to rowing, spread to include cricket, rugby, and association football (the rules of which seem to have been formulated in a meeting held at Wadham in 1866 'for those schools who had no game of their own at Oxford'[49]). The College had a barge from 1886 and acquired a cricket ground at about the same time.[50] By the 1890s athletic fever was at its height, welcomed as a substitute for the rowdiness which had been a major donnish preoccupation 20 years before. The College gloried in the blues of C.B. Fry, in cricket, athletics, soccer, and, very nearly, rugby. Not all students were keen on sport; F.W. Hirst (later editor of *The Economist*) regretted taking part in Torpids in his first year, 'a sort of compulsory patriotism which spoilt one's afternoon and which was very disagreeable in cold weather'.[51]

Wells's College history (1898) concludes with a chapter on sport, 'held by many of us to be one of the great educating influences of Oxford' because of its inculcation of moral qualities and sociability.[52]

A JCR was established, initially as a private club, in 1888.[53] Gaudies, to which all MAs were invited, began in 1881. 'Roll-call' at the lodge (8am) was introduced as an alternative to Chapel in the 1870s; a compulsory parade was considered necessary to make undergraduates get up. Dinner continued its inexorable move to later in the day, to 7pm by 1884.[54] The College was becoming more self-conscious, perhaps again as part of that late-Victorian accent on institutional loyalty and team spirit. R.B. Gardiner published his invaluable Registers of College members in 1889–94; Jackson his great *History* of the foundation and buildings in 1893, J.B. Wells his chattier history in 1898. Wells also founded and edited the *Wadham College Gazette* in 1897. What the twentieth century believed to be 'traditional Oxford' had struggled into existence by 1900.

I have tried to describe the general flavour of College life, rather than listing famous old members. But some mention should be made of the distinguished. Arthur Onslow (1708) was Speaker of the Commons from 1728 to 1761. Richard Bethell came up aged 14 in 1814 (in 'jacket and frill'), got a first in Lit. Hum. and a second in Maths in 1818, was briefly a Fellow, ending up (as Lord Westbury) as Lord Chancellor (1861–5). A future Chancellor of the Exchequer, H.C.E. Childers, was briefly at Wadham. He came up in 1845, while waiting for a place at Merton; Symons refused to let him migrate, and he went to Trinity, Cambridge instead. F.E. Smith (1891 – later Lord Birkenhead) and J.A. Simon (1892),

Above: *Spoof Regulations, 1879, issued following the 1879 'Row' when an attempt was made to tighten College discipline.*

WADHAM COLLEGE,
1892.

KITCHEN CHARGES.

Breakfast.

	s.	d.
Fried Sole, plain or filleted (commons) ...		10
„ Whiting „ „ ...		8
„ Mackerel „ „ ...		9
„ Haddock „ „ ...		8
Kippers, Bloaters, or Herrings, each ...		3
Salmon Cutlet (commons) ...		10
Steak „ ...		10
Mutton Chop ...		9
2 Mutton Cutlets, or Veal Cutlets and Bacon ...		9
3 Sausages and Potatoes ...		8
2 Kidneys and Bacon, and do. on Toast ...		10
Savory Omelette ...		9
2 Buttered Eggs on Toast ...		7
2 Poached Eggs on Toast ...		4
2 „ „ and Bacon ...		8
¼ Grilled Fowl and Bacon ...	1	1
Savory Eggs on Toast ...		7
Porridge (per basin) ...		4
Dry Toast (per round) 1*d*., Buttered Toast do. ...		3
Anchovy Toast (per round) ...		5
Plain Eggs, each ...		2
Milk ½ pint, 1½*d*.; Sugar per lb. ...		4
Coffee, small pot, 4*d*., large do. (quart) ...		8
Tea „ 4*d*., „ „ ...		6

Luncheon.

	s.	d.
Soups, all kinds, (per basin) ...		8
Pickled Salmon (commons) ...	1	3
Soused Mackerel „ ...		10
„ „ (half do.) ...		5
Cold Lamb and Mint Sauce (commons) ...	1	3
„ Beef, Ham, Tongue, Meat Pie, &c. ...		10
„ „ „ „ „ (½ commons)		6
Salad 4*d*., Cucumber 3*d*., Lettuce 3*d*., Potatoes 2*d*., Water Cress 2*d*., Radishes 2*d*.		
Pastry and Sugar (commons) ...		5
Creams 4*d*.; Custards, each ...		3
Jelly or Blancmange (commons) ...		6
Cold Fowl 3/6 with Ham ...	4	6
½ „ 1/9 „ ...	2	3
¼ „ 11*d*. „ ...	1	2
½ Cold Duckling ...	1	10

Game according to Market Prices.
Meat Pies 4/- and 4/6 each.

Dinner.

	s.	d.
Soups, all kinds (portion) ...		6
Fish—Salmon and sauce ...	1	1
Soles and sauce ...		8
Other kinds and sauce ...		6
Entrées of Rissoles, Curries, Patties, &c. ...		6
1 Lamb Cutlet and sauce ...		7
1 Mutton „ „ ...		6
Beef Steak ...		10
Small do. ...		8
Beef, Mutton, Pork, Veal, Meat Pie (commons)		10
„ „ „ „ „ (half „)		6
Roast Lamb (commons) ...	1	1
Duckling, half ...	1	10

All Sauces 2*d*.

	s.	d.
Jelly and Blancmange ...		6
Pastry, all kinds (commons) ...		5
Creams and Custards, each ...		4

Salad 4*d*., Lettuce 3*d*., Water Cress 2*d*., Radishes 2*d*., Pickles 2*d*., Sugar 1*d*.
Vegetables, ordinary, 3*d*.: to order, charged according to Market Prices.

BUTTERY CHARGES.

	d.
Bread—Large commons ...	2
Small do. ...	1
Dinner do. ...	½
Butter—Large commons ...	2
Small do. ...	1½
Cheese, commons ...	1½
Dinner commons of Butter or Cheese ...	1
Ale and Stout, per pint ...	4
Mild Ale, Anglo-Bavarian do., and Cider, per pint	3
Lemonade and Soda Water, per bottle ...	3
Milk, commons, ½ pint ...	1

The Electric Light.

It is desired to call the attention of residents in College to the necessity of care in the use of the Electric Light. The cost of the light will be defrayed by a proportionate charge on the occupants of rooms, and it is therefore the interest of all that there should be no waste of the electric current.

Extravagance in the use of the light will cause unnecessary expense to all others on the staircase, as well as to the extravagant person himself.

It is requested that no light be kept burning, even for the shortest time, when it is not actually needed, and that gentlemen leaving their rooms at any time in the evening will be careful to turn off the light before doing so.

Gentlemen are also cautioned against interfering in any way with the wires or with any part of the electric apparatus.

WADHAM COLLEGE,
24 October, 1894.

Above: *In 1894 regulations were strict concerning the introduction of electric light.*

Left: *The Kitchen and Buttery charges notice of 1892.*

Opposite: *Poster souvenir of Wadham, c.1890s.*

both to become Lord Chancellor, were contemporaries of C.B. Fry (1891). Smith's colourful anecdotes especially helped create the legend of Wadham's 'golden age', though the trio's being at Wadham together was purely fortuitous. Thomas Jackson, already mentioned for his *History*, was an old-style non-academic Fellow, took up a career in architecture, and left his mark forcibly on Oxford: the Exam Schools, the cricket pavilion in the Parks, the High Street front of Brasenose, the Broad Street quadrangle of Trinity, and Hertford.[55] Thomas Beecham was briefly at Wadham, in 1897, before deciding he would rather study music in Germany. But it may be appropriate to end with Francis Kilvert (1859; fourth in Law and History, 1862), the young clergyman whose elegiac diaries of life in the Welsh Marches were discovered in 1937. They contain some fascinating glimpses of Wadham, which he revisited in 1874 and 1876; including a memorable description of the copper beech, and a dinner on High Table, 'an object of my undergraduate ambition realised at length'.[56]

CHAPTER FOUR

'A Liberal Place': 1900–1938

Jane Garnett

In 1898 a French student's memories of Oxford divided undergraduates into three categories: 'les "unvirtuous"' (those chiefly at rich colleges who devoted themselves almost entirely to sport); 'les "virtuous" ou "dull"' (worthy sons of clergy, destined for the clergy); and 'les "populars"' (who were able to find time in the day for five or six hours of work and from whom the most distinguished pupils of Oxford were recruited). Wadham was singled out as one of the three poor colleges (the others being Brasenose and Balliol – 'surtout Balliol') which provided the greater part of the meritocracy of 'les "populars"'.[1] In fact Balliol was well above Wadham in terms of degree results and general academic reputation – and was to remain so throughout this period.[2] In 1900, the *Wadham Gazette* reported disappointment that there had only been two firsts, although arguing that the number of seconds was 'the real test of the industry and teaching of a college'.[3] Wadham was certainly deemed to be a poor man's college, where more undergraduates than usual took their work seriously.[4] The headmaster of Bradford Grammar School told his pupil Umberto Wolff (later Humbert Wolfe, who matriculated in 1903)[5] that Wadham was a good college for him: 'plenty of work, no nonsense, good tutors and decent young men with not too much money to spend'.[6]

In his memoirs, Wolfe portrayed himself arriving at Wadham as a northern grammar school boy longing to break away from his background, and yearning for higher culture. But instead of 'the Public School Boys, the wits

Above: *1913 Torpid: L.W. Collier, L.T. Seymour, W. Lowdermilk, J.L. Dodds, D.S.H. Keep, R.W. Shannon, H.P.C. Burton, E.A. Squire, E.T. Wright.*

Left: *Mock Trial, 1914.*

Below: *A group shot, taken before the College dance in 1914.*

and the poets' of his imagination, he found 'a dreary lot of Birmingham day school boys, who talked nothing but rugger-smut, and couldn't even then get into the University trial games'. The JCR he found to be hearty supporters of the St Andrew's Guild, an evangelical society the members of which were inclined to be 'disgustingly intimate with one's soul'. Whereas public school boys lived in gangs, as if simply moving from one form to the next,[7] there was much more of a process of exploration and establishment of identity for those from grammar schools. Wolfe found his niche in the College Debating Society and Literary Club, where he could exercise his literary pretensions, made friends with one of the first Rhodes Scholars, a South African, and was occasionally admitted to the fringes of smart society outside the College.[8]

The main College clubs continued to be the sporting ones, and Wadham competed in most forms of inter-collegiate sport, which meant that almost everyone had to be in one team or another.[9] Through such team sports – especially rowing – college patriotism was expressed, and

a healthy level of participation was the sign of a healthy college. The Boer War, to which Wadham sent 10 volunteers (including the Captain and Secretary of the Boat Club, a former Captain, three members of the Eight, and two members of the Torpid) was a worthy sacrifice, but 'seriously interfered with college rowing'.[10] In 1903 concern was expressed that men were inclining to the

Above: *College group, 1912. Wright-Henderson is the bearded figure in the centre.*

individual pleasures of tennis or punting, rather than turning up to play in the cricket XI.[11] This was a refrain which was to be repeated.

Wadham had no particular cachet in the University at large. Social cachet was precluded by relative poverty. Snobbishness towards Wadham men continued to be reported.[12] The criteria of university-wide prestige among undergraduates can be measured by the selection of personalities chosen to be *Isis* Idol and written up in the weekly undergraduate magazine. The overwhelming majority of these Idols were blues, intermingled with the occasional President of the Union. Between 1900 and 1914 there were only four Wadham Idols, of whom two were chosen for their sporting prowess: in 1902 G.C. Drinkwater, a rowing blue, and in 1913 Alexander Ziegler, a 15-stone American athlete. Although Wadham had a trickle of blues, it was never a consistently successful sporting college. The other two Idols indicate the beginning of what was to become a slightly stronger trend in the inter-war period: Wadham's association with minor literary and dramatic figures. In 1900 H.M. Tennent, actor, producer, and composer of foxtrots, was chosen. But he was also a hockey blue and had stroked the College

Eight. In 1911 Kenneth Hare, poet, and apparently notable only for being a poet, was a rare bird in gaining University status on that basis.[13] The *Gazette* loyally recorded the College's Idols as a mark of the credit to the College which they represented.

Wadham men were not in general noted contributors to Union debates in this pre-war period. Most were members of the Union in order to use the excellent library (not until 1919, as a war memorial, was the College Library opened to undergraduates), to write letters (which were posted free), and especially to use the washrooms which had running hot water not available in most colleges before the First World War (although it was rumoured that there were baths somewhere in Balliol).[14] Debates within College, however, took place with increasing regularity, and were almost exclusively in this period on subjects of current political importance.

Patrick A. Wright-Henderson (Warden 1903–13) commented in 1909 that there was a greater spirit of earnestness about in Oxford. Movements of all kinds – ecclesiastical, political, philanthropic, social – were numerous and vigorous, and Christianity had come back into fashion. The increased number of foreign students, including Rhodes Scholars, helped to create a less insular atmosphere.[15] Wadham had a shortlived Society for the Study of Social Problems (revived in 1919), in the tradition of Samuel Barnett and Edward Urwick, Wadham men who were involved with Toynbee Hall and the mission to the working classes. This was no doubt particularly encouraged by Joseph Wells, who was active in the university extension movement, the Workers' Educational Association (WEA) and other areas of social reform. In 1910 the Maitland Society for the discussion of political economy and history began, encouraged by the new History Lecturer Reggie Lennard. In 1906 a *club français* for the University was established in Wadham (and attracted some attention in the London press).[16]

College numbers continued to expand. In 1908 there was a record entry of 36, which brought the total nearly to 110, creating an accommodation crisis. In 1909 the custom of sharing sets (on a strictly voluntary basis) had to be revived for the first time in a generation.[17] The criteria for entry to the College still reflected very literally the concept of the College as an extended family. It was a matter of pride that of the freshmen in 1906, nearly a quarter came to Wadham by hereditary descent. 'Happy is the college in which the "generations" are "linked each to each" by such ties.'[18]

Wadham men, the majority of whom had read Greats, History, Theology or Law in the 1900–14 period,[19] left to take up a wide range of occupations. Wells wrote a letter to the *Daily Mail* in 1912 in response to a series of articles attacking English public school and university education as fitting a man for nothing but teaching and the civil service. Wells cited the career destinations of the 155 men admitted to Wadham from October 1903 to June 1908: 37 had been ordained (5 as Nonconformist ministers); 29 had gone into various branches of the Home, Colonial and Indian Services; 20 had gone into teaching; 18 had gone into Law; 12 into business; 7 had become

university teachers and researchers; 4 doctors; 2 musicians; one each into the army, farming (abroad), journalism and the stage; 22 were uncertain, but most of these were from abroad and had gone home. Wells argued that there was a rapidly increasing number of men going into business or the administration of the Crown colonies.[20]

Of the pre-war Fellows of Wadham who did not continue after the war, the most distinctive character was perhaps J.A.J. Drewitt, the half-blind philosopher, who was clearly an inspirational figure to his students. Humbert Wolfe commented that 'his manner was so acutely nervous that he instantly put the most timid pupil at his ease … But behind the manner was hidden one of the great philosophical minds of the last fifty years'. His only published philosophical work was a short article on the distinction between waking and dreaming, and he devoted his main academic energies to a work on Homeric stresses which he never completed.[21] The favour of his company late into the night was a mark of having made it intellectually in the College in the 1900s. Drewitt was a

DANCES
In the cloisters

Four-twenty
    Passepied . . . . Batistin
    Bourrée . . . . Purcell
Four-forty
    Canaries . . . . Purcell
    Gavotte . . . . Mozart
Five
    Valse . . . . Chopin

TOYNBEE HALL.

THERE WILL BE A

MEETING

IN THE HALL OF

Wadham College,

On SUNDAY, Feb. 12th,

At 9 p.m.

The Rev. P. A. WRIGHT-HENDERSON

IN THE CHAIR.

Speakers:

The Rev. Canon Barnett,
Warden of Toynbee Hall.

W. C. Steadman, Esq., M.P.
Of the London County Council.

R. Hutchison, Esq., M.D,
Of the London Hospital and Toynbee Hall.

A. Sidgwick, Esq.
Corpus Christi College.

PRINTED BY SLOPER & CO. LTD., OXFORD.

Left: *A poster, advertising a Toynbee Hall meeting in College, 12 February 1899.*

Bottom: *Advertisement for 'Dances in the Cloisters', c.1910.*

Right and below: *The menu, for a private dinner given by Lionel Collier (1912) and Neil MacLeod (1911) in May 1914. Both served in the War; MacLeod then stayed in the Army, while Collier became chief film critic of the* Picturegoer.

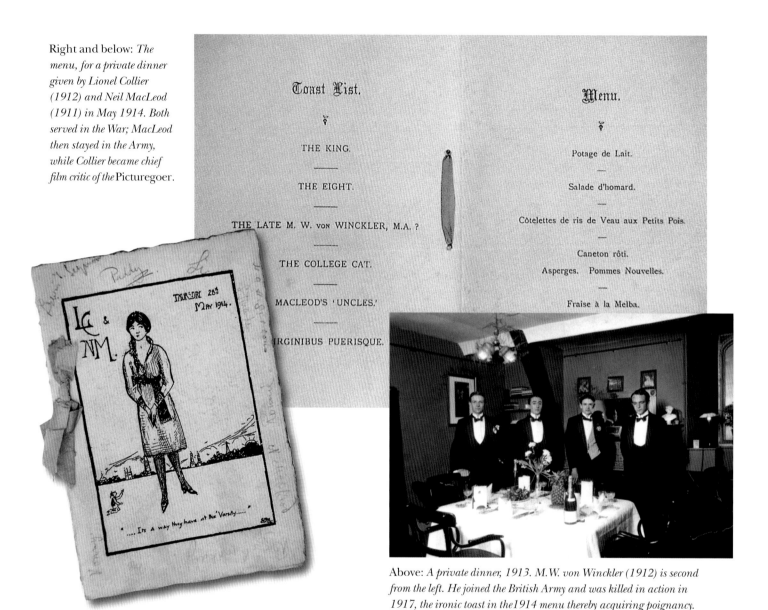

Toast List.

THE KING.

THE EIGHT.

THE LATE M. W. von WINCKLER, M.A. ?

THE COLLEGE CAT.

MACLEOD'S 'UNCLES.'

IRGINIBUS PUERISQUE.

Menu.

Potage de Lait.

Salade d'homard.

Côtelettes de ris de Veau aux Petits Pois.

Caneton rôti.

Asperges. Pommes Nouvelles.

Fraise à la Melba.

Above: *A private dinner, 1913. M.W. von Winckler (1912) is second from the left. He joined the British Army and was killed in action in 1917, the ironic toast in the 1914 menu thereby acquiring poignancy.*

great chess player, who retired in 1919 to play chess, and who died in 1931 falling from a train on his way to a match.[22] The Great War represented to him a tiresome delaying factor in the games of chess which he conducted by post with German intellectuals. Although there were now intervals of months between move and move, this correspondence was maintained resolutely throughout the war.[23]

It was to Wells, as recently elected Warden (1913), that the main challenge fell to maintain the College through the First World War. Numbers immediately halved, and at one point in 1917 there were only eight undergraduates in residence. Already by September 1914, 30 territorial recruits were billeted in the College, and by 1916 Wadham had become a major centre for the training of officer cadets under the supervision of the Dean and Aramaic scholar, Colonel Stenning.[24] For the few undergraduates remaining (some of whom were foreign students), the atmosphere became increasingly claustrophobic.[25] Although, as Wells commented approvingly, the cadets

The Titmice.

Smoking Concert, February 12th, 1914, in
Mr. Burton's Rooms, Wadham College.

Programme.

1. SONGS : (a) 'Through the old city's silence' (from Song Cycle,
        'A Lover in Damascus ') - Woodforde-Finden.
        (b) 'A voice by the cedar tree' (from Song Cycle,
        'Maud' - - - - - Somervell.
        MR. N. P. LEWIS.

2. PIANOFORTE SOLO : 'Polichinelle' - - - Rachmaninoff.
        MR. D. C. THOMAS.

3. SONGS : (a) 'The Song of the Nightingale' - - Brahms.
        (b) 'Weep you no more' - - - Roger Quilter.
        MR. R. J. MACKAY.

4. SONGS : (a) 'When dull care' - - - Leveridge.
        (b) 'The Pretty Creature' - - - - S
        MR. PHILIP BELL.

5. MUSICAL MONOLOGUE AT THE PIANO : 'Etiquette'
        MR. J. G. MONTEATH, B.A.

6. SONGS : (a) 'The Gentle Maiden' - Somerve
        (b) 'The Earl of Moray' - - - Tra
        MR. ERIC DUNSTAN.

7. SONGS : (a) 'I like your old French bonnet ' - Bach (?).
        (b) 'Glorious Devon ' - - - - - German.
        MR. PHILIP BELL.

8. SONG : 'Jean, Jean '
        MR. J. G. MONTEATH, B.A.

9. PIANOFORTE SOLOS : (a) Valse in A flat, Op. 42 -
        (b) Study in F, Op. 25 - - } Chopin.
        (c) Polonaise in A, Op. 40 -
        MR. D. C. THOMAS.

10. SONG CYCLE : 'Indian Love Lyrics' - Woodforde-Finden.
        (a) 'The Temple Bells.' (b) 'Less than the dust.'
        (c) 'Pale Hands.' (d) 'Till I wake.'
        MR. ERIC DUNSTAN.

11. SONGS : (a) 'Jim' (who ran away from his nurse
        and was eaten by a lion) - } Liza
        (b) 'Henry King' (who chewed little bits Lehmann.
        of string and was cut off in fearful
        agonies) - - - - -
        (From Hilaire Belloc's 'Cautionary Tales.')
        MR. R. J. MACKAY.

' ...oved the mountains ' - Löhr.

Left: *The programme
of a Smoking Concert
organized by the Titmice
Club.*

Below: *The Titmice Club,
1913.*

were taking on the College identity and wearing the College colours,[26] this did not prevent them from expressing their scorn of the rump of undergraduates.

One pre-war Fellow, E. A. Webster, joined up and was killed in 1917.[27] For the others, life continued in a straitened way, and they now shared the SCR with some of the officer-instructors of the cadets. These included Robert Graves, who was to retain an affection for Wadham, and even when at St John's after the war, felt Wadham had his primary loyalty.[28] So far as possible, elements of communal life remained, and were in some respects intensified. Dinner in Hall was maintained (from early 1917 undergraduates shared High Table with the SCR), and College breakfast was introduced for the first time (to continue after the war).[29] The excellent College Chef, Mr Tuck, was granted exemption from military service, as was the Butler until 1917.[30] Chapel services

were amalgamated with Hertford, and took place there, for the quaint reason that the Principal of Hertford was senior to Wells.[31] The influx of cadets speeded up an improvement in bathing arrangements. A complete hot-water system was installed in the Old Brewhouse at the east end of the back quad, and three baths were set up, the Warden bearing most of the cost himself.[32]

Wells kept the *Gazette* going right through the war, and wrote to Wadham men at the front, enclosing it sometimes with more practical gifts, like oil of birch for repelling flies. He also wrote to people's families, asking for news and passing it on to others. The replies give some sense of the sustained quality of his kindness, and of the important role that it played in maintaining the familial spirit which he saw as fundamental to the College. Wells was convinced that it was crucial that the University and the Colleges should carry on, and this judgement was vindicated in numerous letters. One letter went so far as to say: 'The *Wadham Gazette* is delightful. It breathes the old world air of Colleges and cathedral squares. If I could, I would tie it to a shell, and send it to the Boche, to show how little their efforts can ruffle Oxford.' As at all such times, traditions acquired a heightened emotional charge: one College man home on leave was horrified to see squads of cadets drilling on the sacred grass of the front quad; another wrote in concern at a proposal that the back quad should be dug up. Here there was a seriousness about maintaining memory unsullied that underlay even the occasional undergraduate facetiousness.[33]

Of course when Wadham started getting back to 'normal' after the war, various changes were either maintained or introduced. In 1919 the extension of the back quad by the conversion of 37 Holywell Street into Staircase 12 began to alter the topography of that part of the College.[34] Various aspects of pre-war etiquette simply vanished – for example, conventions about addressing senior men.[35] Communal meals continued. Their high price and low quality in the immediately post-war period stimulated a campaign led by a 'soviet' of ex-servicemen in 1919, who were commissioned by the JCR to address the rather disconcerted Fellows.[36] Hopes for the revival of dinner and breakfast in rooms (lunch and tea were still provided there) were expressed in the Debating Society on 3 February 1920 on the motion: 'that in the opinion of this House the affairs of the College should be in the hands of a joint committee of Dons, Undergraduates and College Servants'.[37] The College was not radical enough to include the last category, but in that term a 'Bolshevist Committee' consisting of three senior and three junior members was appointed.[38] It is not clear how long it lasted, but its formation in the first place seems characteristic of Wells's flexible form of conservatism.

The inter-war period was one during which Wadham began slowly to blossom. This process was generated partly by a conjunction of personalities among the senior members of College, partly by structural factors and changing expectations in the University at large.

The introduction of University Lecturerships in the mid-1920s began to make it less necessary for tutors, especially in the poorer colleges, to take on extra coaching, although they might still be teaching many hours in college. Reforms of the scholarship system, and the increasing number of LEA and school Exhibitions (in the 1930s half the undergraduates in Oxford were receiving some sort of aid), together with the increasing number of good secondary schools, began to produce more organized competition by the 1930s.[39] In the 1920s it was still relatively easy to get into a poor college as a Commoner by Warden's prerogative. Sir Philip Magnus was an example of someone who came up on the train on a Monday, the term being due to start on the Friday, had an interview with the Warden and was admitted.[40]

In Wadham the sale of land at Southrop (although at too low a price), the sale of land to Rhodes House (at a good price), and the bequest of £70,000 for scholarships by Sir Algernon Methuen (which started to come through in 1935), helped to give the College a boost and enable it to elect more Fellows and offer more help to undergraduates.[41] Although the cost of living was greater for undergraduates than before the war, in Wadham rent was not raised, and College dues were only a little higher.[42] Wells's role in pointing out Wadham's needs to old members – and drawing attention in the *Gazette* to regrettable failures to give to the College – was important.[43] He had also noted in the past a moment when Wadham had been unable to keep a Lecturer (Ernest Barker) who was offered a Fellowship by a richer college.[44] Wells also gave generously himself to improvements in the fabric of the College.[45]

Wells's personality was clearly important in establishing the post-war tone of the College, underlining what was to be increasingly the characteristic sense of 'community without conformity'. He and his kind if somewhat formidable wife (and after her death, his niece) welcomed undergraduates into the Lodgings, and he was regarded with great affection. As Henry Phelps Brown (1924) put it: 'Wells was clear in his own mind that it was a great thing to be a member of the College, not because it conferred a mark of distinction, but because it

Above: *Troops drilling on the grass of the front quad.*

brought the opportunity of forming friendships that would prove lifelong.'[46]

The ethos of the College in the 1920s and 1930s seems to have been mutually tolerant. One undergraduate recalled Wadham as a liberal place, free of rules (unlike, for example, Queen's). Bowra was not rule-oriented as Dean (from 1922 to 1933), and there was little pressure over exams (except that exerted by Lennard).[47] In another sense the College seemed to be free of any particular reputation or character. Nor did there seem to be a great gulf between aesthetes and hearties. Most people continued to lead a 'less exciting but more industrious life' somewhere in between.[48] The aesthetes – in the 1920s especially the literary trio of Cecil Day-Lewis, Rex Warner and Charles Fenby – found their main centre of gravity outside the College. But both Cecil Day-Lewis and Rex Warner were noted rugby players, and were proud of this.[49]

Certainly sport continued to be an important element of College life. An undergraduate's first visitors would be a deputation from the Boat Club. If he refused to join that, he was expected to volunteer to do something else 'for the College'.[50] The Boat Club was the most pampered club, as it was in most colleges. Wells continued to articulate particularly forcibly the rationale of boating: 'It is emphatically the corporate sport where the individual is merged in the team, and the long period of training culminating in one strenuous week teaches the lesson of sacrificing the present for the future, which is the basis of all that is important in life.'[51] This tradition, which

Above: *Frances Mary Crawley, Mrs Wells (d.1925) by G.C. Drinkwater, 1910. She was prominent in working for women's colleges in Oxford, and in the infant welfare movement.*

Right: *Joseph Wells (1855–1929), Fellow 1882–1913, Warden 1913–27, by Glyn Philpot, 1924.*

continued, more or less, faced greater challenges in the inter-war period – not least from the motor car, which Wells felt distracted people from both academic work and College sport.[52]

At a University level, Wadham produced impressive bouts of distinction in cross-country running in the 1920s (to which Harold Harley and Henry Phelps Brown contributed), and also in golf. These of course were sports which could more easily be combined with scholarship, which did not require such long training, and in which the lack of a background in a major public school mattered less. They were also more individualistic, and golf was made more feasible by the advent of cars.[53] But there continued to be intermittent patches of relative success in rugby and rowing, and the whole College patriotically went down to watch Eights. Two of Wadham's rugby blues who made it to be *Isis* Idols in the period up to 1938 were also Scholars.[54] On 8 November 1926 a motion was put to the College Debating Society that 'it is better to obtain a blue than a first'. Vere Ducker proposed

Left: *Twenty-first birthday party for James Furniss (1925), held in 1928 on Staircase 2. Back left: William, a very popular scout. Extreme left, seated: H.B. Arber (1924), later Domestic Bursar.*

the motion and Henry Phelps Brown opposed it.[55] The motion was lost 6:8; perhaps not a completely unrepresentative indication of the slight edge of intellectual seriousness, combined with a general appreciation of the prowess of those who did achieve sporting success.

There was certainly never any question in Wadham of hearties roughing up cello players or members of the Labour Club. 'We felt ourselves all (including the dons, four of whom were bachelors) to be members of Wadham College. This conferred a kind of citizenship that protected each and all of us, even those of us who were not "the right sort".'[56] This sense of community incorporated College Servants, whose success in intercollegiate sport seems to have been more consistent than that of the undergraduates, and was felt to be a credit to the College. Green and Duke won the Servants' Bowls Championship regularly for more than a decade.[57] As well as sporting clubs, particularly popular were the play-reading society and the Wadham Book Club, both of which actively involved senior members. There was an Olympic Club, which sported blue waistcoats and whose rationale was to

have dinners and get drunk, but this catered to a very small portion of the better-off members of the College.[58]

Political differences did not create polarization within the College either. At the time of the General Strike, there was no official College line (or even a semi-official one such as that which operated in Brasenose, where all but eight undergraduates volunteered as strike-breakers).[59] Individuals made up their own minds. Some went to Hull to drive trams (Bowra, as Dean, having given them *exeats*). Others went to Holywell Street to help Douglas Cole work for the trade unions. Others supported the Master of Balliol's promotion of the Archbishop of Canterbury's scheme for mediation. Wade-Gery lent his car to this group. Some, like Charles Fenby, stayed in College and worked. There was a sense of perplexity and potential radicalism, but no one was sufficiently politicized for this to outlive the Strike.[60] By the early 1930s there was a higher level of political awareness and involvement generally. Charles Fenby (by then editor of the *Oxford Mail*) deplored the fact that political buttonholers had taken over by 1934 from sports representatives, distracting from the cause of creative literature in Oxford.[61] The focus of this activity was mostly outside the College. The Union rose in popularity as a debating forum again, and the College Debating Society lapsed into a succession of frivolous motions. Wadham seems to have gone on being a collection of individuals – from Michael Foot to George Devine – who committed themselves to different things outside the College, without ignoring the College. The encomium on Michael Foot as *Isis* Idol in 1933 – much less formulaic than most – in many ways gets the emphasis right. It stressed how popular his election as President of the Union was, because 'He was never "the Union man", but always Michael Foot, an Exhibitioner of Wadham and a leading light in the Liberal

Club, who was always good company, who played for his College and his native village at football, and who also made the best speech at the Union'.[62]

There was a spate of new Fellows in the immediately post-war years. In 1919 Wade-Gery (Ancient History), Lindemann (Dr Lee's Professor of Natural Philosophy), Jacks (Classics) and Lennard (who had been a Lecturer in History before the war) were installed; in 1920 Frank Brabant arrived as Fellow in Philosophy and Chaplain; in 1922 Bowra was elected to replace Jacks (who had gone to be the youngest ever Headmaster of Mill Hill) as Classics Tutor and Dean; and in 1924 Lord David Cecil (History)

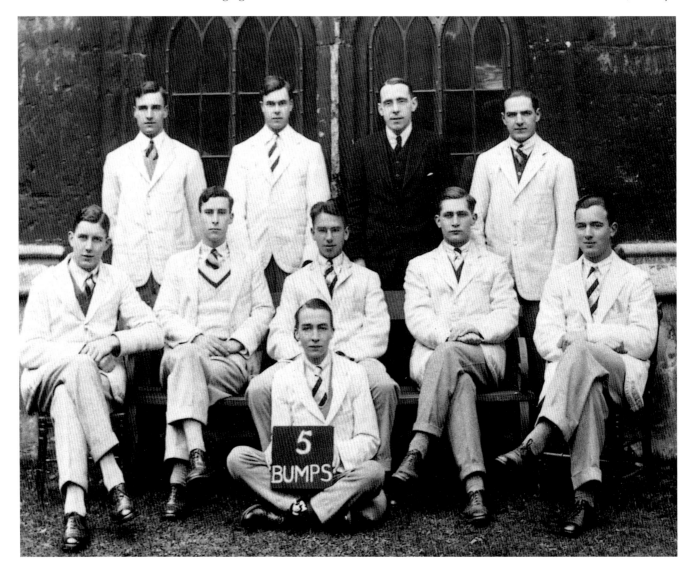

THE ISIS

October 18th, 1933

ISIS IDOL

No. 823.

MICHAEL FOOT (Wadham),
President of the Union.

No election to the Presidency of the Union has been so popular as that of Michael Foot, but few people thought to congratulate him. His election was too obvious for that.

It was no easy task to follow two brothers who had been Presidents, but when Michael made his maiden speech, in October, 1931, it was clear that the Presidency of the Union was to be merely the earliest of the honours he was to win. Prophecies are always risky, but when people went about after that memorable speech saying that 'of course Michael Foot would be President,' nobody dreamed of contradicting them. It took him only four terms to reach office and six to become President—in record time.

It seemed to fall into his hands; but even those who had had to struggle for office, and those who had fallen in the struggle, did not for a moment grudge him his success. The size of his majority testified to his popularity, and his speeches proved that it was deserved.

It is difficult for the Union man to avoid pitfalls, but Michael Foot avoided them all. He was never 'the Union man,' but always Michael Foot, an Exhibitioner of Wadham and a leading light in the Liberal Club, who was always good company, who played for his College and his native village at football, and who also made the best speech at the Union, whether it was a serious debate or Eights' Week.

You are entitled, of course, to know something of his past. He was born on July 23rd, 1913, an event which so delighted Mr. Lloyd George that he presented him with a cup for being a National Health Insurance Baby. He was educated at 'Forres,' Swanage, where he was Head of

[Photo] [Gillman.

the School, and at Leighton Park, where, besides being an Exhibitioner and a sportsman of distinction, he learned the pacifism and hatred of regimentation which have so influenced his political ideals.

He describes himself as 'an uncompromising Radical.' He hates the jingoism which he attributes to the Tories as much as he dislikes the attack on individual liberty which he believes to be inherent in Socialism, but he never sneers at the views of his opponents. That is why his friends come from all parties. The three main tenets of his faith are a genuine pacifism and conscientious objection to the use of arms, a hatred of poverty and inequality, and a passionate belief in liberty and democracy. He is, in fact, in the best tradition of Radical beliefs, with a sympathy and a tolerance which make him loathe oppression, and which, if they were not confined to the Michael Foots of this world, would make it impossible.

The best way in which the Union speakers can congratulate their new President is to follow his example in their speeches—to obtain a thorough knowledge of their subject, to strive to understand their opponents' point of view however much they may dislike it, to hit hard but never to lose their sense of humour. He is a great colleague. He will be a great leader. Would that there were more Michael Foots.

It was unnecessary to congratulate him on his election because it could hardly have been otherwise. In the same way, it is needless to wish him a happy and successful term of office. We are confident that it will be all which he himself could wish.

Opposite: 1st Torpid, 1925. Back row (l. to r.): M.A.V. Fleming, B.W. Chafy, Revd G.F. Graham-Brown (coach), G.V. Kidder. Front row: D.E. Benbow, G.E.P. Collins, H.T. Fawcett, V.T. Ducker, H.B. Arber. On ground: W.F.P. Chadwick.

Left: *Michael Foot, as Isis Idol in 1933.*

remained the main subjects, History increasingly so, but the range of subjects developed over the period. From about 1922, English had become well-established in Wadham and the University, and PPE and Modern Languages were to be important schools by the 1930s.[63] Although Wadham had a reputation as a Law college, there was no Law tutor until Bill Hart was elected in 1926.

Bowra's election as a Fellow was very close because of a traditionalist pro-Greats versus a modernizing pro-science split in the Fellowship.[64] There was certainly a breeze of change in the College, and an increased commitment to the goal of a broader education. In the summer of 1920, the *Gazette* reported that Lindemann had been giving a course of lectures on scientific method to Greats tutors and lecturers in Oxford: 'a new departure in Oxford of a most admirable kind'.[65] In Michaelmas 1921 a scheme was instituted whereby freshmen were invited, twice a term, for their first three terms, to take to the Warden or one of the Fellows an essay which had no bearing on their Schools subject.[66] This imitation of the Balliol scheme, introduced by Jowett in the late nineteenth century and to be maintained by Lindsay in this period, was clearly part of Wells's broader humanist intent for the College. It is not

and Keeley (Physics) were elected Fellows. Lindemann and Nathan (an ex-captain of the Boat Club) each contributed half the cost of Keeley's Fellowship. Only Dixey, the entomologist and Tutor in Physiology (also Bursar) and Stenning (later Bursar and Warden), both of whom had graduated from Wadham, remained from pre-war, apart from Wells who continued as Warden to give tutorials. It was a varied and committed and, at least in part, a stimulating body. Greats, History, and Law

clear how long the scheme lasted, nor how successful it was. One of the first batch of freshmen remembered taking his essay to Lindemann, who apparently took not the slightest interest in it.[67]

Lindemann, who migrated to Christ Church in 1922, although remaining a Fellow of Wadham, was clearly a remote figure to undergraduates. A prevailing image was of him walking through the quad in his bowler hat and being driven away from the College in a large car, to Blenheim or some similar haunt of the aristocracy.[68] He was clearly a significant gadfly on the Governing Body and enjoyed attacking Greats students.[69] At the other end of the spectrum of pretension was Keeley, known as 'the plumber's mate' because of his moustache, who passed silently in and out of College without impinging on many undergraduates, but who was regarded with great affection by those who did know him.[70]

Frank Brabant, the Chaplain until 1931, was a saintly but accessible figure, who was happy to talk to undergraduates about theological problems, and was a good friend of an agnostic anti-clerical like Wade-Gery.[71] He was often to be seen on the towpath offering encouragement. Attendance at Chapel was variable: very poor on weekdays, although reasonable on Sundays.[72] Brabant seems to have aroused loyalty and to have tried hard to represent the Chapel as the heart of the College, even in a period of generally declining religious earnestness.

The dominant characters of what was still the most distinguished subject were Bowra and Wade-Gery – great friends and collaborators, but intellectually and in person an exercise in contrast. Bowra, while being a brilliant talker and an inspiring teacher, particularly of poetry, was a flat writer and a dull lecturer. Wade-Gery wrote much less, but with great style, and his lectures on the Peloponnesian War were so good that even people not reading Classics would go to them.[73] He was a stimulating and dedicated tutor, good at drawing people out. Both men shared an interest in modern literature. In the 1920s Wade-Gery had on his shelves the first Paris edition of *Ulysses* and an English translation of Proust.[74] He and Bowra shared an attraction to Yeats, and introduced their

pupils to modern writing. One pupil who went to Bowra for Mods work, early on found half the tutorial being spent, not on his dull proses, but on a wide-ranging discussion of English literature.[75]

Wade-Gery was eccentric in appearance: unconventional in dress, he hated wearing a tie and never wore socks.[76] Undergraduates recalled him engaged in digging and laying out the flower-bed in the back quad, and were surprised to see a don doing manual labour.[77] His rooms on Staircase 6 were light and white, furnished simply with furniture from the William Morris workshop. They entranced the young Alan Bullock, who had come from the north of England (from Bradford, like Humbert Wolfe), and who said that he had never seen a white room before.[78] After his marriage (and up to 1937), Wade-Gery lived in Appleton, but still dined in College frequently (as did all the married Fellows), and indeed chose the menus with Mr Tuck, who was a great friend. When Wade-Gery left Wadham to go to New College as Professor in 1938, he was sorry to leave. Wadham was a friendly home: New College simply an academic institution.[79]

Bowra as Dean lived in rooms on Staircase 4. There was 'a forest of Tang horses, Ming vases and staring Bodhisattvas to pass through before reaching the small inner study on the left'.[80] These rooms were the forum for Bowra's smart parties, but also for entertaining ordinary undergraduates. Some undergraduates felt in retrospect that, as Dean, Bowra made less effort than he was to make as Warden with uncongenial undergraduates, and that he too obviously favoured the gifted or beautiful.[81] Others put the emphasis slightly differently, and remembered him as being kind to everyone, but specially interested in some.[82] As Dean he did apparently invite every undergraduate in turn to dinner on High Table.[83] He certainly also did his bit by the Boat Club, buying up second-hand furniture for them to burn whenever victory celebrations loomed, and rushing back from dinner out of College to offer them port in his rooms.[84] The non-sporting, non-artistic, non-intellectual undergraduate probably did miss out on Bowra's private hospitality at this

Opposite: *Self-portrait by T.C. Keeley.*

Right: *Maurice Bowra (1898–1971), Fellow, Dean and Warden 1938–70, by Henry Lamb, 1951–2. Lamb also painted Evelyn Waugh and Lord David Cecil, and was the brother-in-law of Anthony Powell and Elizabeth Pakenham (Lady Longford).*

Opposite: *Lord David Cecil.*

period. But he might not have felt very inclined towards it. Even Cecil Day-Lewis, who was taken up by Bowra and who was very grateful to him for civilizing him and introducing him to interesting people, sometimes felt ill at ease and thought Bowra was best taken in small doses.[85]

A more ill-assorted duo, although in a way the perfect foil to each other, were the two History Tutors in the mid-

1920s: Reggie Lennard and David Cecil. Lennard was a medieval economic historian, also – like so many of his generation – committed to putting his historical training to work on contemporary problems of political economy.[86] He was also keen to build up research in social history, and produced in 1931 *Englishmen at Rest and Play*, an innovative collection of essays by Wadham men on

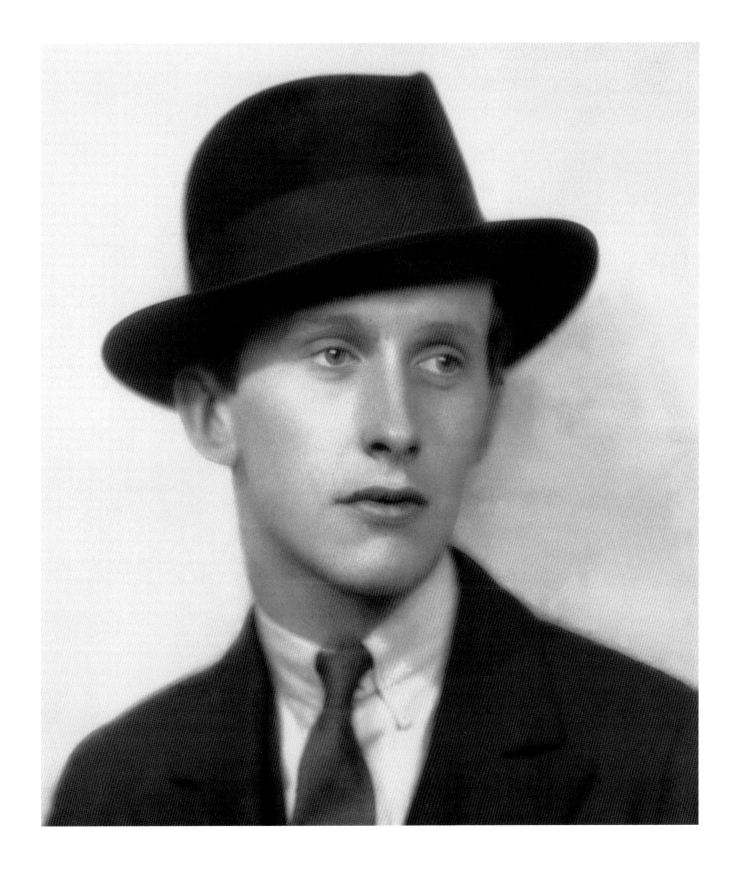

Left: *A reading party at Wythburn in the Lake District, New Year's Day, 1929:*

L to r: R.V. Lennard, C.R. Cheney, J.S. McIlvride, W.P. Baker, R.F. Bretherton, W.H.S. Cowley, F.H. House, A.R. Woolley.

Opinions of Lennard's teaching varied: some found him stimulating; more found him lucid, but rather dull and pernickety, delighting in small points and not taking the wider view. He rarely engaged directly with the essay which had been read out, and seems generally to have failed – curiously – to convey much of the colour and substance of historical experience. Perhaps in veering away from political history, he was too weighed down by his reverence for Vinogradoff, the rigorous historian of the medieval manorial system (whose picture sat on the piano in his home). He also taught too much, which contributed to a certain weariness in tutorials. He was unusual in this period in encouraging pupils to take postgraduate degrees. His influence spread wider than the historians: he invited Wadham men to his cottage in Lower Heyford at weekends (often encouraging the organization of concerts in local villages) and took reading parties to the Lakes, gathering around him decent, able young men – often athletes, especially runners – who shared his love of the English countryside and the byways of history. He laid great stress on the qualities of good fellowship and civility. Clearly he irritated some of the Fellows, notably Bowra, but in fact managed to promote his reforms *vis-à-vis* the entrance procedure and the extension of the Fellowship effectively.[90]

Very different was David Cecil, a charming and gentle literary man, who would take up something which had been said in an essay to develop the thought in a wonderfully imaginative way, drawing out of pupils what they had only half-thought. Henry Phelps Brown, who was taught by him, has vividly described him: 'It was his friendliness, as much as his wit, that made him outstanding as a conversationalist. He looked for response, and

different aspects of the history of leisure.[87] The *Gazette*'s review commented that, at the end of Lennard's own chapter, he made an 'eloquent plea for that humaner sort of history which seeks, not the mere rise and fall of generals and statesmen, but the colour and substance of human experience'.[88] He was passionately committed to raising standards in the College, and evidently had a very good eye for potentially talented pupils who could be picked up from other colleges' lists. He worked the new system well. He encouraged pupils before they came up to read widely, not to 'get books up', and urged them to spend time in Germany studying the language.[89]

because his interest was unforced, he obtained it. Those who talked with him caught the spark, and began to feel that they too were talking well.... He conveyed a fresh and immediate conception of the past.... When one came down into the quad after an hour with him, to meet Peel or Palmerston walking there would not have seemed remarkable.'[91] Elizabeth Longford commented that he nearly always discussed people rather than ideas: 'what made them tick – or fail to get themselves properly wound up'. He could also be very funny – so much so when she first met him that she 'laughed her complexion off her face'. While Bowra to her was the best of all talkers, David Cecil was the best of all conversationalists.[92] He must have been an inspiring teacher. His literary interests preoccupied him more and more, however, and in 1928 Russell Bretherton (Wadham, 1923) was elected to a Fellowship to help out with History teaching. In 1930 David Cecil resigned his Fellowship altogether in order to be able to write. In 1936 Bill Deakin was elected as a further supplement to the History team, Russell Bretherton taking greater charge of PPE. Other arrivals in the 1930s were Ian Gallie (to replace Brabant in Philosophy), and Jack Thompson in Mathematics (E.A. Milne was also a Fellow as Rouse Ball Professor of Mathematics). Humphry House came briefly as Chaplain, but, despite Bowra's efforts to keep him as English Tutor, he left when he lost his faith.

The Senior Common Room, particularly in the mid- to late-1920s, was a lively community, in which affinities developed through close association with the affairs of the College. The image of Keeley and David Cecil redesigning the lighting in the Hall together is an attractive one.[93] The inter-war period had seen a large influx of young Fellows mostly from outside the College. Opportunities were beginning to arise for improving the College's academic reputation and raising its profile in the University at large. The basis for the commitment to grasping these opportunities seems to have been laid in many respects by Wells. Although he was amiable, Stenning as Warden seems, for example, to have had little of the day-to-day contact with undergraduates which Wells managed so well, nor to have been very close to the Fellows. His

Above: *John F. Stenning (1868–1959), Exhibitioner, Fellow and Warden 1927–38. A photograph taken at his ninety-first birthday party.*

Wardenship simply seems to have gone with the trend, and the real energy came from the Fellows. This energy was beginning to bear fruit. By 1938, when Stenning retired, and Bowra was elected Warden,[94] the College was a rising place. By the end of this period, for the first time since 1910, Wadham just surpassed the average of all the men's colleges on an inter-collegiate analysis of Schools results.[95] In 1933 there had been four firsts in Natural Sciences.[96] Balliol was still ahead, but the foundations had been laid for Wadham's development in the period after the Second World War.

CHAPTER FIVE

The Bowra Years: 1938–1970

A.F. Thompson

In 1938 the Senior Tutor, Maurice Bowra, was elected Warden by a narrow majority of the Governing Body as Stenning's successor in preference to the Bursar, Bill Hart.[1] As was still customary, there was apparently no thought of finding a Warden who was some sort of grandee from a wider world than the Fellowship. Dignified, judicious, and a competent administrator, Hart was the candidate of the College establishment, led by Reggie Lennard, whereas the flamboyant, immensely gifted, if occasionally erratic and slightly disreputable Bowra, already at the age of 40 an Oxford legend, had the support of what he liked to call 'the immoral front' – a somewhat uneasy alliance between the more raffish younger Fellows and two or three well-known moralists, notably Lindemann and Keeley, both of whom had long admired the new Warden's force of personality and sheer panache. Stenning moved out to retirement in the Woodstock Road, from which he was to emerge for 20 years and more to delight High Table with his old-fashioned, gracious and often witty presence, commenting freely on the good looks (or otherwise) of the Fellows present and dining.[2]

Maurice Bowra set about furnishing the Lodgings for bachelor occupation, exploiting in the pursuit of comfort a depressed market in the uneasy summer which ended in the Munich crisis. He bought briskly, cheaply, and at times with a degree of taste, advised as always by his favourite supplier, 'the drunken fudger of Little Clarendon Street'.

On the eve of the Second World War, in the words of Ian Crombie, then an undergraduate at New College, Wadham was regarded by most outsiders as 'a small, friendly and undistinguished college, neither a brain-college like Balliol nor a brawn-college like, in those days, B.N.C. In truth the College did not stand out in sporting activities … but it was by no means academically dim'. A Fellowship of considerable distinction, whether young or middle-aged, tended 'a very decent proportion of intellectually able undergraduates and very little dead wood'. This was the result of the inter-war campaign, led by Lennard, to recruit applicants of all-round capacity, whatever their origins, and the effects were now being felt, both in the Schools and more generally in terms of College life. The happy accident of recent donations for scholarships, notably the bequest of the publisher, Sir Algernon Methuen, underpinned the search for quality, both human and scholastic, and kept Wadham 'in the van among Oxford colleges from pre-war days in preferring the ability of its applicants above their provenance'. Nevertheless the College remained poorly endowed, if not poverty-stricken by comparison with

Left: *A detail of the statue of Maurice Bowra by John Doubleday, 1977.*

from those denounced by Humbert Wolfe before 1914. The furniture was likely to be battered, the carpets threadbare, and the exclusively coal fires dusty and smoky. Whatever may have happened in other colleges there was little of *Brideshead* lingering in Wadham. Nevertheless, hot water for shaving, as well as breakfast, was brought up to rooms by male scouts, who could be prevailed upon to look after their 'gentlemen', at a price, later in the day. Lunch was usually a matter of bread, cheese, and beer from the Buttery, and it was normal to dine in Hall. At all times plumbing was primitive, and having a bath meant braving the draughty horrors of the old brew-house behind the Kitchen. Happily the traditional earth-closets alongside Love Lane had been abandoned, and the more enterprising undergraduates luxuriated in the recently installed Fellows' lavatory, where there were large baths available for all interlopers.

That Wadham was 'friendly' seems to have been the universal verdict. In those days, however, there remained a somewhat schoolmasterly distance between teachers and taught, reflected in the traditional wearing of gowns for tutorials, the normality of collars and ties, and a tendency for undergraduates to be addressed by their surnames only. Tutors often dispensed a glass or two to their pupils, if at times in desperation; but entertainment was largely left to the ever-hospitable Warden and the Dean, Jack Thompson, then at his most relaxed. Their sherry parties were renowned as convivial occasions which did much to diminish the gap between juniors and seniors.

Within the Junior Common Room itself the evidence suggests that an easy co-existence was maintained between the academics, the aesthetes, and the hearties – a crude if convenient categorization, but one which may obscure the fact that good scholars, for example, could be talented sportsmen as well. At any rate the atmosphere was cohesive rather than divisive, and this sense of a common identity in a small community, shared alike by seniors and juniors, survived six long years of a disruptive war. After 1945 a large majority of those whose courses

some, for years to come. There was therefore a problem: when would the available finances permit an increase in the Fellowship to provide adequate tuition for abler undergraduates over a wider range of subjects, not least the up-and-coming sciences?

After Munich Wadham was still undoubtedly 'small', at a time when several other colleges had more than twice its numbers. In that Michaelmas term there were some 107 undergraduates in residence, together with a dozen or so pursuing 'graduate and other special courses', making a total junior membership of about 120, less than a fifth of the figure in 2009. Nearly all of those taking Schools lived in single sets in College for two years, an objective the Governing Body had set itself in the early 1920s. Even if they were one's own, rooms often remained bleak and unprepossessing by latter-day standards, little different

Above left: *Jack Thompson, Fellow and Tutor in Mathematics 1936–75, Dean, Keeper of the Gardens and, above all, a highly successful Estates Bursar who put Wadham on its financial feet after the War.*

Above right: *Ian Crombie, Fellow and Tutor in Philosophy 1947–83, Librarian, Senior Tutor and Sub-Warden.*

had been cut short returned to take their degrees, together with many of the officer-cadets, briefly resident in College, to whom the Warden, always mindful of his own miseries in 1917–18, offered a place if they were still alive once the fighting was over. Aided and abetted by the Fellows, especially the newcomers who had also suffered in the services, these two groups of undergraduates coalesced to strengthen a tradition of corporate loyalty that has persisted.

Attitudes in 1939 were very different from those of 1914, when disasters like a major war were quite unexpected, not least in the groves of academe. There were some preparations for the bombing which never materialized. An air-raid shelter was constructed under the Hall and, much to the general disgust, slit-trenches were dug in the Fellows' Garden, while essentially cosmetic protection was provided by the boarding-up of key statues and the removal of the better Chapel windows. What nobody had foreseen, remembering the early stages of the Great War, was how gradually undergraduate numbers would decline, at least until 1941, and how far the College could be full to overflowing with migrants from St Thomas's medical school in London, many from its neighbour, Keble, dispossessed by the Foreign Office, but above all by relays

of short-stay officer-cadets from the Army, Navy and Air Force. Most of these were taught something at least by the Fellows still in residence, and enjoyed what remained of the Warden's hospitality now that any sort of wine became more and more difficult to come by. Sobered by shortage, Maurice Bowra spent his days writing learned but unreadable books, and his evenings at the cinema with Keeley and his dog.[3] Like Wells before him, he also corresponded with those away at the war.

By 1945 the College was more than ever dilapidated, inside and out, and the efforts of a dwindling band of elderly servants had been reinforced by a substantial measure of self-service in rooms and Hall. Whatever their dreams of better things, 'the returning warriors' – the Warden's phrase – rarely complained of being crammed into double or even triple sets, however uncomfortable, especially as lodgings were an available alternative now that the wartime migrants from bigger cities began to go back home. Demob suits did their best for formal occasions, though dinner jackets could always be hired and often were; on a lower level, a tweed jacket and grey flannels might have survived the war. For the most part, however, those returning relied for everyday purposes upon what they had managed to loot from His Majesty's Government, from string vests, badly needed in the appalling winter of 1947, to tattered anoraks in faded camouflage and the ubiquitous duffel-coat or, for the grander ex-officers, a 'British Warm' greatcoat in all its glory. What was probably hardest to bear was the descent from the lavish, if ill-cooked, plenty of food in the services to the starkness of civilian rations in the immediate post-war period, particularly as an old-fashioned Kitchen found it difficult to cope. Something, if not much, might be salvaged by ingenious buying in the Covered Market, coupled with a little bribery, and it was always possible to move on from Hall to the nearest British Restaurant for a cheap second supper.

Demobilization, initially a little slow but rapidly accelerating, meant a dramatic increase of those in residence. The peak was probably reached in Michaelmas term 1947 with some 350 undergraduates, reading one or other variant on the Schools made possible by wartime changes in the normal University regulations. In addition 30 or 40 were lurking about, doing 'graduate and other special courses', not always assiduously. Since there were still only eight Fellows actually teaching undergraduates, as in 1938, this threefold rise in numbers created large problems, though these were mitigated by the temporary presence in Oxford of many able men awaiting permanent appointments whose performance as tutors was often admirable. Tutorial Fellows, even so, had a hard time, glad as they were, like so many of their pupils, to be survivors of the war and able to enjoy the revelry of that dissolute epoch. Having heard 'the chimes at midnight' and beyond, they faced a teaching commitment far above that of pre-war days and, until the later 1950s, roughly twice what is expected nowadays. Not surprisingly, that other

obligation on academics, the pursuit of scholarship, tended to get neglected or forgotten, especially by those Fellows caught up in administration. The back-up for these part-time bureaucrats was minimal: for years to come the College officers, apart from the Senior Tutor, Keeley, who could use 'the day and night nurses' from the Clarendon, but including the Warden, who wrote far too many of his own letters without keeping a carbon, were serviced by a single secretary, while the two Bursars had to reply upon a couple of hard-working clerks who somehow satisfied the auditors.[4]

If numbers had more than trebled, accommodation in Wadham itself and the clawed-in Holywell houses had only increased by some 50 per cent, much of it cramped or antiquated, though heating and plumbing were being

Left: *In the summer of 1941 G.M. McInnes, Reader in Imperial History at Bristol University, organised holidays in Oxford colleges for people from Bristol, one of Britain's worst-bombed cities.*

In the Gardens: They Rest and Play
Everything is done for the Bristol housewife, staying in Wadham College. All she has to do is rest and look after her children.

greatly improved so far as building restrictions would allow in the years of post-war stringency. Hope had emerged of creating new rooms, but this was postponed until the Goddard Building was opened with 30 single sets in 1953, followed by the takeover of the hotel section of the King's Arms in 1962, which, mercifully, spared most of the ground floor for its long-established convivial purposes, even though the tenants prematurely abandoned their bar-billiard tables. Meanwhile, there remained powerful arguments for reducing the inflated size of the College, for academic as well as social reasons. Given the burden on weary Tutorial Fellows, it was agreed in 1949 that 'perhaps the ideal figure for membership is about 250'. In fact, the undergraduate total rarely fell below about 275, and the tendency was for the number of graduate students to increase, even before the dramatic rise in the 1960s.

Admissions were gradually brought under some sort of control. Traditionally, Heads of House had great power in this area, and Maurice Bowra used his freedom to considerable effect during and after the war. Having survived a damaging session at White's or the Athenaeum with the likes of Cyril Connolly and Evelyn Waugh, legend has it that he frequently recruited young men, often of promise, on the train from Paddington. Whatever its products, a tough-minded group of Tutorial Fellows was not prepared to allow this dominance to continue. When the Warden was given leave to be Charles Eliot Norton Professor at Harvard in 1948–49, a great honour, there was a palace revolution in his absence, somewhat unfair in that he was sending his colleagues generous food parcels at a time when they and their families longed for a little luxury. Henceforward admissions were essentially determined by those who would have to teach the young they had chosen, usually through the annual Scholarship Examination. Over the next 40 years and more, as a series of changes in the inter-collegiate arrangements for entrance proliferated, Wadham adhered to a simple principle: those to be taught must be selected by those who will teach them.

In the recent past the College, with its vaguely West Country reputation, has had in fact few connections with the home of its founders, though Dorothy Wadham's Petre

estates in Essex remain a crucial part of the endowment. For Scholarship purposes there was only a meagre award from King's School, Bruton. Much more important, in both financial and academic terms, were the Philip Wright Exhibitions, confined to those from Manchester Grammar School, for long the greatest of scholastic powerhouses, which produced many talented entrants. Together with the large Methuen bequest, this meant that a poorly endowed college was relatively rich in awards, something which gave the Tutorial Fellows real power to select men of ability and personality by shopping around among candidates for any college until this freedom was first restricted in the 1960s, and then destroyed in the 1980s, when entrance awards were abandoned throughout the university. It was therefore no longer easy to exploit the misjudgements of the self-satisfied, notably Balliol, to the great advantage of Wadham, as had been the case for at least a quarter of a century. On the other hand this was no longer necessary. Given the rise in its reputation over the past generation, the College could attract so many good first-choice applicants that it had become an exporter rather than an importer of the talented. The number of Fellows available (and ambitious) to make use of these opportunities slowly increased.[5]

Left: *Maurice Howse (1914–87). He joined the College staff in 1933 as assistant to the JCR Steward. In 1947 he became College Steward, a newly created post which he held until 1981.*

Above: *Visit to a College farm in the 1950s. Back (l to r): Pat Thompson, Duncan Stewart. Front: Bob Williams, Maurice Bowra, Lawrence Stone, Ben Arber.*

The gaps left by Wade-Gery and the Warden were soon filled. Thereafter, from the election of Bob Williams in 1955 until the mid-1960s, most of those added to the Governing Body were scientists or mathematicians, which gave a much better balance between the arts and sciences.[6] What made this possible was partly the ability of the University to provide a growing number of jointly financed appointments with colleges, and partly the success of that idiosyncratic but most effective of Estates Bursars, Jack Thompson, in boosting Wadham's endowment income by astute investment now that the permitted range had been extended beyond the old limitation to land and gilt-edged securities. Quite apart from the contribution he was also able to make to continuing improvements in accommodation, the Bursar could find scope for the occasional luxury, most notably the return of Humphry House to a Senior Research Fellowship, thus righting an ancient wrong. Sadly, House died prematurely, but not before his magisterial presence, as he alternated manically between the deepest gloom and the wittiest frivolity, had earned the esteem and affection of all his colleagues.[7]

In many respects the 1950s seem in retrospect to have been a halcyon period for juniors and seniors alike. Undergraduates were apparently contented in general but critical on matters of detail, especially at the expense

Right: *Pelican on the roof of the Old Library.*

Opposite: *Maurice Bowra photographed in the Warden's Garden, one of a series of 'Oxford characters' taken by Norman Parkinson for* Vogue *in 1951. Parkinson later wrote: 'It was many years ago – but I remember him so well – he hopped about on that lawn like a puffed up robin redbreast on a chilly day. Lovely man.'*

of successive Domestic Bursars. Grants were adequate and parents rarely failed to pay their share; dress remained conventional, coupled with a distressing though declining tendency to address one's tutor as 'sir'; and in the early years at least attendance at Chapel was often substantial. In the aftermath of war athletics had flourished through the skills of men like Philip Morgan, Gordon Philo and Charles Wenden, together with the majestic, impossibly tall members of the Mara family from Fiji. Now most blues were won in rugby under the leadership of the redoubtable John Currie, who acquired more than twenty caps as an English international second-row forward living up to the low standards of decency expected of such mammoths.[8]

Culturally, there was also a renaissance, promoted in many cases by those who could combine academic success with literary or theatrical expertise. How far this was a by-product of a sharp-eyed, rigorous process of selection is a nice question; but few colleges could match Wadham's good fortune in attracting so remarkable a 'nest of singing birds' as that of the 1950s and early 1960s. Their distinguished precedessors, Lindsay Anderson and Tony

Richardson, had given their time largely to the OUDS; now loyalty back home was the order of the day and most agreeable were its results in the plays and revues then so frequent. In roughly chronological order, respects must be paid to the services of John Gross, Michael Barnes, Julian Mitchell, Hamish Carmichael, John Caute, Melvyn Bragg, Alan Coren, Simon Brett and Stoddard Lincoln – the New Yorker who rediscovered and staged John Eccles's opera, *Semele* – in adding to our gaiety, still an unambiguous term in those far-off days. None of this prevented them or their contemporaries from producing greatly improved results in the Schools, led initially by Mathematics and Modern History successes, which were the basis of the College's modern reputation as a high-powered educational institution.

Meanwhile the Fellows were also enjoying themselves. Tutorial loads were slowly lightened and salaries modestly increased. Food at High Table, whatever the suffering of those lower down the Hall, was delectable and wine, brilliantly if improbably selected by Reggie Lennard, was still absurdly cheap by present-day standards. The cooking was done by two outstanding Chefs who were,

alas, disastrous managers of the Kitchen and lacked the control of costs required. Henry Millin – poached by Maurice Bowra from Corpus in 1942 as worthy to succeed the renowned Tuck – regularly produced menus of two- or three-star Michelin quality. The successor he had trained, Gilbert Humphreys, may gradually have shed a star or two, but this did not deter even the most epicurean of guests from accepting an invitation to dine at Wadham. They knew (or had learnt) that an excellent meal was likely to be followed by an always lively and often scintillating session in Common Room, dominated by the Warden, then in his prime as a conversationalist and raconteur. Not surprisingly, a group of nine or ten Fellows turned up on most weekday evenings, leaving their unfortunate wives to cope with the children and subsist on cold shape in the gloomier recesses of North Oxford.

Essentially, this central group of Tutorial Fellows ran the College and determined its policies. This was not apparent to outside observers or indeed old members, since Maurice Bowra continued to talk of 'my College', like any immodest Victorian squire asserting his prerogatives. The reality was different. After the palace revolution of 1948–9 over admissions, the Warden's powers were slowly eroded, especially after his unexpected accession to the Vice-Chancellorship in 1951, when his predecessor, the drunken Stallybrass, fell out of a train at Didcot. He was to remain a splendid chairman of the Governing Body and its committees, always doing his 'homework', as he called it, assiduously; his gift for identifying the best of the candidates for any Fellowship was usually undiminished, though once or twice he had to back-pedal at high speed; and even as Vice-Chancellor he continued to entertain all undergraduates in the Lodgings, and could recognize at once those whom he met (and tackled) during his daily perambulations of the front quad. Naturally the Warden was still *primus inter pares*, but his traditional authority had been greatly reduced if not destroyed. Henceforward, by an implicit bargain, power was assumed by the concerned Fellows, while Maurice Bowra acted as the front man and publicist for the College, claiming whatever he chose to allege, a role he was to perform to perfection, in Oxford and beyond.

The Fellows who mattered were still less than a dozen in the early 1960s. Temperamentally, they were a sociable if quarrelsome group, energetic, and fiercely defensive of their own bailiwicks, while at the same time sharing a basic solidarity in wanting to promote the betterment of Wadham in every way and by any means. These characteristics were best displayed in that curious, probably Edwardian, survival, 'Wednesday Breakfast', when the Tutorial Fellows met weekly during term time at 9 o'clock. By the Warden's dubious definition, only those 'actually engaged in education' attended, which meant the exclusion of the Professorial Fellows. Over a lavish, old-fashioned breakfast, crucial decisions, quite improperly, tended to be taken in a manner which often reduced meetings of the Governing Body to little more than brief rubber-stamping occasions. Among the marginalized Professors, Edgar Milne (who also acted as Librarian), a brilliant if eccentric Mathematician, and the Musician Jack Westrup, were both liable to fall asleep.[9] This was not true of 'the Prof', Lindemann, long since Churchill's Lord Cherwell, a bowler-hatted, vegetarian autocrat of scabrous tendencies, who emerged from Christ Church, crossing the front quad without respect for its grass to intervene, at times to effect, in his reedy, always plaintive tones.[10] Milne's successor, Charles Coulson, a devout Methodist, very rarely spoke, but was respected for originating the College's policy of judiciously admitting a series of worthwhile entrants from the Third World, financially supported by a very liberal-minded Junior Common Room.[11]

By now, however, the days of an informal, relaxed, and unstructured *ancien régime* were numbered, as 'the swinging sixties' and their aftermath in the 1970s created new pressures for change. The Robbins Commission, whose statistician was a future Warden, Claus Moser, stirred up the whole world of higher education, and this was followed in Oxford by the Franks Commission, a meticulous investigation into every hole and corner, majestically presided over by the greatest of 'the great and the good'.[12] Wadham came well out of Franks and the consequential internal enquiries. It was hardly necessary to remind the College of what was well known: that it needed more Tutorial Fellows to service its under-graduates and more accommodation for them. Meanwhile the young, influenced by these restless times, were developing novel demands of their own, like students everywhere in Western Europe and North America. Protests (and posturing) began in 1968–9. The peak of confrontation came later, largely because of the respect in which the Warden, a robust defender of free speech and reasoned argument, was held. In the interim the fellowship continued to grow, and at an accelerating pace. By 1965 its numbers were twice those of 1938 and 1948, and by the early 1980s this total had again doubled to 40 and more. Though notorious gaps were filled, the proportion of full-time Tutorial Fellows tended to decline. Happily, this was offset by the willingness of others – Senior and Junior Research Fellows and Fellows by Special Election – to do at least some teaching, from which Oriental Studies and Modern Languages in particular benefited, while the Biological Sciences eventually secured proper recognition.

Not least because of sheer numbers, there was a new formality (and pomposity) in the conduct of business. 'Wednesday Breakfast' lost first its pivotal role and then its pleasures, as breakfast in the old style gave way to a tepid cup of coffee over modest problems in the early dawn (actually, 8.45), admittedly, as always, an excellent moment for truncating redundant discussion. Henceforward the Governing Body became, as the statutes require, the arena where all important issues are discussed and decided, though some committees, notably the long-established Estates (or Finance) Committee, with its restraining, Treasury-style approach, and the new Academic Policy Committee, inclined to be nervously expansive, retained considerable authority. As the burden of business built up year by year, generated at least as much from without as from within the College, the tide of paper rose inexorably, and the office staff and their pretty if expensive machines had to be augmented, which added to the load any conscientious Fellow had to cart to meetings of the Governing Body, whether or not he had managed to read the ever-thickening mass of minutes and memoranda beforehand.

An issue which inevitably arose in this epoch was how far, following an ancient Oxford tradition, the academic could also be an administrator, thus closing a gap which is only too apparent in higher education's structure elsewhere, on the other side of the Atlantic in particular. For the foremost of College jobs, the Estates Bursarship, Wadham decided to retain part-timers, often to their discomfort from lively criticism. Jack Thompson and his successor Peter Carter somehow survived attacks on their management of affairs, whether financial or aesthetic.[13] In other directions the increased burden became more tolerable by subdivision, notably for the Senior Tutor. Once the academic Almighty, he dissolved into three persons, as some of his functions were delegated to the Tutor for Admissions and the Tutor for Graduates. In only one area did the full-timers take over. As the amateurs wilted under the strain, Ben Arber was appointed simply as Domestic Bursar in 1958.[14]

Meanwhile the number of undergraduates was creeping up, averaging 300 or rather more in the 1960s, but the largest increase, in those hopeful years for anyone looking to an academic career, came in graduate students, from at home and abroad, and especially the United States. Before long they totalled over a hundred. This ratio of roughly three to one was regarded, a little nervously, as manageable so long as something tangible could be offered in return for their University-enforced membership of a college, particularly as even the most eligible, such as Rhodes Scholars, could seldom hope for more than a single year's residence in College. As a result, the Middle Common Room was established in 1962, initially under the King's Arms, but six years later this social centre moved into altogether more sumptuous quarters in the front quad. There, for a decade or so, the Warden and a handful of Fellows lunched frugally with the graduates once a fortnight; they in turn could draw upon the advice of the Tutor for Graduates and their College Supervisors, whose role was to do what they could to offset the shortcomings of those expected to direct their research; and the best of them, especially the Senior Scholars recruited in open competition, have gone on to distinguished careers, in Oxford or elsewhere. These innovations might have proved divisive, but in practice they have strengthened the links between the three levels of a usually harmonious academic community.[15]

For the undergraduates, the bedrock of any college, this was a period which saw the mingling of traditional preoccupations with the rise of a new radicalism, which drew upon the dubious notion that Wadham had to live up to its rarely substantiated reputation of being full of iconoclastic left-wingers. Conventional games were played conventionally, with most blues now being won in soccer rather than rugby, with cricket, as always, the laggard; and something of the cultural zest of the 1950s and early 1960s was maintained, while essay societies flourished. The scholarly (or ambitious) continued to labour for good results in the Schools, pressed on by their equally ambitious tutors, who, however, could be tolerant of probable thirds – and even fourths, so long as that splendidly exclusive category lasted – if they had other talents to justify their survival. This tolerance helps to explain why the College, having moved on to the higher levels academically, never came top of the Norrington Table, that statistically defective construct, which purported to determine the ranking of colleges, although it was nearly always in the top quartile.

Nevertheless, change was in the air by the mid-1960s. Ever since Maurice Bowra's days as Dean in the 1920s and early 1930s, old-fashioned discipline had been humanely applied. Now it began to disappear, even before the raising of the revolutionary barricades, and largely evaporated during the 1970s under the influence of a novel youth culture, which tended to promote alienation from rather than assimilation into existing institutions. The notion of *in loco parentis* ceased to be acceptable, but not without leaving a considerable residue of problems with which Tutors have struggled to deal in their role as counsellors. A few crimes still remained: flagrant disregard of academic obligations, gross abuse of Library requirements, and any defacing of the renovated stonework all featured prominently on the shrunken list. Symbolic of this time of surrender by the old guard was the opening of the gate twenty-four hours a day, which brought to an end the time-honoured

practice of climbing-in, often on the last lap through the Warden's Lodgings, where the penalty for being caught was more likely to be verbally ingenious than financially damaging. Already another symbol of the past, the wearing of gowns for tutorials and in Hall had been abandoned, while blazers, tweeds and grey flannels were giving way to leather or denim jackets, jeans and, eventually, trainers. Consequently more and more undergraduates became indistinguishable from their old enemies, the young of Cowley. Most embarrassingly, those of middle-class and public-school origins could be heard talking in what they supposed to be working-class accents of their hopes for root-and-branch reform, of what precisely seldom being too clear.

Little of this was welcome to Maurice Bowra, but, being a true libertarian, he floated with the fashionable tide and escaped the worst excesses of a difficult time by late retirement, which restrained the would-be reformers, and an early death. In appreciation of his services, which had given tone and a distinctive style to the College over nearly half a century, his Wardenship was renewed, as was then possible, for two years beyond the normal retiring age of 70. Increasingly deaf, with his remarkable powers fading, he hated leaving the Lodgings after 32 years, and died in his sleep a mere 12 months later in a modest set of rooms behind the King's Arms, suitably after a day spent adorning two lavish weddings and a brandy-laced dinner party.[16] By any test Maurice Bowra was a striking, indeed unique personality, described by the Cambridge-bred Noel Annan as 'the greatest don of his era', and even by his enemies in Oxford as something of a Shavian 'life force'. Nevertheless, that brash, apparently self-confident exterior masked an uneasy and complex character, and in old age he remained convinced that he had failed to meet the standards he had set himself long ago and became curiously resentful of what he saw as a lack of recognition, despite the innumerable honours, national and international, bestowed upon him. His many books were stately, bland, and even boring, revealing little or nothing of his sparkling conversation on the astonishing range of topics he covered. The exception to this generalization is his literary and scholarly monument, *The Greek Experience*

Above: *Maurice Bowra and Charlie Chaplin at the Encaenia Garden Party, 1962, when Chaplin (at Bowra's suggestion) was given an Honorary D. Litt.*

of after-dinner speakers to clubs and gaudies. Especially in view of his other preoccupations in the University and the great world, such a performance required appropriate back-up and this he got for much of his Wardenship from two Fellows in particular, whose devotion and efficiency had to survive a good deal of exasperation: the ever-reliable, monosyllabic Keeley – as Humphry House discovered, it was dangerous to address him as 'Tom' – and Jack Thompson, the sharpest of minds on the Governing Body but not always the most outgoing and articulate of men. As Sub-Warden and Senior Tutor, for long the only Tutorial Fellow in Science, the laconic, apparently dour Keeley did for Wadham in the Bowra years even more than he had done for 'the Prof' at the Clarendon, by acting as the hard-working second-in-command, never afraid to say what he thought, gruffly and to the point.[17] More important still was Jack Thompson, who provided, as the ingenious and astute Estates Bursar, much of the financial support essential to the underpinning of Wadham's post-war rise to prominence, to which he also contributed as the most successful tutor in Mathematics of his day. Somehow he found time and energy to take a major part in University affairs, notably at the Oxford University Press, and his singular services were eventually recognized by his appointment as Pro-Vice Chancellor, the first person in modern times not Head of a House to be so honoured.[18]

Wadham's post-war resurgence had been remarkable. A body of Warden and Fellows, still small enough to be cohesive, was united by a sense of distinctiveness for which Maurice Bowra was the vigorous, if not always accurate, mouthpiece. In terms of its role as an institution for teaching undergraduates, the years 1945 to 1960 represent the classic period in the College's history. The College's purpose seemed clear: to recruit the 'best' undergraduates (with little debate as to what constituted the best) and to give them a challenging and liberating education, if not always as academically rigorous as in later days; indeed, with a good deal of tolerance for the vagaries of the young (men, of course). From about 1960 those certainties were beginning to be challenged. To misquote Bob Dylan, 'the times they were indeed a-changing'.

(1957), written with clarity, passion and sensitivity as a last tribute to his first love, the study of the Classics.

In College what really mattered was the sheer power of Maurice Bowra's exuberant, witty, and invariably booming presence, which enlivened every sort of gathering, formal or informal. A superb if managerial host, committed to 'tanking up' after a well-organized day, he was also a very rewarding guest, at the humblest as well as the most ostentatious of tables, and in his prime the best

CHAPTER SIX

Since 1970

Cliff Davies and Jane Garnett

Above: *Stuart Hampshire (b.1914), Warden 1970–84,*
by Lawrence Gowing, 1981.

James Lunt, Major-General and Domestic Bursar, wrote in 1994 that colleges were like regiments: 'they recruit much the same sort of people and do much the same sort of thing, at the same time insisting on their difference from every other college or regiment'.[1] It is true that since the 1960s (when Lord Franks saw Oxford moving from being a confederation of colleges to a collegiate university[2]) colleges have become less autonomous. Admissions procedures have become increasingly transparent and standardized. The University's voice in joint appointments with college fellowships has grown. The financial autonomy of colleges in relation to the University has decreased. Colleges have got bigger. Faculties play the key role in defining what is to be expected in teaching and in research. Pedagogical approaches have received much more critical attention. The university system as a whole has come increasingly under public scrutiny, embodied in a complex range of regulatory structures. The incidence of maverick eccentricity within colleges has been correspondingly reduced. Yet – just like regiments – colleges still pride themselves on their distinctiveness and have a strong sense of individual identity. Such a sense of identity – necessarily subjective and constructed – is reinforced through being rearticulated and acted out by successive

Left: *The Women's Eight at Christ Church Regatta, Michaelmas 1975. Daphne Dumont (bow), Bryony Cottrell, Miranda Stone, Jackie Prince, Martine Ingerhousz, Mary Wilson, Julie Curtis (captain), Beverley West (stroke), Nickie Lawson (cox).*

generations within the College, as well as through the perceptions of members of other colleges.

Wadham is still marked out in the University in ways which have contributed since 1945 to a progressive image: one of the first five colleges to go mixed (in 1974), it established a reputation for taking more state-school entrants than the average. Even before the Second World War the College was seen as friendly and welcoming; it has continued to be seen as characterized by lack of pomposity, impatience with formality or gentility, tolerance, egalitarianism and directness in social relations. Nearly every respondent to a questionnaire sent out to old members in 2008 remarked on these qualities. Such a progressive image creates high expectations, which have (inevitably) sometimes been disappointed in practice – in part as a result of the complacency which can too easily arise from taking such a reputation for granted. Yet the very existence of such a reputation has been fundamentally constructive; its persistence has continued to offer the potential for challenge and creative adaptation.

Undergraduate teaching, the traditional core function of a college, has been maintained, in spite of pressures on the system from an increasingly research-orientated academic culture. Undergraduate selection is still largely done by the tutors who will teach the individual students, although now according to a common procedural framework across the University. The tutorial is still dominant, with more variety of format from the traditional one-to-one model to groups of two or three students. Tutorials have also increasingly been supplemented by classes, both on a college and faculty or departmental basis. Written work is more regularly taken in and subjected to critical scrutiny. Standards of presentation of student work have become more professional, as has the production of tutorial bibliographies or problem sheets. Easier communications – photocopiers, then electronic media – have played their part. So, too, on the part of tutors, has the belief that high academic standards are appropriate for students as a whole, not just for those aiming at an academic career. Newly-appointed tutors are offered training in pedagogical methods, organized by faculties and departments. Students are invited to provide termly self-assessments as well as feedback on the perceived qualities of teaching as well as learning. Several of the respondents to the 2008 questionnaire regretted the lack of such pedagogical self-consciousness in their day. There were comments even from the late 1940s about the lack of advice in the run-up to finals; from the 1960s, 1970s and 1980s about the lack of opportunity for student views on the structure of learning to be heard, and lack of guidance on how to study; about some tutors being humane, informal ('have a glass of sherry'), even inspiring, but not necessarily demanding or rigorous enough. In these respects, whilst there will always be a variety of experience, the tutorial system has shown itself capable of developing its pedagogical potential. Its

Right: *Jane O'Brien, Lodge Porter 1978–91: Wadham's first woman Porter.*

Far right: *The cover of the first issue of* Dorothy's Lip, *a magazine written and produced by Wadham women. This issue was edited by Emily Burnham, Josephine Crawley Quinn and Sharon Mascall.*

Opposite: *Students outside the Bowra Building, 2008.*

rationale – of fostering independent thinking and writing under tight time-pressure, and enabling serious discussion of that work – has remained the same. The life-skills acquired were consistently noted in the 2008 survey. The interest of tutors in fostering the personal as well as intellectual development of their students has also remained fundamental to the tutorial relationship.

The real expansion of the Tutorial Fellowship came in the 1950s and 1960s, with the aim of providing tutorial provision in (almost) all subjects, and somewhat greater specialization within subjects. The number of Tutorial Fellows rose only from 25 to 33 between 1971 and 2007. The large expansion of the fellowship since 1971 (from a total of 37 to 59) has been due to an increase in Junior Research or other forms of early career Fellows, Senior Research and Professorial Fellows (who hold primarily University posts), and full-time administrators (only the Domestic Bursar in 1971, now joined by a full-time Senior Tutor, Finance Bursar, and Development Director). Of course many of these, especially the JRFs, have contributed to undergraduate teaching, but essentially the change reflects the greater attempts to bind those with

research posts in the University, especially in science, into the collegiate system, along with the insatiable demands of modern administration.

Student numbers increased gradually. After the post-war bulge the annual intake of undergraduates fell back to about 80, giving a total of about 260 in residence in the 1950s, and rose to about 130 a year, 450 overall, in 2007 (there has been an increase in four-year courses). There were already 63 graduate students overall in 1954; this increased to about 100 in 1970, and 166 in 2007. In that year Wadham was the largest college in terms of undergraduate numbers, and the second-largest (to Balliol) for undergraduates and graduates combined. At that point in fact a decision was taken to stem this gradual expansion, and indeed slightly to reduce overall numbers, on the ground of enhancing the intellectual and social quality of College life for students and staff. The issue of student numbers in the University as a whole continues to be a complex one, especially in the light of growth in the graduate community. Graduate students were rather out on a limb in the 1950s. Their separate Middle Common Room was founded in 1962, and the office of Tutor for Graduates (Pat Thompson the first holder) was created in 1964. Successive Tutors for Graduates along with MCR officers have worked to promote the interests of graduate students. The system of college advisers is well established, and provides a structure of support in College for students whose academic supervision is organized at a faculty level.

Over the period from 1970 the College has become much more international in composition. From about 1990 there has been a smattering of non-UK undergraduates, especially from Europe. From 1979 to 2006 about four Hong Kong students a year were awarded scholarships to come to Wadham, supported financially by Dr Lee Shau Kee. Hardly any of these hundred or so students would otherwise have been able to study in Britain, and they achieved some outstanding results, especially in Engineering and Mathematics. About half the

graduate intake have taken their first degree outside the UK (and about half of the rest at universities other than Oxford). There have been some special scholarship schemes, linked to particular parts of the world, and Wadham along with other colleges has had Rhodes and Marshall Scholars. Graduates from universities in Japan were funded by Dr Shoichi Okinaga, President of Teikyo University, from 1990; from 1992 to 2008 he also supported a distinguished series of JRFs in Japanese Studies. Recent University and College policy has been moving to focus new resources on schemes defined in the widest possible terms. From 1984 Wadham has had a relationship with Sarah Lawrence College in Bronxville, whereby between twenty and thirty-five visiting students come for a year to Wadham. Their tuition has always been separately organized by the programme director (appointed by SLC), but the students have integrated with Wadham students and have

collaborated on joint projects, most recently to establish a transatlantic literary magazine – *Call and Response* – which on a termly basis is written and edited by students on alternating sides of the Atlantic. A number of SLC visiting students have come back to Wadham as graduate students. Since 1996 a small group of Wadham students has gone over to Sarah Lawrence for three weeks each spring to gain reciprocal experience of their system.

The most striking change has been amongst the academic and non-academic staff. In 1974 only three of the then Fellows had originated from outside the United Kingdom (from France, Iran, and New Zealand). Of 37 Fellows appointed between 1997 and 2006, twenty were of non-UK origin. The non-academic staff have also become more culturally diverse over the last decade. In 2008 exactly the same proportion of non-academic staff as of the fellowship originated in other parts of the EU (1 per cent), and 7 per cent from other parts of the world (the corresponding proportion of the fellowship was 13 per cent). As has been the case in most Oxford colleges, the arrival of staff from eastern Europe (predominantly Poland, Lithuania and Bulgaria) has made a particular contribution to this diversity; Chinese, Asian, African and Caribbean staff are also significantly represented.

Wadham has prided itself on taking a large proportion of its UK undergraduates from state schools (at least by comparison with Oxford generally). The three-year average for 2005–7 was 64 per cent state-school offers for undergraduate admissions, compared to the Oxford average of 53 per cent; even so, Wadham was by that point only fourth-highest of the colleges. Getting to the social reality behind these figures is more difficult, given that a large proportion of the intake from the maintained sector come from a similar social background to the 'independent' intake. Answers to the 2008 questionnaire show some striking results. The sample is too small to be statistically significant, and the categorization of 'parental occupations' is necessarily broad-brush, but a clear overall impression emerges.

The balance between those students with a parent who had attended university and those who had not has swung decisively towards the former over the years, with the tipping-point in the 1970s. This reflects the fact that a far smaller proportion of the population were graduates in the earlier years and that families could be comfortably middle-class without a graduate bread-winner in a way which has become less likely today. Even so, the proportion of students coming from 'non-traditional' social backgrounds

Group A: those with a parent who had attended university.
Group B: those with non-university parents of professional or generally upper-middle-class status.
Group C: those with non-university parents of lower-middle-class (shopkeepers, clerks) or working-class background.

Entries	Total	Group A	Group B	Group C
1940–9	51	11	16	24
1950–9	47	10	23	14
1960–9	76	29	24	23
1970–9 (M)	31	11	13	7
1970–9 (F)	17	10	4	3
1980–9 (M)	25	13	8	4
1980–9 (F)	16	8	8	0
1990–9 (M)	13	6	5	2
1990–9 (F)	16	13	1	2
2000–4 (M)	7	6	1	0
2000–4 (F)	12	8	3	1
TOTAL	**310**	**125**	**106**	**79**

Right: *A Wadham family history over the 20th century: Harry Sherwood and his wife Bessie (Batts), 1940s. Harry was born in 1888 in Wadham Cottage, the son of the College Gardener and Lamplighter, Albert Sherwood. He worked at Pressed Steel and was a union activist; his granddaughter Maggie Jackson became a teacher. In 2000 her daughter Hannah came to Wadham from a comprehensive school in Norwich to read Greats, having no idea about the family connection with the College.*

is startlingly high; and this includes a sprinkling of 'labourers', 'factory workers' and 'cleaners'. Wadham was much more a vehicle for social mobility from the 1940s to the 1960s than it has since become.

In this Wadham conforms to wider social and educational trends. The year in which the highest number of Oxford undergraduates as a whole came from the state sector was 1969 (62 per cent).[3] As recent research on participation in higher education shows, socio-economic and educational problems in Britain have led to increasing and often unbridgeable gaps in academic achievement before children even reach post-compulsory education. By 2005–7 private schools were achieving twice as many 'A' grade A levels per pupil. Over the last ten years the changing government policy on student fees and grants has hugely increased the problem of student debt. Academically elite universities like Oxford and Cambridge have been particularly frustrated by these trends, despite greatly enhanced commitment over the last ten to fifteen years to promoting wider access. Wadham's established reputation for social breadth has been fortunate in enabling it to continue to attract academically able students from a good range of types of school or further education colleges. Nearly all respondents to the 2008 questionnaire, whether from a state or private school background, commented on this aspect of Wadham as having been a factor in their application to the College. But there is renewed work to be done – on a College as well as University basis – to diversify

access (nationally and internationally), especially in an increasingly tough financial climate.

The admission of women has obviously been the most striking change in the composition of the College in the period since 1970. The possibility was first seriously raised by New College, which indeed passed a resolution in favour in 1965, although with an insufficient majority to authorize a change of statute. The University's Franks Commission (1964–5) conceded the case for an expansion of the number of women admitted, following a large increase in the number of women taking A Levels. The subject was a good deal debated in the student press and in the dons' *Oxford Magazine*. There were similar moves at Cambridge, where three male colleges admitted women students in 1972. In fact a majority of Oxford men's colleges seriously explored the possibility in the run-up to the change by five colleges which took effect in 1974. Wadham was part of a trend, with a determination to be at the head of it, rather than (as subsequent self-congratulation too often implied) daringly radical.

The process began with a *nem con* motion in the JCR on 4 December 1968 (in a house of 55).[4] Again, this was typical of several colleges at about this time. It was part of a series of motions calling into question the division between Scholars and Commoners, demanding a say in the planning of the new building, and an appeal procedure for disciplinary decisions. Where the Governing Body might previously have treated such motions with amusement or contempt, the mood in that year of continental student revolution was to be as flexible as possible. It had already conceded the case for a 'twenty-four hour lodge', obviating the ancient sport of climbing in (or out). A committee of five was therefore established to investigate the possibility of Wadham becoming a mixed college. Three representatives of the JCR (Andrew Hodson, John Knight, from Harvard, and David Nightingale) were joined by two Fellows, Ray Ockenden and Tim Binyon. Ockenden had been elected in 1967, Binyon in 1968, so were among the most junior of the fellowship. This suggests a belief that any findings might be easily kicked into touch. Maurice Bowra, however, seems, perhaps surprisingly, to have been accommodating, explaining to the principal of St Hilda's: 'I think my J.C.R.,

Left: Observer *feature* 'Room of my Own', 17 February 1985.

like other J.C.R.s, desire change for the simple reason that most of them have been brought up at home with girls around them, and find it very odd, if not unnatural, to be severed from them; this may seem peculiar to us…'[5] The committee produced in the event a very reasonable and well-argued report, which was well received by the Governing Body. This had a majority of Fellows elected in the 1960s, while their elders, the College 'establishment' of the time, were of the generation which had prided itself on its progressive thinking; any lack of enthusiasm by some of the latter group was masked by the difficulty of finding opposing arguments which did not violate their own principles. The issue featured prominently in the long-drawn-out and hotly-contested election for the Wardenship which was also taking place during 1969. Stuart Hampshire's enthusiastic support helped secure him the support of the younger Fellows and gain his victory.

Ray Ockenden suggested to Hampshire that the issue should be placed at the head of the agenda at Hampshire's first meeting of the Governing Body, in October 1970. At a special meeting a fortnight later, 16 Fellows voted in favour, four against (with eight abstaining and, apparently, nine absent) on a motion that 'the College should become multiple sex', also rejecting implicitly any notion of a 'quota'. The Warden was instructed to call a meeting of interested heads of colleges, which began to explore the technicalities from December 1970. In 1972 the University approved a scheme by which five men's colleges would admit up to 100 women undergraduates each year. In the event, when the first admissions took place, in 1974, the quota was apparently disregarded, Wadham alone taking 27 women (in a total undergraduate admission of 97).

By 1974 the five colleges conducting the 'experiment' had become known as the 'Jesus group', apparently because the Principal of Jesus was about to become Vice-Chancellor. During the proceedings a large number of colleges had dabbled with the possibility of making the change, only to drop back for various reasons. Nevertheless Stuart Hampshire had been the driving force behind the move, and his tactful handling of the interested parties, especially the women's colleges, had been crucial in bringing about a successful conclusion. Wadham's decision was vindicated by the scramble of the majority of colleges onto the bandwagon at the next

Above: 'Clothes line' designed to illustrate the proportion of men to women undergraduates admitted that academic year at Wadham (57 socks to 43 tights). Installed for International Women's Day 1993.

opportunity, in 1979. In that year Duncan Stewart, the most articulate opponent of going mixed at Wadham, became the first male Principal of Lady Margaret Hall.

The effects on Wadham were less dramatic than many had feared, but none the less substantive. There was some increase in civility. Michael O'Day, the Assistant Gardener, commented on how much more polite and friendly the student body became after the arrival of women (and how much less destructive of the borders in the gardens).[6] Although Wadham did not, at this time, foster the rowdy or boisterous male behaviour still apparent in some other colleges, it still seemed a very male-dominated environment to several among the first generations of women. Some avoided the bar for this reason. Following on the establishment of all-women consciousness-raising groups (and a 'Men against Sexism' group) in the early 1980s, the SU Women's Officers in the later 1980s were very active in working for improved facilities for women in College. A policy on sexual harassment was defined and put into place at this point, signalling a more general cultural shift in attitude. Arguments that the first five colleges were anxious

to improve their academic standards was hardly applicable in Wadham's case. Keith Thomas credits Wadham with having achieved 'the most striking rise' of any college, 'from 21st in the 1940s to seventh in the 1960s'.[7] As it happened, only one of the first intake of women achieved a first (Judith Bunce, in Biochemistry), perhaps an indication that there was a degree of strain in their situation, although this apparent academic anomaly was dramatically put right by their immediate successors. The joint-committee report had suggested that 'sporting life' would be adversely affected, consoling itself with the thought that 'the emphasis on sport in Wadham is less strong than in many other colleges'.[8] In the event, Wadham women promptly formed an VIII, which went on to win the Christ Church Regatta in Michaelmas 1975, beat the University's second women's crew in Hilary 1976, and came top of the women's division in Trinity 1976. This unexpected boating prominence helped win over many of the (relatively few) old members who had opposed the change.

The number of women undergraduates in Wadham kept up when co-residence became general in Oxford in 1979. In 1981, for instance, there were 32 women out of 114 entrants. The spectacular rise in the women's entry took place in the 1990s: in 1997, of a total entrance of 136, 81 were women. The 2007 figure was 63 out of 131. The reluctance of women to tackle the more mathematical sciences was crumbling by the 1990s, though they remained a distinct minority in Physics and Engineering. The proportion of women among graduate students grew more slowly, although women made up 23 of 56 admissions in 2007. Women's presence was even slower to establish itself in the fellowship; partly because of a less rapid turnover. The first was Ruth Padel, literary critic and poet, elected to a one-year Junior Research Fellowship in 1975. The first Tutorial Fellow was Christina Howells, in French, elected in 1979, followed in 1986 by Tao Tao Liu (Chinese) and 1987 by Jane Garnett (History). The first woman Tutorial Fellow in a science subject was Giulia Zanderighi, in Physics, elected in 2007. In 2007 there were 18 women in a Fellowship of 58; they comprised eight Tutorial Fellows, two administrators (Domestic Bursar and Senior Tutor), three Senior Research Fellows and five

Junior Research Fellows. In 2008 Sallie Lamb became Wadham's first woman Professorial Fellow.

The other great change since 1970 has been in College accommodation, both in quantity and quality. James Lunt used to claim, with only a degree of exaggeration, that when he arrived as Domestic Bursar in 1972, Wadham conditions would not have been tolerated by an army private. An American graduate student who arrived in 1962 commented that it was like living in a castle, a pleasure which wore off rapidly in winter. In 1976, even after the conversion of the King's Arms, the takeover of Holywell houses, and the first miniscule Gillespie, Kidd and Coia building, Wadham accommodated 174 students: 95 first year undergraduates, 53 other undergraduates, and only 24 graduates. By 2007, with the new library building (1977), the Bowra Building of 1991–2, and the Merifield development off-site in Summertown (1997), the total accommodation rose to 350 undergraduates (out of 446), and 84 (of 166) graduates.[9] The same period saw a large extension of catering facilities, and the building of the large new College Library (1977). The questionnaire elicited pretty consistent complaints (though particularly vehemently from the 1950s to 1970s) about the College food (the improvement recorded by some in the early 1980s being qualified by specific memories of the mushrooms *à la grecque*, rock-hard baked potatoes on Sundays and the SU vote to ban the rum baba), in spite of valiant efforts by Domestic Bursars, Catering Managers and Chefs.

It is difficult to document something as intangible as College atmosphere. Nevertheless, the 2008 questionnaire produced some vivid and telling material. Almost all claim to have applied to Wadham because of its 'progressive', 'left-wing' reputation, with frequent reference to a lack of 'stuffiness'. There are repeated references to social and intellectual radicalism, to ethical engagement, to a lack of conformism (without undue pressure to be nonconformist). One student who matriculated in 2000 observed that it was the College about which everyone else in the University had a view – the opposite of a grey college – that it was relaxed, political and activist. This has never meant, however, a uniform passion for student politics, or indeed homogeneity in type of political allegiance.

Duncan Enright, writing in 1994 about his time as Student Union President ten years earlier, claimed that the SU banner had fallen apart after twenty demonstrations in one year. Wadham's politics showed 'discipline and energy', as opposed to Balliol's energetic indiscipline. But the left-wing image per se was misleading. About fifty students on average attended SU meetings (although controversial issues could always pack the JCR). What most characterized Wadham was a determination 'to be bloody-minded and different'. In general he saw some decline in student activism from about 1970, with a revival in the 1980s, particularly during the miners' strike of 1984–5.[10] One respondent remembered the fund-raising activities then, and the fashion for pretending to be working-class. Middle-class intellectual socialism had always had the potential to irritate the genuinely working-class, and one student at Wadham in the mid-1970s reckoned that 'we were all academic Marxists and never joined anything'. The introduction of tuition fees in 1998 gave a more focused edge to some aspects of student discontent. But Wadham involvement remained strong in more altruistic

Opposite and above: *Wadstock. Robin McCleery (above), then Dean, playing with Dot's Funk Odyssey, 2007.*

Below right: *Visit of Nelson Mandela to Wadham in 1997. Here accompanied by Farhan Nizami, Director of the Oxford Centre for Islamic Studies, and former Wadham doctoral student in History (matric. 1979).*

aspects of protest, rising (along with student engagement more broadly) from the late 1990s. There was a significant Wadham presence in the 2003 demonstrations against war in Iraq (and in the 2009 ones over Gaza), as well as in protests relating to government policies on armaments, on asylum-seekers, and on environmentalism and climate change. Wadham has hosted the Oxford Radical Forum – two days of workshops and seminars involving high-profile members of the radical left – in 2008 and 2009.

Wadham acquired a Student Union (in place of an institutional JCR) in 1977, and is still the only college to have made the change; the difference is recondite, but symbolic. Concern for minorities (women included in that category) is a leitmotif. The first edition of *Dorothy's Lip*, a magazine produced by Wadham women since 1993 noted that 'all the OUSU Women's Officers ever have been Wadham women' and that Wadham had recently set up a Black Women's Group.[11] The SU commissioned a Queer Week in 1996, the origin of the popular Wadham Queer Bop, which became an Oxford institution. So, too, the Trinity Term day-long music festival, Wadstock, has flourished since 1981. From 2004 the headline band has been Dot's Funk Odyssey, which formed initially for

Wadstock, and has since become established. Although the unofficial designation of a 'Ho Chi Minh quad' in the 1970s has faded a little from popular memory (although still flagged up in the publicity for the Oxford Radical Forum in 2009), the singing of 'Free Nelson Mandela' has persisted as the winding-up ritual of college bops, to the amusement of President Mandela when he visited the college in 1997.

One striking feature of the College over the last forty years has been the prominence of the Chapel. As with politics, religion has been very much a minority pursuit, but one with a prominent profile in college. This has been due to a succession of young, open-minded, non-judgmental Chaplains who have made themselves accessible to the whole College, students and domestic staff, believers and unbelievers alike; in striking contrast to the evangelical 'missions' of pre-war and immediately post-war years. The tradition (since 1931) of short-term appointments was broken in 2007 when Harriet Harris was given a permanent appointment.

The Chapel, liaising closely with the SU and also with staff, has been active in the organization of voluntary and charitable work. Giles Fraser, Chaplain 1997–2000, together with Professor John Hirsh, then Keeley Visiting Fellow, set up the Tower Hamlets reading project, whereby

students from Wadham go to a primary school in East London once a week to help children with their English. Under Harriet Harris's and John Hirsh's aegis this project has expanded into other London primary schools, involving students from other colleges in the University – and has also stimulated related activities in Wadham – working with schools both in Oxford and London. The Oxford-based element has been enhanced by the establishment of a fund to commemorate Robin McCleery, Tutor in Biology, who died in 2008. In a new register, such involvement picks up on the voluntary work of earlier generations of Wadham students – in the 1890s at Toynbee Hall (established by Canon Samuel Barnett, Vicar of Whitechapel, Wadham 1862), in the 1950s with the Bullingdon Youth Club, and from the 1960s with the JACARI (Joint Action Committee Against Racial Intolerance) scheme to visit immigrant children in their homes and help them to learn English.

For a substantial number of students, of both sexes, sport has been a major activity. Stuart Hampshire's verdict on rowing has a wider resonance: 'Wadham rowing is a fitful and occasional triumph over impediments, and is the opposite of grimly professional.'[12] There have been improvements in facilities. The old ground in Marston, bought in 1908, was sold for housing in 1977. Its replacement, on land in Summertown, fortuitously close to the later site of the Merifield flats, came into use in 1982.

The Cricket Club applauded its 'superb pavilion backed up by a square … ranked second only to the Parks by a recent Blues captain'.[13] The College barge was sold in 1973 as too expensive to repair. (It sank soon after.) Wadham rented space in OUBC boathouse until the opening in 1989 of a new boathouse, shared with St Anne's and St Hugh's. The Boat Club generates the most nostalgic resonance among old members, judging by the provision of funds, advice, and general support by the Boat Club Society, founded in 1975 by a veteran of the glory days of the 1920s, the Revd Vere Ducker. Cricket perhaps runs it closest. Competition triumphs generally have been few. The achievement of the women's VIII in 1976 has already been mentioned. The men's football team won 'cuppers' in 1999, achieved a double in cup and league in 2000, and

Above and opposite top: *Wadham sport.*

Bottom: *Theatre programme for* Jungle Town, *a production at the Oxford Playhouse by a group of Wadham undergraduates in 1992.*

reached cuppers finals again, although to go down, in 2002. The cricket and rugby teams also won their respective 'cuppers' in 2000. This millennial spurt did not last long, sporting reports reverting to a succession of promotions to or relegations from the first divisions.

Other activities have ebbed and flowed, in volume as well as character. The 1950s were a particular golden age for drama and film-making in College, focused on a conjunction of gifted individuals. Another such moment occurred in the late 1980s/early 1990s, and since the 1990s the existence of the Moser Theatre has encouraged a wide participation in theatrical activities. Music has flourished, especially promoted during Claus Moser's time as Warden. The appointment since 1989 of a graduate organ scholar (the result of an inspiration for use of the Brookman trust fund by Estates Bursar Patrick Martineau) not only invigorated the musical life of the Chapel but also benefited concert-giving generally. From 2009 the appointment of a Fellow director of music (Philip Bullock, who was Brookman Scholar 1996–8 and 1999–2000) will enhance this coordination and encouragement of musical life in the College. On a practical level, the establishment of the Beecham Room and the bands room for music practice has been important (a student in the mid-1980s remembered a terrible piano by the laundry and the ban on playing electric guitar). Self-electing elite groups, a prominent feature of earlier years (essay society, dining clubs) fell out

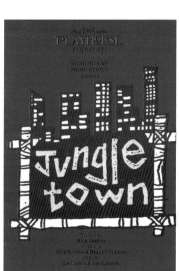

of fashion. One exception has been reading parties. Fostered by Reggie Lennard between the wars, they were revived in 1971 by Ray Ockenden, who remained their main organizer for over thirty years. Parties have gone to Lamledra House in Cornwall, the family home of Jenifer Hart (former History Fellow at St Anne's). Selection has been largely a matter of (discreet) tutorial recommendation, and has done a good deal to boost the academic self-confidence and aspirations of participants, to the occasional resentment of those passed over. Since 2007, through the generosity of the Robinson family, there has been a parallel reading party for graduate students on the Edge Barton Manor Estate in Branscombe in Devon, which was once the dower house of the Wadham family; Dorothy Wadham died there in 1618. Within the College, subject groups get together for informal talks and dinners, and, since the 1970s, the MCR has organized MCR/SCR evening seminars hosted by the Warden. In 1980 the Law Society was founded to bring together students and practitioners, and in 2007 a Medical Society was set up on an analogous basis.

A fundamental aspect of Wadham's identity has been the significance placed on good and easy relations across the whole College community. In 2009 this was symbolized by a performance in a packed Holywell Music Room of Haydn's 'Nelson Mass', involving students and staff (both academic and non-academic), on the initiative of a third-year Classics student, and with the support of the

Some of the College staff, 1993: Clockwise, from top left: Mike Smith, Head Chef; Gwen Parsons, Assistant Butler, and Virginia Parrott, member of SCR staff; Colin Smith, Barman; Mike Roche, Hall Supervisor; Bill Henwood, Lodge Porter.

Some of the College staff, 2009: Clockwise, from top left: Neil Mahon, Head Chef; Gary Cook, Head Butler; Ann Kidd, Deputy Hall Manager; members of the Works Department (from left: Bruce Mortimer, Fred Pledge, Jo Ridley, Jack Kenyon, David Clements, Bob Thomson, Kevin Dawson); Theo Rnjak, Tutorial Administrator.

Left and above: *A group of College Scouts and General Assistants with the Housekeeper, 2009.*

Brookman Organ Scholar; and by a lunch provided and cooked by the SU for the whole College – students, Fellows and non-academic staff (including the Chefs). On a more day-to-day basis, students' experience of the College has been framed by the supportive relationships which they have had not just with their tutors but (and often even more) with members of the College's non-academic staff. This comes out very strongly from the 2008 questionnaire.

Long-standing Scouts have been remembered fondly. Students as late as the 1960s recalled Ned Blackwell, who had fought in the First World War, and who, as one student radical put up his Lenin poster, remarked that he remembered him. His remedy for all illnesses was a double rum. His brother Nick, who had run an ice-cream shop on the Plain before the Second World War, also worked for the College in Hall. Barbara and Arthur Church, and Barbara's sister Gwen Parsons were another family group who worked for the College in a variety of roles over a long period. Willie Coates came to Wadham as a teenager to work in the JCR around 1960, then became a Scout and carried coal up for fires in Fellows' rooms on Staircase 2 until into the 1990s; he ended up as Head Scout, and died in 2000. A reminiscence of the 1950s recalled a Scout worrying that the student was

not working hard enough. Scouts have continued to be concerned about the students in their care.

The Porters have been much loved. Always knowing who people are, and empathizing with their interests and problems, they have performed a crucial pastoral role. In the words of one recent student, they have been 'the glue that held the College together'; another student who came up in 1997 said that she had applied to Wadham because the Porters were the friendliest people she had met in Oxford on her first visit. Other key figures over the last thirty years have been the Gardeners, the Works Department, the Barman Colin Smith ('the college patriarch'), successive Groundsmen (and in earlier years the JCR Steward), as well as the Librarians. Sandra Bailey, who arrived in Wadham in 1986, felt that in her early years her pastoral role was particularly important, as there were fewer other structures of support. Wadham's 24-hour Library opening enabled people to camp out with duvets, and in other respects to think of the Library as home. Her predecessor, Irene McCollin, having masterminded the transfer to the new Library, had pursued a very similar policy, whilst in the best Wadham tradition holding left-wing discussion groups in the Library office. In more recent years the system of tutor as

The Lodge before and after:

Left: *The Lodge in 2008: left to right, Jim Doyle (Porter 1998–2008; Head Porter 2008–); Bill Clark (Porter 1996–7; Head Porter 1997–2008); David Allen (Porter 1996–2008).*

Below: *The Lodge following the restoration of the South Range (2009): Jim Doyle (Head Porter) and Helen Harwood (Porter 2008–).*

well as student peer support has become better established, as well as other resources in the city and University. The Tutorial Office has also become a more regular resort of those seeking advice and support, not just information, and students have also been more closely involved with the Senior Tutor and Tutor for Admissions in discussing student-related issues and access initiatives.

Money has been a continuous preoccupation. Wadham ceased to be one of the poorest colleges, thanks to legislation which for the first time allowed colleges to invest in equities, and to the skill of Jack Thompson as Estates Bursar to 1965 in playing a rising market. However, the demands on the accommodation front, increasing tutorial provision, the provision of Junior Research Fellows, have all created the need to run harder to stay in the same place. In addition, it began to be apparent, even before the Thatcher era, that government would not continue the extraordinary generosity it had shown to students since 1945. An appeal for £200,000 was initiated in 1963, and with it the foundation of a Wadham Society. Secretarial activity was provided by the just-retired Keeley, armed with a card-index and a capacious memory. In 1975 there was an attempt to contact all old members by distributing the *Gazette* free. Not coincidentally this was followed in 1976 by a major appeal to help pay for the 'new' (Library) building. Part-time staff were employed, and attempts made to establish a comprehensive database. 1986 saw the appeal declared an 'ongoing activity', with James Lunt as the first 'Appeal Organiser', part-time but with a full-time assistant. From 2003 the Development Director has been a full-time

professional, and the Development Office employs a staff of six, responsible for relations with old members generally, including the organization of events. Although the initial trigger was the need to appeal for financial support, the ability now to conceive 'development' in broader terms, keeping in better touch and inviting old members back to the College more regularly gives substantive credibility to the ideal of the wider Wadham community.

There have been major benefactions to the College over the last forty years. Parallel to these large benefactions has been the raising of money from old members, in many cases substantial individual amounts, but also the aggregation of many generous small gifts. Without such help, the College would have been unable to transform its accommodation. Its continued vitality in the future, including its ability to sustain the cost of Tutorial Fellowships, to subsidize less well-off students in an age when state support has become much less generous, and to provide scholarships to attract high-quality graduate students is dependent on continuing fund-raising. Wardens have increasingly been expected to play a key role in this process.

Greater involvement with the wider world has been reflected in the Wardenship. Maurice Bowra, although well-known internationally as a scholar, had been very much an Oxford figure. This could well have been otherwise. There was a chance that, but for the premature death of his friend the Labour leader Hugh Gaitskell, Bowra might have headed the national commission on higher education policy in the 1960s. The election of his successor Stuart Hampshire was a breaking of the mould, in that he was the first Warden since John Wilkins was imposed on the College in 1648 not to have been a Wadham Fellow. Hampshire was very much an Oxford figure (Balliol, All Souls, New College), but his career also encompassed London and Princeton. Distinguished as a philosopher, he was very much a man of the Atlantic world and its intellectual journalism. His election split the College, between, basically, those Fellows appointed before 1950, hitherto the College establishment, and their younger colleagues, who formed a substantial majority. The former supported Freddie Ayer, briefly a Fellow (1944–6), an even more famous philosopher. Matters were complicated by Ayer's having been Hampshire's academic patron, and the fact that his first wife Renée had later married Hampshire. When Ayer withdrew, having irreparably alienated the young by ignoring them when he came to be looked over, the establishment substituted as its candidate Jack Thompson, Maths Fellow, an extremely successful Estates Bursar, and a major figure in the University. The younger Fellows were blind to these solid and indispensable virtues, and insisted on the need for an outstanding academic figure. The bitterness of the election reflected both the persistence of the habits of a small Governing Body in which the opinion of each member counted (although expansion was beginning to make that an unrealistic aspiration), and the face-to-face, rather villagey atmosphere of post-war Oxford. The election marked the end of that intensely clubbable atmosphere which Pat Thompson has evoked in the previous chapter. Subsequent elections have been less personalized; and less exciting.

Above: *Claus Moser (b. 1922), Warden 1984–93, by Tom Phillips, 1989. The background is an allusion to 'The Marriage of Figaro', commemorating his term as Chairman of the Royal Opera. The copper beech is that which was in the Fellows' Garden until 1995.*

Some of the warnings of the 'old gang' were, in the end justified. Stuart Hampshire, although always affable and indeed remarkably patient, gave many students a sense of aloofness; the Warden, whatever his good intentions, was no longer a father-figure to all sorts and conditions amongst the student body. This was countered by the warm, though very much behind-the-scenes, involvement of Renée Hampshire with students in difficulties, and her especial encouragement to the first women students. She was also very engaged with the College staff, coming out with boxes of chocolates when people had been ill. Her inclusive garden parties, with string quartets juxtaposed (sometimes hazardously) with donkey-rides for children, were memorable. (Among her achievements was that of having been, it was claimed, the first woman to ride coast-to-coast in the US on a motorcycle.) Stuart seemed also detached in the running of the College, leaving decisions very much to College officers. One Senior Tutor reflected later how odd it was that he never thought to talk over difficult decisions with the Warden. One exception here was Stuart's alliance with James Lunt, Domestic Bursar, cemented on the golf-course; Stuart was fond of reminding his colleagues of his unlikely role as Domestic Bursar of All Souls. In retrospect it is apparent that he had a strong sense of priorities and applied firm direction when it was needed, while having confidence in the general direction of College affairs. Renée died in 1980. Part of Stuart's time as Warden was taken up successfully countering accusations made by some elements in the Security Services about his record in Intelligence, following the Anthony Blunt affair.[14]

The election of his successor, Sir Claus (later Lord) Moser, Warden from 1984, completed the transition which had begun in 1969. Claus had no official Oxford connection (other than a visiting fellowship at Nuffield). A refugee from Nazi Germany, he had been student and academic at LSE, eventually becoming Professor of Social Statistics (1961–70). He had masterminded the statistical presentation which was the bedrock of the Robbins Committee Report of 1963 on the future of higher education. He became head of the government's statistical service, then entered banking as vice-chairman of NM Rothschild and Son. As important, he was chairman of the Royal Opera House from 1974 to 1987. He was (and is) a passionate musician and skilled pianist. He had energy, enthusiasm, and great personal charm. He was a natural and inveterate networker. In spite of his outside interests he took a keen and hands-on interest in all aspects of the College, and was accessible. In different circumstances there was something of a return to the patriarchal aspects of the Bowra period. He saw his role in relation to the undergraduates as being fundamental, and with his wife

Mary he instituted regular student lunches and musical evenings, and encouraged students to drop in to discuss their problems. Many later commented on ways in which he had supported and advised them. Mary, who unlike Renée Hampshire, went out of the front door of the lodgings, was a very visible presence in the College, and helped to implement Claus's other major goal of developing positive relationships across the College. She was the first wife of a head of house in Oxford to be made a member of the SCR.

Ostensibly his successor (from 1993) John Flemming was a very different person; quieter, self-effacing, an Oxonian, from Trinity, then Economics fellow at Oriel and Nuffield, where he was also Bursar. Like Claus Moser he had moved into the wider world, initially with the Bank of England, latterly as Chief Economist of the European Bank for Reconstruction and Development, set up in 1991 to help reconstruct the former communist economies. John, too, was a hands-on Warden. Without Claus's ebullience, he was equally approachable, and offered good judgement and support to Fellows, students and staff who needed his help. His wife Jean maintained Mary Moser's commitment to the College as a whole. One enthusiastic student commended her as 'a master ice-breaker and expert cake-baker'. In College (and indeed University) business John's keen eye for detail did not cloud a steady strategic vision.

Above right: *John Flemming, Warden 1993–2003, by James Lloyd, 2001.*

Right: *Neil Chalmers, Warden 2004– , photograph by Bi Scott.*

His time was tragically cut short; in 2002 he announced that he had inoperable cancer and that he would retire the following year. Obviously in pain, he continued to perform his duties with his usual efficiency and great dignity, dying within days of his formal retirement.

His successor, Sir Neil Chalmers, took up the post in 2004. Jeffrey Hackney, Tutor in Law, took charge in the intervening year as Acting Warden, with his habitual energy and élan. Neil, a primatologist with extensive field experience in East Africa (where he had also taught, and had met his wife Monica), is the first natural scientist to be Warden, with the exception, once again, of John Wilkins. He had been an undergraduate at Magdalen, a graduate student at Cambridge, and taught at the Open University, eventually as Dean of Science, before becoming Director of the Natural History Museum in 1988. At Wadham his time has seen major refurbishment of the older buildings, plans for the conversion of the previous Blackwell's Music

Shop into a Graduate Centre, and preparations for the celebration of the quatercentenary in 2010. It has also seen the appointment of the first full-time Finance Bursar (Ian Thompson) and Senior Tutor (Caroline Mawson), as these offices have become too burdensome to be dealt with in the intervals of a Tutorial Fellow's day.

Of course, there is much more to the College than its Wardens, however distinguished. The College has its own self-confidence and sense of purpose which determines its direction and demands only light steering. Individual Fellows have, in their various ways, made their particular contributions to their subjects, their pupils, and, as College officers, to the development of the institution. The expansion of the Fellowship has, however, made it impractical to try to record the achievements, characters, and continuing eccentricities of individuals. We would refer readers to the booklet, *Tutorial Teaching at Wadham; a History* (2008), edited by Cliff Davies and Jane Garnett, which attempts to chronicle developments in each subject.

College life is formed of intersecting cycles: the three- or four-year spans of an undergraduate degree; the one year or four to five years of a Master's or doctoral student's period in the College; the variable lengths of tenure of academic and non-academic staff. The influx of new students each year is rejuvenating; so, too, is the stimulus of new Fellows. Over the last few years there has been a striking turn-over (and also generational shift) in the Fellowship, which gives a real sense of energy and momentum for the next phase of the College's history.

Far left: *Holywell deck and Staircase 12.*

Left: *Staircase from the Bowra Building.*

Opposite: *Reflections in the front quad.*

CHAPTER SEVEN

The Library

Oliver Pointer

The Library originally occupied the room (now the SCR lunch room) above the Kitchen: kept warm and dry by the rising heat of the Kitchen for the well-being of both books and readers; and reasonably secure from the danger of fire by virtue of the stone vault which carried it over the Kitchen. The fitting-out of the room as a library features in the building accounts, while the foundation statutes spelt out in some detail the ways in which the Library was to operate and to whom it was open: 'only to the Warden and graduates of the said college, each of whom shall have a key of his own'.

Dorothy Wadham herself is supposed to have donated a portion of the first books – though no indications as to which these were remain. It was the library (to the value of £1,000 – some 3,000 volumes in number) of Dr Philip Bisse, Archdeacon of Taunton, which formed the bulk of the founding stock. The majority of these books are recognizable by their distinctive late-sixteenth-century, unadorned, dark brown, almost black, leather bindings. As specified in the statutes, the College and donor's name are found on the front endpapers – an injunction which is still continued. Most distinctive of all is the inscription of the author and brief title on the fore-edge of each volume, indicating that books were originally placed with their spines pointing inwards on the shelves, contrary to modern

Opposite: *An undergraduate working, 2007.*

Right: *Philip Bisse (c. 1540–1613), Archdeacon of Taunton, friend of the founders, who gave the Library some 3,000 books. He was painted at Dorothy Wadham's behest in D.D. robes, 1612.*

practice. This was to enable the protection of books, then still comparatively scarce and valuable, by chaining them to the shelves. Each chain was bolted to the cover of a book at one end and to a rod fixed to the bookcase at the other. An impression of the general appearance of the Library in these early years can still be gained from Duke Humphrey's Library of the Bodleian which retains the type of bookcases then at Wadham: with integral desks designed for use with chained books, set at right-angles to the walls between the windows to allow maximum use of space and natural light. Books continued to be chained at Wadham until late in the eighteenth century, by then an old-fashioned practice, which was necessarily ended by the influx of many thousand books in several large donations. These involved a complete reshelving of the Library with cases that followed the original layout but which bore no trace of chains. At this time the chains were removed, often quite crudely, from the books themselves, which were henceforth shelved spines outward, enlivened with gilt author and title panels familiar to us today.

THE HISTORIC COLLECTION

During the seventeenth and eighteenth centuries the stock of the Library grew through a steady stream of donations. To Bisse's books, predominantly on continental European theology, were added smaller donations: from Warden Wilkins on matters scientific reflecting his interests as co-founder of the Royal Society; from Gilbert Drake, Fellow, on theology; from John Goodridge, another Fellow, who bequeathed his medical library; and from or in memory of several of the early Wardens, and many Fellows and alumni, in the classics, theology, history and topography. These donations created a rounded, typical college library, slightly unusual for its scientific, medical and continental European emphases.

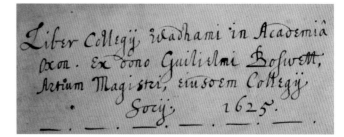

Four large donations in the eighteenth century substantially increased the size of the book stock and gave the Library its particular strengths. In 1720 Charles Godolphin donated about 1,500 manuscripts and books from all periods but predominantly printed in Spain. These had been mainly collected by his relative Sir William Godolphin, former ambassador to Spain. Chiefly of historical and theological interest, they are mostly bound in white vellum, their titles inscribed on the spines in a distinctive contemporary Spanish script. They stand out in marked contrast to the bulk of brown leather bindings amongst the old books. In 1771 Alexander Thistlethwayte donated as many books again, of a more varied subject range, though strong in European literature; while in 1775 Richard Warner, of Woodford Row, Essex, bequeathed his library of 4,000 volumes collected around his twin interests of English literature and botany. A friend of David Garrick, Warner had intended to publish a glossary to

Donor dedication (above) in front of the 11th-century Gospels (above left), a manuscript given by William Boswell in 1625. Boswell also donated the 13th-century Paris Bible, from which this miniature detail (left) is taken. Boswell – the son of Alderman William Boswell of the City Council – was admitted Scholar at the foundation, as part of the deal for the acquisition of the site. He was Fellow from 1622 to 1639.

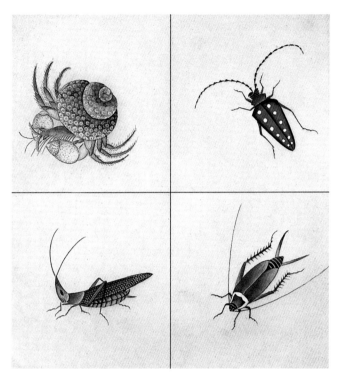

Above: *One of the jewel-coloured studies, from the silkbound volume of oriental plants and insects donated by Warner.*

Above: *One of the finest plates from Richard Warner's personal collection* Icones Plantarum.

Shakespeare's works. To this end he had collected copies of all four early folio printings, together with many other works by Elizabethan and Jacobean writers. His project foundered on the rival proposals of George Steevens.

The great glory of Warner's donation are the botanical items. These include a *Hortus Siccus*, or dried flower book of West Country specimens put together by William Paine in 1729. There are two copies of Warner's own *Plantae Woodfordienses*: one elegantly bound in two volumes with numerous hand-coloured engraved plates of botanical specimens, the other a working edition in one volume, without the plates but interleaved with numerous jottings in Warner's own hand. There are also two sets of large, loose-leaf, watercolour plates of plants: *Icones Plantarum* in four volumes, and *Specimina Plantarum* in two modern folders. These are marvellously fresh and clear, with a depth of colour, feeling and understanding for the subject matter which is quite stunning. Warner also donated a smaller book of hand-coloured plates of oriental flowers and insects, appropriately bound in coloured silks in an

Eastern style. The jewel colours of these illustrations retain all their original freshness. Lastly, in 1783, Samuel Bush, Vicar of Wadhurst, Sussex, bequeathed over 1,000 volumes, a collection strong in eighteenth-century works of all kinds, particularly theology.

Apart from changes to the fittings of the Library and the method of shelving books occasioned by these four last donations, they also mark the start of a gradual change in the way in which the Library acquired its books. Although the Library had always specifically bought a number of books to supplement donations, direct purchases now gradually overtook donations in number. This reflected the increased specificity and seriousness of academic learning that developed throughout the nineteenth century. It put an increasing distance between the reading habits of the academic and the learned cleric or gentleman, from whose personal collections Wadham had so conspicuously benefited hitherto.

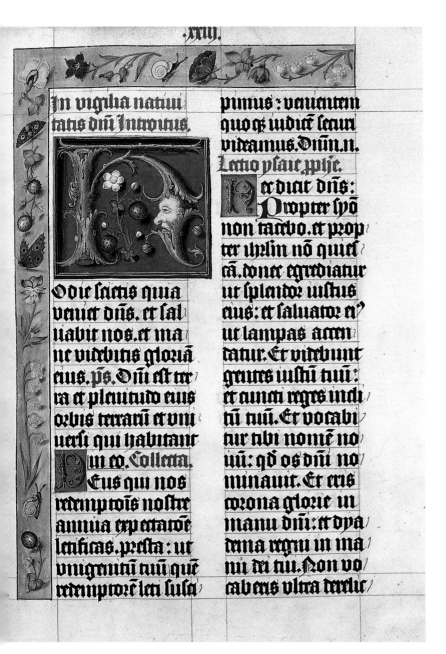

Far left: *The sixteenth-century Flemish missal, illuminated by Francis Weert.*

Left: *The elegant bookplate, of Samuel Bush, one of the four major donors of books during the mid-eighteenth century.*

Below: *Spanish-style lettering on the spines and white vellum bindings, distinguishing the books donated by Charles and William Godolphin.*

There are a number of small general donations from this period: first or early editions of Tennyson, Thackeray and Dickens, together with contemporary editions of Shakespeare and various lives and letters, from Henry King, Fellow 1844–88 and Librarian of the Garrick Club; good examples of nineteenth-century novels, particularly those of Jane Austen and Benjamin Disraeli, from B.B. Rogers, Fellow 1852–61 and translator of Aristophanes.

The majority of these later donations tend to be either of single items related to the College, its Fellowship and their publications, or of small groups of books related to specific research interests of the donors. The latter include the numerous editions of Aristophanes collected by B.B. Rogers; A.D. Rigby's 1933 donation of his collection relating to the French Revolution; two fine sets of Rousseau's works and, in 43 volumes, Voltaire's works, donated in 1842 by G.H. Rogers, Fellow and subsequently Chaplain; a donation of a complete run of the *Philosophical Transactions*, volumes 1–131, 1665–1841, in memory of Robert Braithwaite-Batty and in recognition of Wadham's founding role in the Royal Society; R.B. Patch's impressive collection of eighteenth-century mathematics; and the collection of nineteenth-century social and economic history, including early editions of Cobbett, left by F.W. Hirst, Gladstonian editor of *The Economist*.

By far the largest and most significant donation from this period is that of B.B. Wiffen, a Quaker much interested in the history and contemporary propagation of Protestantism in Spain, received in 1867 largely as a consequence of the presence of the Godolphin donation already at Wadham. The printed books, many annotated by Wiffen, date from the sixteenth to the nineteenth centuries and include early Spanish translations of major Protestant Reformers, which are scarce due to the activities of the Inquisition. There are also manuscripts concerning Juan de Valdes, an early Reformer, and much correspondence between Wiffen and evangelists in Spain and Britain.

Below left: *Page from Qur'an, Iran (Shiraz?), c.1550. Calligrapher Nizam ad-Din Ahmad Al-Shirazi. Illuminations in gold and polychrome, two double page arabesque frontispieces.*

Below: *Hafiz, Divan (collection of poetry). Kashmir, 19th century. Illuminations and illustrations in polychrome. This MS formed part of the Caro Minasian collection which came to Wadham in 1972 from Isfahan.*

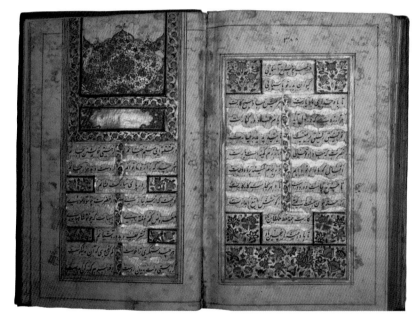

Donations also reflect the quickening of intellectual endeavour at Wadham. There are a number of books donated by Warden Symons, in particular a run of the University theological Bampton Lectures 1780–1833 with oddments 1865–70; his successor, John Griffiths, editor of Elizabethan homilies, donated his small but scarce collection of original editions; while many books written, reviewed or simply read and then given by Warden Wells are to be found throughout the Library in a wide variety of subjects. The bulk of Maurice Bowra's personal collection came to the Library upon his retirement, including his collection of modern first editions – many bearing personal dedications from authors and editors. Of similar significance are the first editions and manuscript drafts by Humbert Wolfe, alumnus, poet and civil servant, whose work was enormously popular and influential in the inter-war years, donated in part by the author and in part by Lady Maufe.

THE LIBRARY NOW

Books purchased by the College specifically for the use of undergraduates in University courses came increasingly to be the main method by which the stock of the Library grew and continues to grow – now at the rate of about 800 new books a year. This increasing inflow of new stock soon made it impossible to retain the entire library in the original room. Older books, particularly those of antiquarian value, were periodically removed to secure stores around the College, many being kept in the Antechapel. In 1955 the main portion of the books in everyday use by students was moved to a new, purpose-built site in the Goddard Building, occupying what is now the Junior Common Room. Some of the older books remained in the Old Library, which also became the law library, while others were placed in store.

This solution was itself overtaken by increasing student numbers and the size of the book stock. In 1972 the move was made to the present Library with space for both the main library and law library on three floors. Whilst the Library's attractiveness derives from the sense of space, there is increasing pressure on shelf-room, although this has partly been mitigated by the decreasing need for hard-copy periodicals. Despite digitization, books in humanities and social sciences continue to be well used, and the Library provides a popular environment for work. The distinctive cataloguing system, derived from

Above: *Despite the removal of chains, the late eighteenth-century refit of the Library followed the original layout designed to accommodate chained books. In the window is a bust of Lord Westbury, appropriately presiding over the room in its period as a law library.*

Right: *The interior of the new Library.*

Right: *The view from the Library over the Cloister Garden.*

Below: *The Librarians, 2008: Francesca Heaney, left, and Sandra Bailey, right.*

Cheltenham Ladies' College (allegedly much admired by Maurice Bowra) remains in use.

The top floor of the Library also houses a significant Persian collection related to the substantial Iranian donation to the building. This includes Persian books, around 800 Arabic and Persian manuscripts and some 900 Armenian printed books, donated by Dr Caro Minasian. A catalogue of the manuscripts is currently

being prepared. The Persian collection continues to attract valuable donations, and is of major importance.

From the cavernous basement storage area an environmentally suitable security stack was created, into which all the older books were collected from around the College. Thus the 'division' between the main Library and the old book collection, which arose gradually out of shortage of shelf space, was effectively formalized. The old book collection, 17,500 volumes, has been reclassified and recatalogued, but it still forms part of the College Library and is open for consultation by all members of College. There are some 90 manuscripts and 55 incunabula or books printed before 1500. In addition to the outstanding items already mentioned, further treasures include an eleventh-century manuscript of the Gospels, with outline miniatures; a Bible with coloured initials from thirteenth-century Paris; a mid-fifteenth-century French *Book of Hours* with fine, though slightly damaged, colour miniatures; a Flemish *Missal* of 1521 by Francis Weert with fine colour miniatures and borders; an early manuscript copy of Sir John Gower's poem *Confessio Amantis*; and a scarce six-volume Chinese story book probably dating from the sixteenth century.

CHAPTER EIGHT

The Gardens

D.J. Mabberley

*with contributions by Matthew Kempshall,
Andrew Little and Michael O'Day*

Compared with the gardens of other Oxford colleges, the gardens at Wadham are extensive, yet unpretentious, a series of large lawns with trees and more intimate sheltered corners. For more than three centuries they have been admired: today they hold some trees of international importance and are some of the most conspicuous assets of the College. But it has not always been so.[1]

BEFORE THE WILLS GARDEN

The Augustinian Friary which occupied Wadham's site was founded in 1268: with later additions, it covered some five acres, much of the ground probably given over to market gardens and orchards. Three centuries later it was gone, save for some of its perimeter walls. A map of 1578 shows the area completely cleared and subdivided by more walls into plots for market-gardening. The City acquired the whole site in 1587 for £650, from a number of investors who had speculated in monastic land after the Dissolution. The southern and western edges were let to various townspeople including a publican and shopkeepers, but the bulk was left as orchards, 'groves' and other gardens. North of these holdings, the rest of the property was let to a butcher, Richard Kenner, whose land included that on

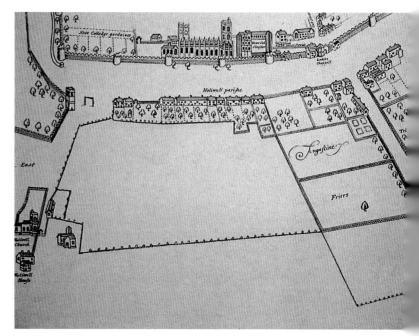

Above: *The site of the College, from Agas's map of 1578.*

which the front quadrangle was built, as well as a 'grove' of two acres to the north, which Kenner sublet to a market gardener, John Burrowes of Holywell.

Dorothy Wadham bought the site from the City for £860 after some haggling, for £1,000 was the original price (see page 14). She sublet 'The Grove' to Burrowes for 36

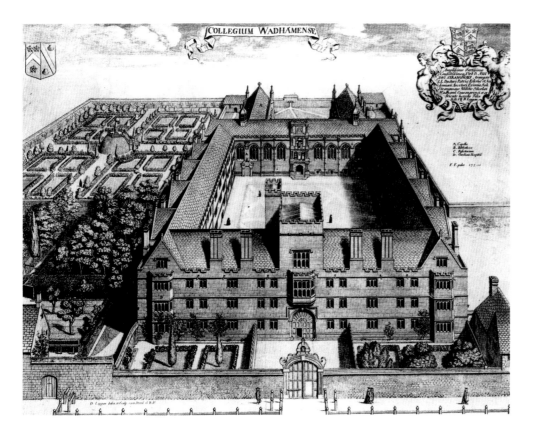

Left: *An engraving from David Loggan's* Oxonia Illustrata *(1675).*

Below: *The water-works at Enstone, below, constructed in 1636 and restored in 1674.*

years from Michaelmas 1611 at a (high) rent of £8 per annum, but she possibly had the future needs of the College in mind, for the tenant was required 'to leave the ground well and sufficiently furnished with apple trees pear trees and other fruit trees thereupon to be growing of the growth of 20 years fit for an orchard at the end of 36 years'.[2] Otherwise, for the immediate needs of the College, ground for gardening comprised only the two plots in front of the Lodge, both now grassed, the northern one being for the Warden (the Lodgings being what is now Staircase 1), possibly the southern for the Fellows: they were walled. The area between the Chapel and the Kitchen was the Cemetery, and the College precincts were bounded by lanes running east to west directly north and south of the front quadrangle. How this modest start led to the spacious gardens of today is not known in any precise detail. In general, only the most directly financial matters are recorded in the College archives: much on what the Warden and Fellows should pay the Gardener and general statements of expenditure

on changes. But we are fortunate in that most of what was known of the Gardens and their development before the end of the nineteenth century was set out by Jackson in his *History* (1893). Jackson saw the Gardens at their most extensive, following massive expansion by Warden Wills at the end of the previous century. Since 1871 there have been some contractions, in particular of the Warden's purlieu – eventually to the advantage of the Fellows, who gave up their own original garden to access for undergraduates and, indeed, the general public.

In 1640, before the expiry of the lease on The Grove, Warden Estcot took in about half of the western part of it for his own use: this more or less corresponds to the piece which is all that is left of the Warden's Garden and it may have been the show-area of the market garden. It came to have arbours and urns, and a talking statue usually said to have been designed by Warden Wilkins, but this Italian idea could well have been the work of Thomas Bushell, who from 1643 ran the mint in Oxford for Charles I. Bushell had created a 'surprise-garden' at Enstone Wells,

Above: *Wadham Cottages, which date from the early seventeenth century, with later additions.*

where incautious visitors were likely to be soaked by sudden jets of water or pelted with soot; Wadham's statue seems to have been the only Oxford exercise in such japing. Evelyn saw it during his visit in July 1654, noting in his diary that it 'gave a voice and uttered words by a long and concealed pipe which went to its mouth, whilst one spake through it at a good distance'.[3] Evelyn was obsessed with horticulture, which he considered intimately related to natural philosophy; his host seems to have agreed.

Four years before Evelyn's visit, Wilkins had presided over the acquisition of the rest of The Grove, which became the Fellows' Garden and which is open to students and the general public today. The market gardener retreated to the next field northwards, moving into the adjacent farmhouse-like Wadham Cottages, as they are now styled, which were occupied at the end of the seventeenth century by the Buddard family, also market gardeners. Wilkins noted that the expenses of setting out the Fellows' Garden came to £72.13s. This sum reflects the cost of laying out so elaborate a design as that shown in Loggan's print of 1675, which conceals the fact that the garden to contain such a regular pattern is far from rectangular! There were parterres and clipped hedges of yew and box in four groups of four around a fashionable mound with steps and a

platform surmounted by a (voiceless) figure of Atlas bearing a globe 'curiously gilded'. Around the edge, the walls held a variety of espalier fruit-trees. Evelyn tells us of Wilkins's transparent apiaries 'adorned with a variety of dials, little statues, vanes etc.',[4] while Plot noted another Wilkins contrivance, 'whereby, of but few Gallons of *Water* forced through a narrow *Fissure*, he could raise a *Mist* in his *Garden*, wherein a Person placed at a due Distance between the *Sun* and the *Mist*, might see an exquisite *Rainbow* in all its proper Colours'.[5]

In 1720, the walls of the Warden's and Fellows' Gardens were repointed, raised and repaired. Ten years later it was agreed that the trees against the walls were to be taken up and replanted the other side of a grass walk, though there seem to have been some misgivings about garden expenditure at this time. Despite changing fashions, however, the overall garden design persisted, though altered somewhat and, if Williams's engraving of 1732 is to be trusted, made yet more intricate. There was an obelisk in the centre of each group of four parterres and a summerhouse at the foot of the mound, but as Parks Road appears lined with ramrod trees of Escherian precision, the rather fussy clinical design with topiary in the shape of balustrading, sundial, and what seems to be a

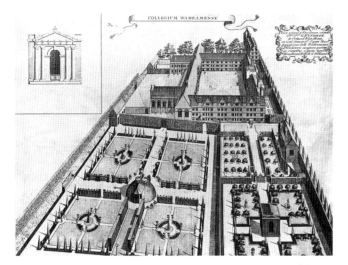

Above: *An engraving from W. Williams's* Oxonia Depicta *(1732).*

Below: *A watercolour of the Cloister Garden by Edward Dayes,*
engraved for the 1795 University Almanack. Dayes taught Girtin and
had an influence on his painting and on the early work of J.M.W. Turner.

camomile seat, urns and tubs of plants in the Italian style, may be somewhat fanciful. Nevertheless the espalier fruit-trees are still drawn faithfully. The Warden's Garden had a Doric temple in the middle of a parterre separated off from the ground nearer the lodgings by a hedge and gates across the middle, while the enclosed gardens in front of the College were also parterres.

In 1753 it was agreed to build a wall along the original northern boundary of the College, and the Fellows' Garden was somewhat remodelled following the collapse of Atlas in a storm and the clearing away of the mound (the gardener got an extra £18 for his pains). The expenses of all this, and of the digging away of ground in what is now the back quadrangle to a level lower than the floors of the ground floor rooms, were paid for by Thomas, Lord Wyndham. In 1777, the Cemetery, which had been little used for its original purpose, became a

second garden for the Fellows and a second wall separated it from the lane along its northern boundary, running east 'to an outbuilding containing a tool house and certain necessary offices for the Fellows', as the gentle Jackson put it.[6] It was agreed that the Cloisters were to be fenced with iron bars from the Library, and the Fellows were issued with keys, though they had to return them to the Warden when they intended to be away from Oxford.

But all this lasted for less than 20 years for, in April 1795, it was decided that the walls between the Fellows' two gardens be taken down and the 'necessary houses' be replaced, the wood-and-charcoal house being partly converted for the Fellows' use and a 'New Common Necessary House' built elsewhere. Moreover there was a devastating remodelling of the Gardens themselves, bringing them much into the form we have today. Warden Wills had brought in the Duke of Marlborough's gardener, Shipley, alleged to have been a 'pupil' of Lancelot 'Capability' Brown. Shipley marked the trees to be felled; all that remained of the cross walls and tool shed were taken away, the timber and stone sold to help defray the expenses. Later in 1796, Thomas Knibbs was elected Manciple and Gardener. By 1801, his salary was raised to £40 a year in recognition of the extra work engendered by the changes.

Clearly all did not approve of the overdue revolution (the changes were typical of garden fashion of half a century and more before). Among Warden Griffiths' papers is a sketch-plan of the garden just before the alteration. The whole of the garden walls had been 'covered with Fruit Trees – productive Vines on the Coping, and below Peach Trees, Nectarine Trees and Apricot Trees – There were Espalier Apple trees (beside the Walks across the Garden) which abundantly supplied the Common Room with Non-Pareils and other good Apples'. In addition, the Garden had a row of lime trees running north-south and separated from the eastern wall by a bowling-green.

Above: *The Fellows' Garden, a photograph taken in 1978, showing the cedar which was felled in 1988.*

Right: *An engraving from Edmund Hort New's* A New Loggan View of the Oxford Colleges *(1910).*

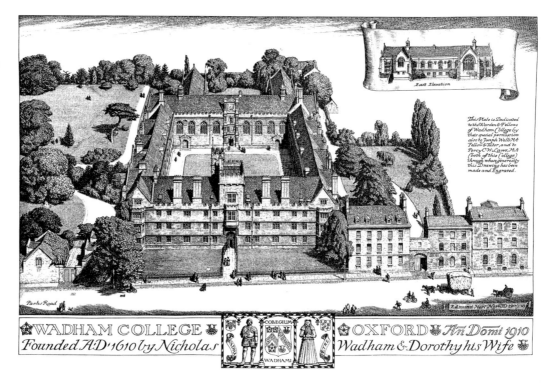

WADHAM COLLEGE
Founded AD 1610 by Nicholas

OXFORD An Domi 1910
Wadham & Dorothy his Wife

THE WILLS GARDEN

It seems that some of the limes survived into the twentieth century and, of Shipley's plantings two cedars of Lebanon, which figure in the *University Almanack* for 1819. One of them, with 110 rings, fell on 25 April 1908 after a heavy late snowfall (cedars are notorious for succumbing thus), leading the Warden to utter a few appropriate words from Sophocles, while the Sub-Warden, not to be outdone, 'relieved his feelings' in a Latin epigram. The tree had been the scene of some scandal, for a Scholar, who went on to become a bishop, was once found in it in 'scanty raiment'. When it fell the cedar's girth was 2.9m. Its fellow was then 2.6m. This was the mushroom-shaped specimen which leant towards the window of the Antechapel until 1988, when it was felled as unsafe. A photograph published in *Country Life* in 1905 shows this tree with a rather more orthodox, if straggly, shape. The curious modern profile was achieved by lopping before 1909, when E.H. New prepared his modern 'Loggan' of the College, faithfully depicting it as it was to the end. Some of the timber was used to make the handsome chest, built by Waywood,

Witney, in the Antechapel. Until recently, the one surviving tree from Shipley's time was the enormous but declining copper beech (girth 5.7m 1992), planted when it was a novelty. By 1905, *Country Life* considered it 'the finest in England' and it had a girth of 3.5m in 1912. It was the focal point of the garden, and provided a backdrop for many theatrical productions. Sadly it had to be felled in 1995. In 1912, the garden was more crowded than it is now, for, besides the old limes, there was a redwood, *Sequoia sempervirens*, a paper mulberry, *Broussonetia papyrifera*, and a tree of heaven, as well as the extant *Magnolia acuminata* (0.9m girth then, 2.3m in 2009), 'all among the finest of their kind in Oxford'[7].

Warden Wills, who at the time was the College's greatest benefactor since the foundation, had a lease of the Merton lands north of the College and south of what had been known for a century as the 'New Parks'. This was four acres of land occupying a corner of the old earthworks put up during the siege of Oxford in the Civil War. At the time of his taking on the lease, it comprised Wadham Cottages and market gardens. 'The Warden's Close' was walled, there previously being a ditch and hedge planted by him;

Above: *A photograph of the copper beech, taken in the 1930s by T.C. Keeley.*

Right: *The cowshed and the surviving apple tree in the Fellows' Private Garden.*

Wills was said to set to with the haymakers (allegedly as an economy), and the 'cowshed' set into the earthworks in the east side is believed to have housed a milch-cow, though the most northerly part was, at least to begin with, still let to a market gardener. Wills's generosity extended, in 1795, to his giving the lease of 'Haines's garden' to the College 'in trust for the use of the Warden of Wadham College for ever': the College acquired the freehold in 1834. The College grounds now extended up to what is now South Parks Road, where, at its junction with Parks Road, a blocked-up doorway in the wall marks the Warden's gate into what were then open fields of the New Parks. So highly thought of was the perk of such a garden, that when it was curtailed on the resignation of Warden Symons in 1871, his successor protested that the major attraction of the post had been removed.

Wills's successor, Warden Tournay, is held to be responsible for the landscaping of the Close and for modifying (or recreating?) the northern and eastern earthworks. He also removed a walled, treed area (like that still in front of St John's in St Giles) between the College and the then much narrower Parks Road. The trees and strip of 'shrubbery' up the east side of Parks Road to South Parks Road seem to have been maintained, at least later, by

the University Chest, but in 1923 the College took over the strip, apparently transferring part of it to the City. In 1933 the College declined the offer to repossess this strip and agreed to convey what remained to the City, with the City undertaking to maintain trees thereon.

Meanwhile, the gardens in front of the College had been given up and the high walls surrounding them (possibly in part dating from the Friary) removed in 1805. They were replaced by a 'Gothic palisade' in 1806, and these in turn by lighter ones in 1822, only to be completely removed a century later, when, in June 1925, a committee was formed to consider the front of College. It proposed replacing the railings with a three-foot wall but if that was too costly with post and chains, though later it was agreed to have a kerb with grass up to it and bicycle racks flanking the approach to the gate. New's engraving and another

Above: *A watercolour, by Augustus Pugin, engraved for Ackermann's* History of the University of Oxford *(1814). The fence of piers and railings was described by Jackson as 'a poor design of "carpenter's Gothic"'.*

Left: *William Tuckwell commented in 1900 that 'Matthew Arnold's leap over the Wadham railings used to be familiar to many who had never read his books'.*

Below left: *Jackson's unrealised proposal for a new gateway and balustrade to replace the railings, 1872.*

Below: *Albumen photograph, c.1866.*

photograph in *Country Life* for 1905 show that there were two large trees in front of the College, a plane near the Lodgings and a service tree, though in 1927 the shrubs on the west face of the Lodgings were removed.

Shortly after the clearing away of the walls, the centre of the front quadrangle was turfed (1809), the necessary scything which ensued, with planting of shrubs under Trinity's wall, prompting an increase of £2 a year in the Gardener's wages. The surrounds were gravelled (renewed June 1769) and it is likely that the whole quadrangle had always been surfaced thus, but it is unclear whether the regular paths across it in Loggan's and Williams's engravings are anything more than artistic licence. It must also be remarked that the College did not possess a motor-mower until the 1930s.

In 1731, the Warden had been allowed to fell the first row of trees in 'the grove' to the south of the College to make way for a coach house (albeit at his own expense) and the next year it was proposed that all trees in 'the grove' be felled. In 1874, the Warden's stables and stableyard and some cottages were demolished; their adjacent gardens were taken into the College, throwing the southern boundary back 25.3m. The Warden's stabling was moved to the building north of the present Lodgings, now perversely known as 'The Old Stables'. Largely at the instigation of Jackson, the area, now known as the back quadrangle, formerly Holywell quadrangle, thus came into a recognizably modern shape, bounded by the Friary wall, now the edge of 'the deck'. Like the front quadrangle, it was laid to gravel and turf, but New's engraving, which shows the weeping lime there, has it bisected by a path from the gate in Parks Road to Staircase 4.

In 1918, the huge sycamore (2.2m girth in 1912), which darkened the rooms too much, was felled, but its stump was not removed until 1925 when it was agreed to erect a wall along the east side of the back quad to hide the buildings beyond, to level the quad, to have two paths across, and, in addition, to fell a large holly.

Above: *An early nineteenth-century watercolour of the Warden's Garden.*

THE TWENTIETH CENTURY

Contemporary photographs show that there were climbing plants on the walls of the Lodgings, Staircase 3, the Chapel and the Old Library, while New's engraving shows two small trees next to the Cloister (one survives) and possibly the Lombardy poplar, which stands to the north of the New Library. There was a tennis-court in the Fellows' Garden, where the bowling green had been, but the mulberry near the Chapel was not yet planted and another cedar (recently lost from the eastern side of the garden) had not yet grown to any significant size.

At the beginning of the century, the Warden's Garden had a number of greenhouses, one housing a Black Hamburgh grape which survives: tradition has it that it was planted in Napoleonic times. The largest greenhouse was demolished in 1903 but this still left two. At this time in Oxford, this Garden had 'by far the best collection of trees outside the Botanic Garden'[8], largely due to Wills and probably his successor, Warden Tournay. One survivor is the tulip tree near the Lodgings (girth 3.3m in 1912, 4.4m in 2009). The holm oak (4.4m in 1992) was felled in 2009, and the huge Judas tree, a medlar (both planted in the early nineteenth century), a monkey puzzle and many others have also gone. In the land acquired by Wills to the north the only tree surviving until recently was a Lucombe

oak (1.9m girth in 1912, 3.1m in 1985 when felled). A giant redwood survived until at least 1951, when it featured in the background of Warden Bowra's photographic portrait (see p.79), a diseased purple beech planted before 1817 was removed in 1977–8, and a great yew fell in 1990.

The greatest loss was deliberately brought about, however, through the sale of the northernmost half of Wills's new land to the Rhodes Trustees in the 1920s. In 1919, an offer had been received from the Trustees for part of the Warden's Garden as a site for Rhodes House and, although a lease arrangement was mooted, the freehold was sold to them at £10,000 an acre with the College having first refusal on any resale. The Trustees offered to respect trees standing on the site and proposed a door or grille to be left in the wall separating their land from the remains of the Warden's Garden: this proposal was declined by the College, though the new wall was breached in 1983 to enlarge, for one afternoon only, the entertainment space of Rhodes House on the occasion of a garden-party attended by Elizabeth II. The North Walk along the old fortifications among the celebrated trees listed in Gunther's *Oxford Gardens* was lost in the building of Rhodes House, and many other trees he mentions must have been felled at the same time. The old path running north from the gateway in the wall of the Fellows' Garden was cut off, and only in 1984–5 was its course curved once more to the northwest corner of the College's domain, now to emerge in the Fellows' car park (proposed 1954, opened 1956 and extended 10 years later) north of Wadham Cottages.

With the change of Wardens in 1938 a committee was set up to decide how to divide the Warden's Garden further to give the Fellows a private garden once more. Twenty pounds was to be spent on the alterations; but £25 was spent on an advisory report alone. In March 1939 the Fellows' Private Garden was so designated and it was ordered to be kept locked, just like its predecessor! The Fellows regained their privacy (and later a tennis court) in the private eastern portion, the Warden retaining the western, still employing his own Gardener.

The Warden's Garden was bounded by a north-south beech hedge and, later, a similar device was used to cut the Garden further, the first hedge being removed, for, again with a change of Warden in 1970, his Garden was returned to the size it had been in 1640 (less, of course, the plot in front of College), the southwestern part of Wills's acquisition being rejoined with the southeastern to make the present Fellows' Private Garden. Nursery beds, sheds and greenhouses persisted for a time. The last relic, an absurd round flowerbed in the middle of the lawn, was turfed over in 1984. Now an ancient apple tree in the eastern part is all that remains of Wardens' kitchen gardening in Wadham.

The Second World War halted all garden development. The new Private Garden was converted to an allotment for growing vegetables for the College; there was also a .22 rifle range used by the Home Guard there. Three air-raid shelters were dug in the back quad while another three were excavated in the Fellows' Garden. The latter were later lined with concrete to make static water tanks, though they were never used and were removed at the end of the war.

After the war, the appointment of a full-time Gardener was postponed, as was the abolition of the vegetable patch. It fell to Jack Thompson, Keeper of the Gardens (1945–75), to begin the restoration of the Gardens, by then in a desperate state of neglect. In 1946 the paths of the front quad were levelled and regravelled, the borders in the back quadrangle replanted, the northern herbaceous border in the Fellows' Gardens grubbed up and a shed in the north-west corner removed to the Private Garden, where steps were added to the rampart and a greenhouse set up (1948). The Fellows' Garden was overcrowded with trees: in August 1946 three holm oaks and three sycamores near the Old Library went, although the lawns were sinking into the old static tanks and the removal of some trees made others prone to gale damage. The Atlantic cedars there were victims in 1946–7 but clearing and replanting went on apace. By 1948 a lime was felled and two more shortly afterwards; in 1951 the first water supply was installed for the garden. At this point there was a part-time Head Gardener with a full-time Assistant, to which post Len Shepheard was appointed in 1950: Shepheard and Thompson together completed the restorations, the most lasting of their original work being that in the back quad. From 1963 Shepheard was assisted by Michael O'Day, who by 2010 will have devoted forty-seven years of service to Wadham gardens. Shepheard retired in 1984 and was succeeded by Andrew Little.

Opposite: *The view into Wadham from Rhodes House.*

The construction of the Goddard Building entailed the removal of a tree of heaven from the site in 1950. The clearing away of buildings nearby led to the tidying up of the now picturesque area around Staircases 13, 14 and 15 and the formation of a workaday JCR quadrangle, which was turfed in 1953 by the University Parks staff for £80. At the same time £836.8s was laid out for paths and lawns in the back quadrangle and an additional Gardener was appointed. In 1954, the predicament of the Warden's Gardener, ill and wishing to retire, led to the taking over of the maintenance of the Warden's Garden by the College; the College also took over the cottage that went with the post. In December 1957, the bed along the front of the Goddard Building was established, and the paths

Above: *The 'white garden', 2008.*

Opposite left: *Pampas grass in the back quad.*

Opposite right: *The back quad looking towards Staircase 9, showing the lime, and, to the right, the border established by Wade-Gery.*

around the back quad (then still referred to as the Holywell quad) were tarred. In the 1960s, Michael O'Day's first job in the morning was to light the coal boiler in the peachhouse where the Fellows' car park now is. The peachhouse was by that stage used to supplement the other glasshouses in providing the large number of bedding plants required for the extensive flower borders, and the wallflowers then massed along the front of the Goddard Building. Such a planting scheme was too labour-intensive for two people, too prone to being trampled by students, and decreasingly fashionable. By the 1980s most of the borders were instead planted predominantly with shrubs. Meanwhile, the twenty holly trees in the Fellows' Garden – another relic of Victorian taste – had been gradually and quietly removed.

More recent work around the New Library demanded realignments in the area beyond the Cemetery, which is now a grove of trees made into a bluebell wood. The incorporation of the Holywell houses led to the setting out of lawns and a few specimen trees in a similarly unobtrusive way. The erection of the Bowra Building created a new, larger JCR quadrangle planted in 1992 with a surround of berberis and a Chinese tulip tree. Between it and the new Staircases 31 and 32 a new, white, scented garden has been planted, with magnolias, roses, olearias, lilacs, jasmine, poncirus, viburnum and philadelphus.

THE GARDENS TODAY

Facing the College in Parks Road is a row of four locust trees, *Robinia pseudoacacia*, and a holm oak, *Quercus ilex*, against the thirteenth-century Durham College Wall of Trinity on the other side of the road; Trinity obtained this strip of land from Wadham on the understanding that trees would be maintained there. The open lawns in front of the College gate contrast with the intimate gardens of the foundation, and even the trees of the early twentieth century have been replaced by modest specimens of ceanothus, japonica and pyracantha on the north and south-facing walls, though the façade itself bears no plants: the front quadrangle is similarly unsoftened, a square of turf.

By contrast, the back quadrangle confronts the visitor with trees and imaginative planting helping to bring together the seventeenth-century buildings with the later additional incorporations. The quad is dominated by a very large specimen of the weeping silver lime, *Tilia tomentosa* 'Petiolaris', on the lawn to the west, scenting the whole College in July and August: grafted, as is usual, this specimen had a girth of 3.6m in 2009 (1.8m in 1912) and has been skilfully pruned to make it one of the finest in Oxford. Farther east, against the deck are two common limes and a cultivar of *Prunus serrulata*, underplanted with Lent lilies, while on the lawn at the east end is a fine female form of the tree of heaven, *Ailanthus altissima* (girth 3.1m in 2009), apparently on the site of a sycamore at the beginning of the century.

Along the south-facing wall of the old buildings is an impressive border of shrubs and herbaceous plants, notable being fine specimens of *Hydrangea aspera*, *Staphylea pinnata* (bladder nut), *Chimonanthus praecox* (wintersweet), *Phygelius capensis* and a corkscrew hazel, *Corylus avellana* 'Contorta', derived, like all those in cultivation, from a single plant discovered in a hedgerow near Frocester, Gloucestershire in 1868. Also here are a chusan palm, *Trachycarpus fortunei*; a loquat, *Eriobotrya japonica*; *Genista aetnensis* (Mount Etna broom); a *Koelreuteria paniculata* (golden rain tree, 1988); and the 'Himalayan honeysuckle' *Leycesteria formosana*, which usually thrives through each winter without dying back, showing how mild the climate is against these walls. The west end is planted up with different cultivars of pampas grass, the biggest bed of them in Oxford.

There are a number of climbers against the deck, the most unusual being a Chinese spindle, *Euonymus kiautshovicus,* propagated from a plant in the grounds of the Radcliffe Infirmary. Near the steps at the east end of the deck is a good specimen of the Judas tree, *Cercis siliquastrum,* and, on the same patch of lawn by the Bursary, a free-flowering form of *Magnolia kobus* (girth 0.9m in 2009) and a *Carpenteria californica.* Most of the adjacent corner is paved, while the backs of the old Holywell Street houses are clothed with *Viburnum tinus*, the tender *Eccremocarpus scaber* (Chilean glory flower) and

Left: *Staircases 14 and 15.*

Below: *Staircase up to the Holywell deck.*

Parthenocissus quinquefolia (Virginia creeper). The northernmost cottage, Staircase 15, has a fine wisteria; to the left, a path leads to the JCR quadrangle.

Against the tall Music Room wall are specimens of *Parthenocissus henryana* and *Fremontodendron californicum*, while on the street side of the Music Room, a tree of heaven (girth 3m in 1992, felled in 2004) and a cypress have been important elements in the streetscape. The newly landscaped lawns to the north of the Music Room have trees planted 1988–92 including *Prunus* 'Kanzan' (1984), presented by an undergraduate, together with a magnolia planted (2009) in memory of Alan Ward, Tutor in English 1950–88. The new JCR quadrangle is surrounded with *Berberis thunbergii* 'Atropurpurea' and a Chinese tulip-tree to the south, all of which were planted in 1992. The 1950s Goddard Building linking this ancient complex to the seventeenth-century front quadrangle is, mercifully, at least partly covered in *Magnolia grandiflora, Garrya elliptica, Vitis vinifera* 'Purpurea' (purple grape), *Fuchsia magellanica* 'Gracilis', ivies and passionflowers, while nearby on the lawn is a specimen of the rare Chinese gutta-percha tree, *Eucommia ulmoides* (girth 0.7m in 2009).

The passageway to the front quad next to Staircase 4 gives an enticing view of the Fellows' Garden through the

passageway of Staircase 3. Until recently this garden was dominated by the great copper beech; a large area of honey fungus also led to the loss of a number of other trees, including a yew, a holm oak, several hollies and a *Cedrus deodara*. The site is now planted with a collection of bamboos, mainly of the species *Phyllostachys* because they are resistant to honey fungus, together with a replacement tree, also resistant, *Platanus occidentalis* 'American sycamore'. The site of the copper beech itself is surrounded in spring by bright blue drifts of *Scilla siberica*, then daffodils and, later in the year, by various dwarf species of cyclamen. To the northwest is a large *Magnolia acuminata* (girth 2.3m in 2009) rejuvenated by somewhat drastic pruning in the 1970s, and between them a grove of fastigiate oaks (1987–8) and a Chinese mahogany, *Toona sinensis*. Nearer to the College is a cedar of Lebanon (1952, girth 3.4m in 2009) with *Hedera colchica* (Persian ivy) at its foot; close to it is a golden yew (girth 1.6m in 2009), a magnificent specimen, and a scholar tree, *Sophora japonica* (girth 1.3m in 2009). Near the Chapel is a mulberry and beyond is the old Cemetery, presided over by Doubleday's controversial bronze of a seated Warden Bowra (1977), the College's first garden figure since the seventeenth-century Atlas and the 'speaking' statue. The small grove of horse chestnuts (one with girth of 3.5m in 2009), purple beech (girth 3.1m in 2009) and self-sown

Above: *The copper beech in 1993.*

Right: *The Gardeners, 2009: Andrew Little, left, and Michael O'Day, right.*

tree of heaven beyond is underplanted with bluebells and native shrubs. Nearer the statue is a Japanese katsura tree, *Cercidophyllum japonicum* (girth 0.8m in 2009), with golden autumn colour, a holm oak, a Lombardy poplar and two yews, one a typical plant, the other a specimen of the unusual 'Adpressa' variety, which differs in its crowded branchlets of smaller leaves.

Back in the original Fellows' Garden, there is an excellent specimen of the rare *Phillyrea latifolia*, the evergreen near the gate to Love Lane, next to a tall ginkgo (girth 1.9m in 2009), and a Canadian maple planted in memory of Peter Derow, Tutor in Ancient History 1977–2006. On the lawn is a Scots pine (girth 1.9m in

Opposite top: *Under the copper beech in the 1970s.*

Opposite bottom: *The northwest corner of the Fellows' Garden, looking towards the 'nook'.*

Left: *The statue of Maurice Bowra, by John Doubleday.*

Below: *The view north along Love Lane.*

2009), a giant redwood (1986) and a purple beech planted in 2000 in memory of George Forrest, Tutor in Ancient History 1951–77, and Wykeham Professor at New College 1977–92. The eastern border, planted with evergreens where once there were apricots and nectarines, is faced by one of the finest mixed borders of shrubs and herbaceous plants in Oxford. There are many unusual plants and fine specimens – the white-flowered *Xanthoceras sorbifolium*, *Cornus mas* (Cornelian cherry), *Fraxinus ornus* (manna ash, 1988), *Sorbus bristoliensis* (1988), *Acer griseum* (paper-bark maple, girth 0.8m in 2009), *Euphorbia characias* (milkweed), *Parrotia persica* (Persian ironwood), *Rosa* 'Aloha', *Paulownia tomentosa* (foxglove tree), clerodendrums, yuccas, mahonias, escallonias. In the northwest corner is a secluded paved 'nook', planted in 1986–7 with cool green foliage plants, rheums, *Sasa palmata* (evergreen bamboo), rodgersias and *Aralia elata* (Japanese angelica tree) behind

a *Magnolia x soulangiana*. In the southwest corner is a particularly good grouping, including *Staphylea pinnata*, *Hydrangea aspera*, and cotoneaster, planned by Jack Thompson. The northern end will eventually be dominated by a grove of incense-cedars, *Libocedrus decurrens* (1986).

Right: *Fellows'*
Garden in the snow,
April 2008.

PRIVATE GARDENS

The Warden's Garden to the west and the Fellows' Private Garden to the north have been open to the public on special occasions since 1981. The most venerable tree is the tallest tulip-tree in Oxford, lopped and with copious flowering epicormics, near the Lodgings (girth 4.3m in 2009). Other trees in the Warden's Garden include a holm oak (girth 3.1m in 2009), in the north border, a purple hazel, roses, and a Judas tree (girth 1.1m in 2009). Against the east wall, the border has the Moroccan broom, *Argyrocytisus battandieri*, hibiscus, escallonias, a fine *Robinia hispida* 'Rosea' (rose acacia) and, at the boundary with the Fellows' Private Garden, bamboos and *Rhus hirta* 'Laciniata'.

The Fellows' Private Garden has, at its eastern end, a curious square building, known as the cowshed, beyond which runs the remnant of the Royalist earthworks of 1642, with a Himalayan birch (girth 1.25m in 2009) and a grove of filberts and cobnuts. In front of this is an old apple tree (Newton Wonder; girth 1.6m in 2009) from the orchard of the nineteenth-century Wardens, a mulberry (girth 1.6m in 2009), a *Metasequoia* (girth 1.5m in 2009), together with a medlar, a quince, a nonpareil apple and other old-fashioned fruit trees underplanted with Tenby daffodils. Near the entrance are a large copper beech (girth 4m in 2009) and a clump of strawberry trees underplanted with meadow saffron. On the lawn are a number of plantings from the post-war period including yet another purple beech; a handsome tulip tree (girth 2.2m in 2009) planted by Warden Bowra; a walnut (girth 1.1m in 2009); a gingko; a paper mulberry (girth 0.6m in 2009); a tree of heaven (girth 1.9m in 2009); a yew (girth 2.8m in 2009); a golden cedar (girth 1m in 2009); a weeping lime (girth 1m in 2009) to replace a Lucombe oak lost in 1985; some maples; a *Paulownia tomentosa* (girth 0.9m in 2009); a *Parrotia persica*, planted as a memorial to Jack Thompson; and a rare Wollemi pine given by the then Keeper of the Gardens, Robin Robbins. Other trees include a Corsican pine (girth 2.8m in 2009) in the northwest corner, while on the earthwork is an oak (girth 3.4m in 2009) and a paper birch, *Betula papyrifera*.

The north end was planted up in 1985 through the generosity of Peter Placito in memory of his father: the border of trees, shrubs, and ground cover includes *Prunus avium* 'Plena', *Davidia involucrate* (dove tree), *Malus hupehensis* (Hupeh crab-apple), *Picea omorika* (Serbian spruce), *Hamamelis japonica* 'Zuccariniana' (Japanese witchhazel), *Magnolia tomentosa* 'Waterlily', *Kirengeshoma palmata* 'Koreana', viburnums and many ground-cover species of *Geranium*. On the wall near the Warden's Garden is the climbing *Celastrus orbiculatus* 'Hermaphrodite' (oriental bittersweet). In Love Lane to the east, along the boundary with Mansfield College, are young specimens of *Sequoiadendron giganteum* (giant redwood) and *Abies grandis* (giant fir), which were planted to replace elms on the bank lost through Dutch elm disease in the 1970s, and, nearer the Library, *Torreya californica* (California nutmeg).

The nursery yard through the pointed arch in the west of the garden has two greenhouses – one containing vines, the Black Hamburgh among them. The yard lies behind Wadham Cottages, the tiny garden in front of which is well known to Oxford citizens for its magnificent clematis and interesting plants at all times of the year: *Nerine bowdenii* (a pink autumn-flowering bulb), *Jasminum fruticans* and, on the house wall, *Hydrangea petiolaris*, all nestling in a sheltered spot lying between a London plane and a lime in Parks Road, on a strip of land released to the City on the understanding that there would always be trees there.

Above: *The raised walk on the top of the old earthworks, allegedly part of the Civil War fortifications thrown up by the Royalist garrison in 1642.*

Above: *Wooden plant labels, in the greenhouse behind Wadham Cottages.*

Left: *The copper beech, winter 1981.*

Below: *Pruning the tree of heaven, 2006.*

Opposite: *The view through Staircase 3 to the Fellows' Garden.*

EPILOGUE

In the accepted view of successful gardening, Wadham's grounds are 'correct' in obscuring their boundaries and in having 'all-year-round interest', though clearly trees have to be planted in anticipation of the demise of the elderly. Although a Victorian rockery and a rose garden in the Warden's Garden have come and gone, there seem to have been no Victorian carpet-bedding, no Gothic fantasies, and except for the 'nook' in the Fellows' Garden, no intimate room-gardens à la Hidcote or colour borders à la Sissinghurst. From gardens which were both utilitarian and at the height of academic and scientific fashion in the seventeenth century, Wadham's landscape has now slid into a 'safe' romanticism of a later period than, but still considered sympathetic to, the old College buildings. We have inherited an eclectic jumble, not exactly an imitation of 'wild gardening' nor a botanical collection but a cottage design in a grand setting, the so-called 'Cotswold Look'. There is therefore no masterplan, simply ad hoc infilling and replacement, screening adjacent modern buildings and fighting the effects of fireblight and honey fungus. Metonymically, however, that historical process also points forward to the development of new planting and a new garden in association with the redevelopment of the Blackwell's Music Shop as a graduate research centre.

CHAPTER NINE

The Buildings

R.P. Martineau

THE OLD QUADRANGLE

The main quadrangle at Wadham was built with extraordinary speed between 1610 and 1613, and on a very ambitious scale; clearly the intention was that it should be only the core of the College, and the Hall and Chapel were built large enough to serve future expansion.[1] Even so the buildings occupied only half the site bought by Dorothy Wadham from the City. The architect was William Arnold, recommended by Dorothy Wadham as 'an honest man, a perfect workman, and my near neighbour'. Although always described, in the style of the time, as a 'master mason', Arnold was in fact an experienced architect, with responsibility for Montacute House and Dunster Castle, both in Somerset, and for Cranborne House in Dorset, built for Robert Cecil, Lord Salisbury (the Lord Treasurer); Arnold was therefore a natural choice for Wadham, both in his West Country ambience and in his Court connections.[2]

The style of the main quadrangle, with its fan vault in the entrance, its battlements and the Gothic windows to Hall and Antechapel, seems traditional. But much of the detail, and in particular the frontispiece to the Hall, with its columns of the four orders flanking statues of King James and of the founders, is classical, while the accent on

Above: *The fan-vaulted ceiling under the tower, in the entrance to College.*

symmetry (down to the provision of a false door to the Hall to balance the entrance to the Chapel) breathes a distinctly unmedieval air. In English terms, Wadham was in fact a very up-to-date building, representative of the Elizabethan synthesis of medieval and classical; though very soon with the advent of Inigo Jones's Palladian revolution, it began to seem old-fashioned, perhaps rather quaint. While the building is largely unchanged, the introduction of sash windows in the eighteenth

Above: The east side of the front quad.

Right: Christopher Wren's clock, set onto the Chapel wall in the front quad.

century, and the replacement of the gravelled court by the present grass sward in 1809, makes it difficult to reconstruct the impression it would have made in 1613. The clock-face on the Antechapel dates from 1671, allegedly a present from Christopher Wren.[3]

The use of the building has changed in detail over the years. Originally the chambers were used as communal bedrooms for up to three students, with the small rooms off functioning as studies or work carrells. But 'chumming' or the sharing of rooms became less tolerable in the eighteenth century. Despite the reduced numbers of undergraduates at this period, the cocklofts or garrets were made more habitable by the insertion of windows looking into the quad. There is evidence,

Left: *The drawing room of the Warden's Lodgings, 1993. Over the fireplace is a portrait of the young Mrs Hody (in 2009 in the SCR).*

however, that some of them had been inhabited, presumably at low rents, and in considerable discomfort, almost from the foundation.

The Warden, who was originally allocated not only the chamber over the gateway but also a large part of the present Staircase 1, was moved to his present accommodation sometime between 1626 and 1640. In 1812 the interior of the Lodgings was remodelled into its modern form of a house, a decision presumably inspired by the 1806 statute allowing the Warden to marry.

THE CHAPEL AND ANTECHAPEL

The Chapel is built on the T-shaped plan common in Oxford colleges. The shape fits in extremely well at Wadham, allowing a completely symmetrical building, in which the Antechapel mirrors the Hall, and the Chapel the Kitchen-Library wing. The axis of the Chapel runs almost exactly east-west; it may be that this explains why the College façade is not quite parallel to Parks Road. Services, of course, were always held in the Chapel proper (corresponding to the 'choir' of a parish church); but the modern accent on liturgical informality has involved some

overspill into the Antechapel. Other activities supposed to take place in the Chapel (e.g. various academic exercises) were probably held in the Antechapel. The election of the Warden, following common prayer, took place in the Chapel itself up to 1872.[4] The elaborate screen between the Chapel and Antechapel (by John Bolton) is original, the high-sided box pews behind it perhaps intended for the College Servants.

The painted glass is of considerable interest. Since the Reformation coloured glass in church had been considered papistical, and while existing glass was often left in place (presumably to avoid the expense of reglazing) new glass was either plain or at best modestly heraldic. The first use of religious glass was by Dorothy Wadham's acquaintance Lord Treasurer Salisbury at Hatfield House, between 1607 and 1612, and his example was followed by King James and taken up in Court circles.[5]

Dorothy Wadham was therefore being daringly up to date (or firmly reactionary, according to viewpoint) in her insistence on the representation of David and the prophets, and of Christ and the Apostles 'that it may a little make shew for what purpose that place was appointed'.[6] A local builder, Robert Rudland, was

Below: *An early nineteenth-century watercolour by J. Eagles, of the Chapel before Blore's 'restoration'. The stalls and screen are shown painted red. Behind the altar is a drawing of the Last Supper by Isaac Fuller.*

Right: *A nineteenth-century watercolour of the Chapel, right, after the 'restoration' carried out by Edward Blore, an early Gothic revivalist who was more admired in Oxford in the 1830s than he was ever to be again.*

Above: *A drawing of the Chapel by F. Mackenzie, engraved for Ackermann's* History of the University of Oxford *(1814).*

Right: *An early nineteenth-century watercolour of the Antechapel.*

Above: *The east window of the Chapel, by van Ling.*

Above: The Entry into Jerusalem, *left, drawn by Martin de Vos and engraved by Hieronymus Wierx to illustrate Hieronymus Natalis's* Meditationes in Evangelia.

Above right: *St Stephen in a detail from the south wall of the Chapel: a dramatic and original treatment of the subject.*

Above left: *Jonah, in a detail from the north wall of the Chapel.*

employed initially but paid off on the foundress's orders before he had completed the work. Some of the Apostles are by a distinguished French glazier, Louis Dauphin, who also worked at Hatfield.[7] The original windows fill the lower lights of the north and south range. The Nativity and Pentecost in the upper lights were bought by Warden Symons at an upholsterer's in Bond Street in 1836; they are also seventeenth-century Flemish work, probably removed from Belgium in the course of the French Revolution.[8]

The great east window was made and installed in 1622 by Bernard van Ling, a native of Emden in Germany who had recently worked in Paris and in London at St Paul's. The cost was £113.17s.5d, paid by Sir John Strangways, Nicholas Wadham's nephew. The window comprises scenes

from the Passion, Resurrection and Ascension, with, in the upper light, Old Testament 'prefigurations' (including a striking Jonah and the Whale). They are largely based on the plates designed by Martin de Vos, in a book, *Meditationes in Evangelia,* of Catholic provenance, printed in Antwerp in 1595; a copy was presented to the Library by Dr Bisse in 1613. Van Ling went on to other work in England (including some at Lincoln's Inn Chapel); his style was

Left: *Stalls in the Chapel.*

Above: *Stone angel in the Chapel.*

continued in Oxford by his brother Abraham, at Lincoln, Queen's, Balliol, and University Colleges.[9]

The wood panelling forming the back of the choir stalls continues the design of the screen, featuring a characteristic Jacobean design of plant and animal life. The rest of the stalls were either drastically modified or provided new in 1832 by Edward Blore. Blore also inserted the stonework around the chancel: unfortunately the Bath stone is extremely fragile and many pieces are now missing.

It is in fact very difficult to recapture the original form of the Chapel's fitments and liturgical arrangements. The present altar rails and the handsome black and white marble floor were put in later, in about 1670. The original communion table was taken away by Blore in 1832 and after many vicissitudes finished up in the Antechapel. A Jacobean communion table, similarly ejected from Ilminster church, was bought in 1889 by Alfred Stowe, the Senior Bursar, and is still in use. The Jacobean pulpit was also ejected to the Antechapel in 1832. Although restored to the Chapel, it is now rarely used, sermons being preached either from the lectern (given to the College in 1691) or from the modern reading-desk.

The Fellows complained in 1764 that sitting in Chapel was 'very inconvenient' because of the rain. Attempts to deal with this culminated in the insertion by Blore in 1832 of new stucco ceilings to replace the original simple board ones. Even Jackson (no admirer of Blore) found it difficult to dispute their acoustic quality and their contribution to keeping the Chapel reasonably warm. The simpler design in the Antechapel was to be echoed in the new ceiling inserted in the Old Library in 1986.

The Antechapel has some heavy mid-Victorian glass, which even the swings of artistic fashion have not yet restored to favour. Largely obscuring the glass in two of the windows is the fine organ by Henry ('Father') Willis, built in 1878. The organ 'stood at first nakedly on the floor of the south transept', but in 1886 it was moved to the west wall and provided with a loft and case by Jackson.[10] The College wisely (or perhaps thriftily) resisted any 'restoration' of the organ until 1985, when extensive but conservative repairs were carried out to what had become a rare period piece.

The monuments in the Antechapel include a very fine (and expensive) commemoration of Sir John Portman, Fellow-Commoner, who died in 1624, aged 19.[11] Next to it there is a representation of a set of books forming a tablet commemorating Thomas Harris, one of the foundation Fellows.

Above: *The organ, of which the loft and case were designed by T.G. Jackson.*

Below: *The monument to Sir John Portman, Bart, who died as an undergraduate in 1624.*

Above: *The monument to Thomas Harris, Fellow, who died in 1614. The tablet is surrounded by a representation of books, set with their fronts outward in the way that they were placed on shelves at that period.*

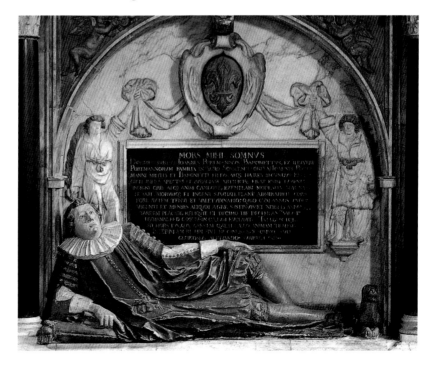

THE HALL

The Hall, large by Oxford standards, is one of the least-altered parts of the College. The screen at the north end is the original one, less ornate than the one in the Chapel, but carved by the same craftsman, John Bolton. The hammer-beam roof, with its carved decorations, is particularly fine. During redecoration in 1985, carpenters' marks were discovered on the elements of the main structure, indicating that the trusses were first made and fitted together at ground level, and then hoisted into place and reassembled.

The Hall would have been 'heated' originally by an open brazier, with the lantern above being open for the escape of smoke. This was changed in 1826 when the present fireplace was installed near High Table, though the Hall would still have been extremely cold (in winter the water used to freeze in the jugs on the tables nearest the screen). At last in 1873 a form of central heating was introduced which also served the Chapel.

The lighting system (low-voltage electric candelabra on the tables, with cold cathode tubes over the cornice to provide reflected light from the ceiling) was installed in the 1920s, a tribute to the unlikely design team of T.C. Keeley and Lord David Cecil.[12] During the 1985 redecoration some real tennis balls were found lodged in the rafters, presumably the result of (undergraduate?) high jinks.[13]

THE OLD LIBRARY

Above a remarkably spacious Kitchen Dorothy Wadham positioned the Library, no doubt to keep the books dry. The room gives the impression of having been constructed in rather a hurry: it was the last part of the foundation building to be put up, and was completed after the master mason Arnold had left. The side window embrasures in particular are very plain, and out of keeping with the general style of the rest of the College, though they admit much more light than would be allowed by the narrower and more rectangular openings found elsewhere.

In 1732, the College resolved to 'replaster' the Library: this can only refer to the major realignment of the walls and ceiling which was revealed in the course of the 1986 works referred to below. The north wall, in particular, was severely out of plumb (some 17.5 cm) and we can surmise from the nail holes that the ceiling was originally boarded (with square edge boards of course), and, having shifted substantially, would have allowed dirt and maybe even rain into the room. The presence of substantial and awkwardly placed buttresses on the north wall indicates that structural problems emerged soon after the original building. The barrel ceiling, which was removed in 1986, was also not original, since it fouled the head of the east window in a quite unacceptable way, and was presumably also inserted in 1732.

The various Library collections were concentrated in the large New Library in 1977. The Governing Body flirted with the idea of establishing a kind of museum or gallery in the Old Library but the pressure to provide a larger room for meetings and meals was irresistible. The opportunity was taken to remove the 1732 cosmetic alterations (the timbers of which in any event were riddled with woodworm), and the window reveals were restored, with new stone heads. The eighteenth-century

work was not completely obliterated, however; the new west wall incorporates the main Library door of that time, with its false-fielded panels and generous architraves. The panelled ceiling and deep cornices are an invention of Robert Potter, the architect responsible for the work, and echo Blore's ceiling in the Antechapel.

Opposite, far left: *A Victorian watercolour of the Hall.*

Opposite: *The Hall, 1993.*

Right: *The Old Library, 2009.*

There remains one enigma. During these alterations, after the eighteenth-century plasterwork 'repairs' were removed, a curious half-egg shaped recess was exposed, to the right of the east window (it does not have a fellow to the left). It seems obvious that this was quite an important feature: the back surface was (and is) painted black, and there is a stone surround with every indication that it supported a carved cartouche (chopped away, presumably in 1732). At the base it seems that there must have been a stone pedestal supporting some kind of emblem or perhaps a bust. The prize (offered by the Estates Bursar in the 1990s) of a magnum of champagne for documentary evidence of what originally occupied this niche remains unclaimed.

EXPANSION

From the first the College used various buildings between the main building and the King's Arms, on Parks Road. One of these was demolished and replaced in 1693–4 by the present Staircase 9, a handsome building in the form of a detached house (its door facing inwards to the quad). Unfortunately there is no authentication of the tradition of its design by Wren.[14]

The next building south, beyond the great gate, was known as the 'Old Building'. Found to be ruinous and dilapidated, it was pulled down in 1801 and replaced by a brewhouse or bakehouse. Three cottages between this and the King's Arms were sold in 1797 to the University, which erected on the site a building for the Press (successively a Bible storehouse and stereotype foundry). This was repurchased in 1828, and both buildings converted into rooms, as Staircases 10 and 11. Undergraduates, not unreasonably, referred to Staircase 9 as 'heaven', 10 and 11 as 'hell'.

The rest of the original site (i.e. the King's Arms and the houses along Holywell) was from the first rented out to provide income. But eventually, in 1876, Jackson proposed a scheme to create a second quadrangle. Some houses, cottages and the Warden's stable were demolished: but Jackson's plan of 'opening out' the quad, on the lines of his treatment of the front of Trinity,

Above: *Building work in the 1950s around Staircase 14. To the left of the photograph is the space where Staircase 15 was to be constructed.*

foundered on the financial difficulties which hit the College at that time.

Not until the 1950s was anything further done to fulfil Jackson's dream. News was received of a benefaction of £250,000 to the University to help finance expansion. The University decided to allocate this among the poorer colleges; Wadham put in a bid for £118,000 and was allocated £35,000. With this it was able to take over a tangle of cottages and outhouses known as Wadham Place and resettle the occupants. Most of the buildings were demolished, save for 35 Holywell Street, a charming seventeenth-century house with twin spiral staircases, now known as Staircase 14. To tidy up the back of the house, Staircase 15, a mock cottage which regularly deceives tourists (and others), was designed on the back of an envelope by the clerk of works, Roy Cozier.

On this site in 1953, a large new building containing a second Library, JCR, and Staircases 16 and 17 was built, to designs by the architect H.G. Goddard, himself an old member of the College. The building is in stone, in the minimally modernist style of the mid-1950s. Originally called the 'New Building', that designation soon became inappropriate and the name 'Goddard Building' has now become canonical by long use.

Top left: *King's Arms yard, 1964, before the construction of Holywell Court.*

Top right: *The Goddard Building from a flattering angle. The Sir Thomas Beecham Music Room is visible in the background, just before the steps up to the Library deck.*

Above: *Staircases 28 and 29, beside the Holywell Music Room.*

Left: *Holywell Court.*

While the Goddard Building alleviated the accommodation problem produced by post-war expansion, it did not solve it. There was increased pressure on colleges to house their students. The old-fashioned landlady, happy to accommodate undergraduates in her spare room during term-time, disappeared, driving students on to the housing market involving 'lets' for a whole year. In 1966 a party of Fellows led by Maurice Bowra reported favourably after a trip north to inspect the work of a Glasgow firm of architects, Gillespie, Kidd & Coia, who were making a considerable reputation with their educational buildings and churches in Scotland. They were commissioned to provide a development plan; the partners principally concerned were Isi Metzstein and Andrew Macmillan. The first part of their proposals resulted in alterations to the Holywell Street buildings in 1970; the creation of Blackwell's Music Shop under a first-floor deck, with the new Staircase 12 above it, and the small hidden Holywell Court, all on the site of the old King's Arms coaching yard; part of the old medieval wall was retained. The development won a Civic Trust award in 1972. Changing tastes resulted in the 'demodernization' of Staircase 12 just 20 years later when a pitched roof replaced the original flat one and sash windows the plate glass.

'Decks' were to be a feature of the Gillespie, Kidd & Coia style, and one carried over by their successors. Their use helps solve the problem of marrying the need for a horizontal layout of public rooms and services to the somewhat inflexible vertical nature of the traditional Oxford staircase. A notable example is the expansion of the facilities of Dorothy Wadham's Kitchens under the deck joining the old building to the Goddard Building.

Gillespie, Kidd & Coia's main proposal was the creation of a third quadrangle, using the Goddard Building as its west flank, fairly open to the north, enclosed at the Holywell Street end by houses and by the Holywell Music Room; while to the east there would rise a massive new building, along the College's boundary with Manchester College. This would involve yet another Library (the one in the Goddard Building was already bulging at the seams with readers and books), as well as residential accommodation. The College approved the plan in principle, and agreed to proceed with the first phase: the New Library and some 33 rooms. Financial problems were eased by a substantial donation from the Imperial Organization for Social Services of Iran:[15] in recognition the College named the Library after the Shah of Iran's twin sister, Princess Ashraf Pahlavi, and dedicated part of it for the promotion of

Above: *The 'streetscape' of the Bowra Building, looking towards New College Tower.*

Left: *The exterior of the new Library.*

Opposite: *The curiously 'naval' outcrop of one of the rooms of the Bowra Building.*

Persian studies. With the Princess's permission it was subsequently renamed after the medieval Persian poet Firdousi. The result, opened in 1977, was dramatic. The mixture of coloured pre-cast and in-situ concrete with stainless steel and oak finishes in an austere split-level design, has created one of the finest working college libraries in Oxford. Above the Library, reached by Staircase 19, is a quasi-Venetian piazzetta, charmingly or infuriatingly introspective according to taste, which, however, presents a rather massive appearance of two stories of near-vertical leadwork to the outside world.

There was a series of consequential changes: the transformation of the Old Library into a Senior Common Room, the removal of the Junior Common Room upstairs to what had been the Library in the Goddard Building, and the conversion of the JCR to a refectory, as an overflow to the Hall. Later, with the opening of the new bar in the Bowra Building (1992), the bar in the Goddard

Building was converted into a music practice room, named after Sir Thomas Beecham; the previous flat roof has been replaced by a copper-clad pitched roof, to match the rest of the building.

For several years the College was unable to proceed with the Gillespie, Kidd & Coia plan. In the mid-1980s when it had again plucked up the courage to attempt more building, architectural fashion had changed and the majority feeling was that a range of further units on the 'Staircase 19' model marching south towards Holywell would be too massive and dominant.

The firm of MacCormac, Jamieson & Pritchard (its principal partner, Richard MacCormac, became President of the RIBA during the proceedings) was commissioned to redesign the projected new quadrangle. The result was the Bowra Building, opened in 1992. The scheme of a ground floor and basement devoted to 'public rooms' was continued; those include a second cafeteria and a bar, a squash court, a lecture room and a theatre (doubling as a modest sports hall). From the open-air deck rise nine residential staircases, squeezing 85 rooms into a restricted site, achieving an intimate but not overcrowded atmosphere. The thrust of the towers balancing the horizontal strips of the windows, the rectangular projections, the uncompromising right angles, are reminiscent of Hardwick Hall, the product of Dorothy Wadham's formidable contemporary, Bess of Hardwick. The 'main street' thoroughfare through the building, with New College bell tower annexed as a scene stopper, has another, intentional, reminiscence, of Siena.

Outside the bar in the Bowra Building is a small terrace with an odd and at first sight unremarkable pattern. In 1974 Roger Penrose (Rouse Ball Professor of Mathematics, and Fellow of Wadham) discovered that it was possible to construct a curious pattern from just two different shapes, each of them a rhombus with angles which are multiples of 36 degrees; the pattern achieves fivefold symmetry and, most remarkably, can be extended to infinity without repeating itself. Extraordinarily, ten years later, chemists discovered a new class of metallic alloys with similar fivefold symmetry, in defiance of the previously accepted laws of crystallography.

in 1998 of a large residential building off-site, about a mile and a half north, in Summertown, close to the College playing field. With a further extension in 2004 it accommodates 147 students in (mostly) four- or five-bed flats. No common room was provided, to discourage separatist tendencies by the inhabitants; though this is being reconsidered. Building off-site was much cheaper than building in the College itself, whilst sparing the College gardens from development. The building, of six blocks, was designed by the Architects' Design Partnership. The exterior design is unremarkable, but the internal spaces function well. When purchased the site was called 'God's Little Acre', but this was changed to Merifield, after the Wadhams' mansion.

While the three new buildings (Goddard, New Library, and Bowra) are the most spectacular recent additions, almost as much accommodation has been added by the gradual takeover of houses in Holywell: most of them old College property converted when leases fell in, others bought from Merton. Their adaptation owes a good deal to the ingenuity of successive Estates Bursars and Clerks of Works (Roy Cozier, John Hanrahan and David Smith). Adaptation and in some cases extension have resulted in five new staircases east of the Holywell Music Room, forming a vernacular foil to the mass of the Bowra Building. Similar adaptation has also spread north of the Warden's Lodgings, where a badly designed two-storey mid-Victorian building – used latterly, until it became too dangerous, as the Warden's garage – was converted and extended into rooms and a cycle shed for the Fellows. This involved the complete refacing of the Parks Road frontage and the insertion of two new (imitation Victorian-Gothic) windows. A major development was the opening

Top left: *The Penrose paving.*

Above: *Merifield.*

THE HOLYWELL MUSIC ROOM

The Holywell Music Room[16] was erected by public subscription, organized by the Professor of Music, William Hayes, in 1742, on land leased from the College. It was built specifically for concerts, and is reputedly the oldest such building in Europe. The design, in the shape of contemporary Nonconformist chapels, is attributed to Dr Camplin, Vice-Principal of St Edmund Hall.

The building has been used continuously for its original purpose, with two breaks. One was for the period 1789–92 on account of rowdiness, and the second occurred in the mid-nineteenth century, when for a few years interest in music in Oxford must have diminished, for it was used for various other purposes, including shows given by a performing horse and a vixen.

The room was eventually let to the University for the use of the Music Faculty, and in 1959 a very substantial restoration was carried out by the University under the supervision of the architects Garden and Godfrey. The interior had been remodelled on several occasions, but there is good evidence that this restoration was in line with the room's appearance in the late eighteenth century. The great chandeliers of ormolu gilt were used at King George IV's coronation banquet at Westminster in 1820:

presented by Warden Tournay, they originally hung in the College Hall. The theory that undergraduates used to swing from them at Bump Suppers seems confirmed by the discovery that the bolts supporting them had been pulled quite halfway through the beams. The present organ (by John Donaldson) was installed in 1985, replacing the original organ by John Byfield which was moved to the Music Faculty's rehearsal hall.

The present 'Green Room' on the west of the Music Room, is yet another example of recent pastiche, dating from 1982. In 2009 conservation and refurbishment work was carried out on the Music Room.

Above: *The exterior of the Holywell Music Room, with new railings, 2009.*

Left: *The Bump Supper, 1914. The chandelier, now in the Holywell Music Room, looms large in the foreground.*

RESTORATION

The story goes that the High Table in the Hall is the same one that was used there during the celebrations of the establishment of the College in 1613. Occasionally, we are told, the top is replaced, and on other occasions the legs have been replaced, but it is still the same table. The story of the fabric is rather similar.

Stonework has always been a problem, especially for the comparatively modern colleges such as Wadham. The architectural styles of the seventeenth century required easily worked stone, and this, together with financial constraints, led to the extensive use of poor quality material from Headington quarry. At Wadham, happily, no substantial alterations or repairs were needed until the early twentieth century, and the first, rather modest, repair programme was instituted in 1920. The very first requirement was to stabilize the roofs, for the large oak wall plates which supported them, having become covered with debris, were quite rotten. Over the years they were all replaced with reinforced concrete beams, and then the outer wall surfaces were replaced with new stone, sawn by hand on site, by the Clerk of Works, Roy Cozier, a mason by trade.

Major repair and refacing work began late in 1957, as a result of the successful Oxford Historic Buildings Fund Appeal (of which the secretary, Ben Arber, was to become Wadham's Domestic Bursar). Under this programme, all the roofs were re-covered and most of the stonework refaced. Gargoyles were replaced and many original features were restored, the carving being done by Edgar Frith of Burford and Michael Black of Oxford. The stone used for the refacing was mainly Clipsham, which had been first introduced to Oxford by Jackson as a sympathetic replacement for decaying local stone. This stone is frequently subject to blue intrusions, which were accepted at Wadham, partly because that reduced the cost, and partly because it relieved the otherwise rather plain elevations.[17]

The only disappointment is that the then Bursar and Clerk of Works travelled the Oxfordshire countryside to purchase (very cheaply) secondhand Stonesfield slates for the re-roofing. They bought them from farmers,

particularly in Great Tew, Little Tew and Deddington, who were only too happy to offload them from derelict cowsheds. This turned out to be a false economy; the College entered the twenty-first century with the burden of having to re-roof the entire old quadrangle. The Hall and Chapel range have now been re-roofed; in addition there has been internal restoration, and the Kitchen has been completely refurbished. In the south range, in addition to

re-roofing, the opportunity has been taken to re-order, yet again, the internal arrangements of the buildings. Modern partitions have been removed, student rooms have been provided with en suite facilities, and new seminar and lecture space has been created. The MCR has been moved to the one-time Blackwell's Music Shop (which had also functioned, briefly and unsuccessfully, as a restaurant). The firm of Lec/Fitzgerald has been commissioned to develop designs for the conversion of this building into a Graduate Centre, to include a study library and seminar room, as well as social space. The plan is to return as far as possible to Gillespie, Kidd and Coia's original design intentions, responding to their spatial sophistication and clever use of light. The change of use will involve re-orientating the building, so that its entrance is from the back quad. An analysis of the original project in 1971 in the *Architectural Review* commended Wadham for having 'sought to find a future for the past and to ensure a past for the future'.[18] This remains the guiding principle of sympathetic development within the College.

Opposite: *Staircase 7, restored in 2009.*

Top: *Blackwell's Music Shop, 1972, now to be restored and converted into a graduate centre.*

Right: *The front of the College on Parks Road.*

The College in 2010

We remarked in the conclusion to the 1994 edition that history warns us against forecasting the future: predictions 'very soon come to seem subtly wrong, quaintly comical, or wildly inappropriate'. Some trends discerned then have in fact proved largely accurate: a 'considerable shift' in both University and College in the balance between teaching and research, an increasing emphasis on graduate studies, and an increasing pressure on senior members not merely to be 'research active' but to prove themselves so.

Then, as now, it was clear that there was a major problem of resources. Reliance on state funding could no longer support the activities of one of the world's leading universities, given the huge increase in the proportion of the UK population attending university and the consequent impossibility of providing for them, through grants and through support for institutions, in the generous way of the 1950s and 1960s. The result has been – unthinkable even twenty years ago – the reintroduction of fees paid by students themselves, coupled with an ever-increasing drive to raise additional endowment funds on the part of the University and of its colleges, to support both research and teaching.

The University and the colleges are working together to raise money for bursaries and scholarships. Within

Wadham we are seeking funds to assist students in financial difficulties, and to provide grants to allow all students to develop their academic and other interests. In a world of fierce international competition for academic talent (one of the most striking developments since 1994), we need resources to underpin the distinctive working environment of Oxford as a collegiate university and to attract scientists and scholars to it. The combined demands of an intensive and very personal teaching system, of engagement with College and University as communities, and of high-level research have become increasingly challenging. To maintain the vitality and rewards of this interrelationship requires considerable capital support.

Accommodation has become somewhat less of a problem than it was still in 1994, thanks to massive building financed by generous benefactions. Even so, what is taken to be an acceptable standard continues to rise; while, as the recent replacement of roof slates in the front quad underlines, the immense privilege of living and working in beautiful and historic buildings comes at a price. Restoration and improvement of facilities are an ongoing part of our responsibility for the future.

Oxford is committed to the maintenance of the college system, and to a high level of undergraduate education. There will be changes, fiercely debated no doubt, in the relationship between colleges and the University, and in the exact ways in which colleges themselves function. Wadham is much larger and more varied than it was fifty years ago, encompassing a wider range of academic and social activity, and in many respects it operates on very different lines. But it continues to work hard to maintain a sense of community.

Contrary to a widespread impression, change in Oxford is nothing new. Classic Oxford, the world of individual tutorials, of sporting prowess, of intense commitment at all levels to 'the college', came about in the Victorian period. A second revolution, the attempt to make Oxford much more inclusive in terms of social class, gender and ethnic origin began in the post-Second World War period and is still far from complete. Change has fundamentally been powered from within (although with some sharp pricks from outside), by a general consensus among tutors and a supporting swell among students. Witness the energy and enthusiasm currently poured by students into 'open days' for potential applicants. Once again, prophecy is hazardous. But the College is in good heart and ready to face whatever challenges present themselves as it embarks on its next century.

Wardens of Wadham

1 Robert **WRIGHT**; 20 April–20 July, 1613. (Bp of Bristol, 1622, Bp of Coventry and Lichfield, 1632. Died 1643)

2 John **FLEMING**; 1613–7 (death)

3 William **SMYTH**; 1617–35 (died 1658)

4 Daniel **ESTCOT**; 1635–44 (death)

5 John **PITT**; 1644–8 (deprived; died, 1654)

6 John **WILKINS**; 1648–59 (Master of Trinity, Cambridge, 1659–60; Bp of Chester, 1668, died 1672)

7 Walter **BLANDFORD**; 1659–65 (Bp of Oxford, 1665, Bp of Worcester, 1671, died 1675)

8 Gilbert **IRONSIDE**; 1665–89 (Bp of Bristol, 1689, Bp of Hereford, 1691, died 1701)

9 Thomas **DUNSTER**; 1689–1719 (death)

10 William **BAKER**; 1719–24 (Bp of Bangor, 1724, Bp of Norwich, 1727, died 1732)

11 Robert **THISTLETHWAYTE**; 1724–39 (died 1744)

12 Samuel **LISLE**; 1739–44 (Bp of St Asaph, 1744, Bp of Norwich, 1748, died 1749)

13 George **WYNDHAM**; 1744–77 (death)

14 James **GERARD**; 1777–83 (died 1789)

15 John **WILLS**; 1783–1806 (death)

16 William **TOURNAY**; 1806–31 (died 1833)

17 Benjamin P. **SYMONS**; 1831–71 (died 1878)

18 John **GRIFFITHS**; 1871–81 (died 1885)

19 George E. **THORLEY**; 1881–1903 (died 1904)

20 Patrick A. **WRIGHT-HENDERSON**; 1903–13 (died 1922)

21 Joseph **WELLS**; 1913–27 (died 1929)

22 John F. **STENNING**; 1927–38 (died 1959)

23 (Sir) C. Maurice **BOWRA**; 1938–70 (died 1971)

24 (Sir) Stuart **HAMPSHIRE**; 1970–84 (died 2004)

25 (Sir) Claus **MOSER** (later Lord Moser); 1984–93

26 John S. **FLEMMING**; 1993–2003 (death)

27 (Sir) Neil **CHALMERS**; 2004–

Notes

The fundamental history of Wadham is by T.G. Jackson, *Wadham College* (Oxford, 1893). This is especially detailed on the Wadham family, the circumstances of the foundation, and on the older buildings; Jackson analysed the buildings themselves and the documents relating to them with a professional architect's eye. J.B. Wells, later Warden, produced his *Wadham College* (1898); partly a popularization of Jackson, it is much more anecdotal and personal in approach, fuller on the eighteenth and nineteenth centuries. Indispensable to Wells and to us are the labours of R.B. Gardiner in producing *Registers of Wadham College* (2 vols, 1889–94), a complete list of members up to 1871, with biographical details when known; the working copy in the College archives contains a great deal of additional information acquired over the years. Biographical details taken from Gardiner (supplemented by such standard works of reference as the *Oxford Dictionary of National Biography*) have not usually been separately acknowledged in the text, but remain the backbone of the relevant chapters. The pages of the *Wadham College Gazette* since its founding in 1897 are also indispensable. Volume numbering of the *Gazette* has been inconsistent over the years; we have compromised by giving only the year number and page reference, e.g. *Gazette* (1907), 163.

The History of the University of Oxford (Oxford, 8 vols, 1984–97), edited by T.H. Aston and others, is invaluable.

References to documents in the College Archives are noted as WA, followed by a reference number or description.

CHAPTER ONE

NICHOLAS AND DOROTHY WADHAM AND THE FOUNDATION OF THE COLLEGE

1. A. Clark (ed.), *The Life and Times of Anthony Wood*, i, Oxford Historical Society, vol. 19 (1891), 259.

2. In addition to Jackson, *Wadham*, and Wells, *Wadham*, see C.E. Mallet, *History of the University of Oxford* (3 vols, 1924–7), ii, 248–62; and *Hist. of Univ.*, iii.

3. Anthony Wood, *The History and Antiquities of the Colleges and Halls of Oxford*, ed. J. Gutch (Oxford, 1786), 592.

4. Sir William Petre was Secretary of State to Henry VIII, Edward VI, and Mary, and remained in favour under Elizabeth.

5. *Hist. of Univ.*, iii, 58.

6. Mallet, *Univ. of Oxford*, ii, 196–8.

7. The fullest account of the foundation, and of the Wadhams, is now C.S.L. Davies 'A Woman in the Public Sphere; Dorothy Wadham and the Foundation of Wadham College', *Eng. Hist. Rev*, 118 (2003), 883–911. This builds on Nancy Briggs, 'The Foundation of Wadham College', *Oxoniensia*, 21 (1956), 61–81, which prints Dorothy's letters to her brother, and on *The Letters of Dorothy Wadham, 1609–1618*, ed. R.B. Gardiner, (1904), the originals of which are in the College archives.

8. For example, see Jackson, *Wadham*, 60, 70, 73, 81, 82.

9. Mallet, *Univ. of Oxford*, ii, 230–1.

10. Richard Bancroft, Archbishop of Canterbury, was Chancellor of Oxford and, on his death later in the year, he was succeeded in that role by Lord Ellesmere, the Lord Chancellor.

11. Presumably James Montagu, Bishop of Bath and Wells, the first Visitor, who according to Nicholas Wadham's wishes retained the office for life although translated to Winchester in 1616.

12. Briggs, 'Foundation', 66–7.

13. *Ibid.*, 69.

14. H. Hurst, *Oxford Topography*, Oxford Historical Society, 39 (1899), 131; W.J. Blair, 'A Monastic Fragment at Wadham College, Oxford', *Oxoniensia*, 41 (1976), 161–7.

15. *Hist. MSS Comm. Marquess of Downshire*, ii, 275.

16. Wood, *Colleges and Halls*, 593.

17. Robert Wright was a Fellow of Trinity, DD 1597, Chaplain to King James, Canon and Treasurer of Wells Cathedral, and holder, among other pluralities, of a rectory in Essex. Although he resigned only three months after his formal installation as Warden, he and the Sub-Warden designate (William Smyth) were active in College affairs from 1611, and were probably responsible for drafting the statutes.

18. Briggs, 'Foundation', 71–7.

19. For example, the Sub-Warden, Dean, Sub-Dean to preside over undergraduate disputations, Bursars, Catechist, and Lecturers.

20. Briggs, 'Foundation', 77.

21. WA 4/31.

22. The Library possesses the copy of the *History* presented by Carew Ralegh, which was repurchased by Maurice Bowra after its disappearance at some unrecorded date.

23. The similitude with 'drones', and the likening in the statutes of the College in the absence of the Warden as 'like a swarm of bees without its governor' recall Bishop Richard Fox's hope in his statutes, to which those of Wadham show many other resemblances, that his own foundation, Corpus Christi – Nicholas Wadham's probable old college – would be like a beehive.

24. It is a moot point whether these were, as reported, Nicholas's intentions; Dorothy seems the more likely source.

25. For admissions and details of members, see Gardiner, *Registers*.

26. Thomas Harris died after only a few months in the College, and is commemorated in the Antechapel by an inscription framed in books, which have their fore-edges forward as they were shelved in those days. See illustration on p.141.

27. King James altered England to 'Great Britain' before the statutes were approved. That the King took the initiative personally is alleged in the College's account of the Walter Durham affair in 1618; see WA 4/31.

28. Briggs, 'Foundation', 75.

29. For example, the foundress's 10-year-old great-nephew, William Petre, in the company of his 13-year-old brother Robert, and the 9-year-old Edwin Sandys, with his 14-year-old brother Henry, in 1641.

30. The most direct impression might be gained from the letters, could they be found, which Thomas Leir wrote during his time at Wadham from 1640 to 1648 to his father, which were said to have been preserved among the archives of the Leirs at Charlton Musgrove; see Gardiner, *Registers,* i, 147.

31. The Warden also had a substantial part of the present Staircase 1.

32. The provision of figurative windows, albeit confined to scriptural subjects, in the Chapel was daringly innovative in the 1610s. See below, chapter 9.

33. There is an entertaining letter (WA 4/27), discovered under the floorboards, from Lady Anne Gower to her undergraduate son in 1618, voicing the perennial parental complaint of his failure to write to his grandmother, and also demanding repayment of a loan she had made to his cousin. There are a few letters printed in J.P. Collier, ed.,

Trevelyan Letters, iii (Camden Society, 105, 1872) from John Willoughby to his father in 1630. Willoughby, a gentleman, did not matriculate but none the less had a Tutor, whom he paid £1 a quarter. He politely requests an increase in his allowance because of the exceptional cost of living and the pressures on him by Bursar and Tutor to pay. He denies spending time at taverns – out of his price range, even if he were, unthinkably, to wish to associate with 'lewd company' – and suggests that a 'turkey pie' would be an acceptable gift to his Tutor. His total expenses seem to have been about £10 a quarter. John Bramston (1626) wrote a voluminous *Autobiography*, ed. T.W. Bramston (Camden Society, 32, 1845), in which he says little of the College except that his Tutor, John Goodridge, was little better as a scholar than the sadistic vicar who had taught him as a boy (pp. 101–3).

34. See the account of Marmion by Derek Jewell and of Gauden by Charles Rosser in C.M. Bowra and D. Jewell (eds), *The Wadham Miscellany* (Oxford, 1947).

CHAPTER TWO

JOHN WILKINS AND THE 'EXPERIMENTAL PHILOSOPHY'

1. Gardiner, *Registers*, i, 162; Wells, *Wadham*, 56.

2. Wells, *Wadham*, 57.

3. *Ibid.*, 60; Gardiner, *Registers*, i, 170.

4. Barbara J. Shapiro, *John Wilkins, 1614–1672* (Berkeley, 1969) and C.S.L. Davies, 'The Family and Connections of John Wilkins', *Oxoniensia*, 59 (2004), 93–107.

5. Gardiner, *Registers*, 189–91; Jackson, *Wadham*, 115.

6. WA 4/102, University Visitors' Order, 20 Jan. 1652. After the Restoration, Wilkins maintained that he had only married under pressure; sceptics attributed his later support for the principle of divorce to this circumstance.

7. WA 4/91, 23 May 1651; Wells, *Wadham*, 64.

8. WA 4/105, University Visitor's Order, 4 July 1654. See Item 4, requiring tutors 'to pray with them [their students] & to take accompt of their time'.

9. The first group had met at Gresham College in London around 1645; see M.M. Purver, *The Royal Society: Concept and Creation* (1967), 161–83. The Wadham group formed after 1648; see T. Sprat, *History of the Royal Society* (1667, repr. 1966), 52–7. Close connections were maintained between the Wadham and Gresham groups, typified by Christopher Wren's appointment to the Gresham astronomy chair in 1657.

10. Wood, *Athenae*, ii, 826–9; Aubrey, *Brief Lives*, 311–14; R.T. Gunther, *Early Science in Oxford*, xi (Oxford, 1937), 90–1 (for John Wallis), 232 and 265 (for Seth Ward).

11. R.E.W. Maddison, *The Life of the Honourable Robert Boyle* (1969), 81, 85.

12. There is an enormous literature on the 'Philosophical Club' – its implications and relationship to the later Royal Society. See, for instance, Charles Webster, *The Great Instauration* (2nd ed., 2002).

13. See C.S.L. Davies, 'The Youth and Education of Christopher Wren', *Eng Hist Rev* 123 (2008), 300–27, summarized in *Wadham College Gazette*, 2009. The room was the great chamber in the entrance tower, originally part of the Warden's lodgings.

14. Christopher Brooke[s] was a professional instrument-maker of some note who married the daughter of the eminent English mathematician, William Oughtred. The office of Manciple could be equated to the modern steward; C.S.L. Davies, 'The Mathematical Manciple', *Wadham College Gazette*, 2003, and 'A Royal Chef for Wadham', *ibid.*, 2006.

15. Aubrey, *Brief Lives*, ed. Dick, xxxviii.

16. A. Chapman, 'A World in the Moon: John Wilkins and his lunar voyage of 1640', *Quart. J. Royal Astronomical Society*, 32 (1991), 121–3.

17. John Wilkins, *Of the Principles and Duties of Natural Religion* (1675); Shapiro, *Wilkins*, 224–50.

18. Rhodri Lewis, *Language, Mind and Nature: artificial languages in England*, (Oxford, 2007), is mainly about Wilkins.

19. 'The Ballad of Gresham Colledge' (*c.* 1663), ver. 8, ed. Dorothy Stimson, in *Isis*, 18 (1932), 103–17.

20. John Mayow, *Tractatus Quinque* (Oxford, 1674). See also J.R. Partington, *A History of Chemistry* (4 vols, incomplete 1961–), ii, 577–614.

21. John Evelyn, *Diary* (ed. E.S. de Beer, 6 vols, Oxford, 1955), iii, 110–11.

22. Christopher Wren (son of Sir Christopher), *Parentalia: or, Memoirs of the Family of Wrens … but chiefly of Sir Christopher Wren* (1750), 230. For the gardens generally, including an alternative suggestion about the origin of their design, see below, Chapter Seven.

23. H.W. Robinson and W. Adams, (eds), *The Diary of Robert Hooke, 1672–1680* (1935), 146.

24. Jackson, *Wadham*, 117; WA 16/1, Bursars' Accounts.

CHAPTER THREE
DECLINE AND REVIVAL: 1660–1900

1. Statistics prepared by Valerie Jobling for the History of the University; WA 110/18.

2. Wadham was unusual, though not unique, in having this as a statutory requirement; *Hist. of Univ.*, v, 233.

3. In fact, many Fellows held ecclesiastical livings worth a good deal more than this; the trick appears to be that the 'official' valuations were those tabulated in 1535; see J.G. Doolittle, in *Hist. of Univ.*, v, 245–6.

4. Edward Stone, Bursar, is important in pharmaceutical history for having noticed the therapeutic effects of willow-bark, a stage in the evolution of aspirin; but did so in the course of parochial duties at Chipping Norton, not in any academic milieu. See *OxDNB*.

5. Gardiner, *Registers*, i, 453–4.

6. Another Wadham man, Samuel Parker (1657), Bishop of Oxford, was one of James's nominees for the Presidency of Magdalen, and was imposed over widespread protest in October 1687. He died the following March, so re-opening the whole issue.

7. Wadham acquired its portrait of William III to celebrate the Revolution, and that of Lovelace which looks down on the Hall from the gallery, with an inscription about William redeeming 'the Nation from Popery and Slavery'.

8. C.E. Doble and others (eds.), *Remarks and Collections of Thomas Hearne* (Oxford Hist. Soc., 11 vols, 1885–1921), i, 291.

9. WA 4/123 A (complaints to Visitor); WA 6/8 (the unconstitutional statutes); WA 4/123 B (Dunster's protest).

10. Maurice Cranston, *John Locke* (1957), 437.

11. *Hist. MSS Comm. Duke of Portland*, vii, 252. By electing Baker the College reportedly lost its chance of a large benefaction from Thomas Lindsey, Archbishop of Armagh, and another from Robert Doyley, both ex-Fellows anxious to win the College back from the Dunster fold; see W.R. Ward, *Georgian Oxford* (Oxford, 1956), 104–5.

12. *A faithfull Narrative of the Proceedings in a late Affair between The Rev. Mr. John Swinton and Mr. George Baker* (1739); copy in the College Library, and another in Bodley (Gough Oxford 50 (3)); see also a hilarious verse adaptation *College-wit Sharpen'd …the Wadhamites – a Burlesque Poem* (1739) in Bodley (Gough Oxford 50(2)).

13. *The Penguin Book of Comic and Curious Verse*, selected by J.M. Cohen (1952), 262; no source quoted.

14. Jobling statistics, WA 110/18.

15. V.H.H. Green, in *Hist. of Univ.*, v, 313–4; and more generally, Lawrence Stone, 'Size and Composition of the Oxford Student Body, 1580–1910', in Stone (ed.), *The University in Society*, 2 vols. (Princeton, NJ, 1974), i, 3–110.

16. WA 110/18; nearly all Wadham Servitors in the 1790s moved rapidly into Bible Clerkships, helping to run the Chapel, rather than performing more menial duties in Hall and Kitchen. Two Servitors in the 1790s entered themselves as sons of gentlemen.

17. See *Hist. of Univ.*, v, 237–55. Wadham's Bursars, for instance, who were nominally paid £2 over the stipends of £20 to which they were entitled as Fellows, received from 1767 a further payment of £22 in return for surrendering certain perks believed to encourage over-charging and a cosy relationship with suppliers; WA, Convention Book, 2/3, 103–4.

18. *Hist. of Univ.*, v, 328.

19. Wills was noted for hay-making in his shirt-sleeves in the 'Warden's Close'; G.V. Cox, *Recollections of Oxford*, (2nd edn., Oxford, 1870), 168.

20. Gardiner, *Registers*, ii, 105–6; WA 10/2/10 for copies of the will. The property was valued at £27,000 in 1853. The Fellowships in Medicine and Law were not teaching Fellowships, but opportunities for Fellows to equip themselves for the professions; for instance, John Andrew (1850), who held the Wills Medical Exhibition while a Fellow and went on to a distinguished medical career at St Bartholomew's.

21. Wells, *Wadham*, 159. Tournay never recovered from a serious illness 'which incapacitated him from the discharge of many public duties' shortly after being elected Warden; see obituary in *Gentleman's Magazine* 1833, ii, 276–7.

22. Mary C. Church, *Life and Letters of Dean Church* (1894), 10–11.

23. Wells, *Wadham*, 164. In fact Symons missed the highest honours, getting an 'egregie' rather than a 'maxime'.

24. J. Cooper, in *Gazette* (1902), 262; also Tournay's obituary, cited above. Cox, *Recollections*, 196, talks of Tournay's 'generous tournament' in campaigning for the 1806 Act of Parliament which removed Dorothy Wadham's statute prohibiting the Warden from marrying, though having no intention of making use of it himself. E. Boys Ellman, *Recollections of a Sussex Parson* (2nd edn., Hove 1925), 206–7, recalls Tournay's relative, Anne Maude Harvey, 'who for his sake spent her long life of upwards of eighty years in single blessedness'. The archives contain a letter from her home town of Dover recalling Miss Harvey's devotion and quoting Tournay's alleged remark when, in 1806, his friends congratulated him on his new freedom to marry: 'I took the oath and an Act of Parliament cannot absolve me from it'.

25. Gardiner, *Registers*, ii, 343–8.

26. Church, *Life and Letters*, 13.

27. Ellman, *Recollections*, 82, 83, 85. Childers (see Spencer Childers, *Life and Correspondence of H. C. E. Childers*, 2 vols, 1901, i, 13–14) claimed in a letter to his mother to attend 17 hours of lectures and to be working hard at Maths under a coach; he also rowed. Church, too, though encouraged to read for honours by his Tutor, found private coaching useful; Church, *Life and Letters*, 15.

28. Maclaine Letters: Bodley MS Top. Oxon. d. 482.

29. B.H. Jackson (ed.), *Recollections of Thomas Graham Jackson* (Oxford 1950), 25–6; Wells, *Wadham*, 196–9.

30. For a hostile account see Frederic Harrison, *Autobiographical Memoirs,* 2 vols (1911), i, 83: 'an obsolete formalist, a miserly, clumsy pedant'. There are balanced accounts by P.A. Wright-Henderson, *Glasgow and Balliol and Other Essays* (1926), 62–9, and by Wells, *Wadham*, 173–93. Maclaine tells how the Warden gave him 'much good advice' in a 'kind and fatherly manner'. Jackson, *Recollections*, 32, for the 'elephant leg' story, which Jackson ascribed to Symons's 'entire want of humour'.

31. Ellman, *Recollections*, 101. However, Maclaine seems to have had no difficulty in attending the sermons.

32. Wells, *Wadham,* 165. For Allies see Mary H. Allies, *Thomas William Allies* (1907).

33. Of the Positivists, see the excellent account by Michael Ayers in *Tutorial Teaching at Wadham*, eds Davies and Garnett, (2008), 12–3. There are biographies of almost all the leading figures. See especially T.R. Wright, *The Religion of Humanity*, (Cambridge, 1986) and Martha S. Vogeler, *Frederic Harrison* (Oxford, 1984) and accounts in *OxDNB*. Interestingly, of the supposedly secular generation of 1861 matriculands, 16 out of 25 entered the Church; compared to 10 out of 19 of the 'evangelical' 1831 entry.

34. Harrison, *Memoirs*, i, 95. Harrison himself and Thorley, future Warden, were the beneficiaries of this coup.

35. Symons argued that a Royal Commission was improper, since colleges were private institutions. Wadham, he claimed, was under no statutory obligation to take Commoners; everything done for such students by the Warden was done out of benevolence and 'without any pecuniary consideration whatsoever'; i.e. the government of the College, writing letters to parents, 'daily correspondence' about admissions, and superintending 'their examination at the close of *each* term for several *entire* days'; see Public Record Office, 30 22 8D ff. 1243–6. I am grateful for this reference and for a copy, to Mr J.M. Prest of Balliol.

36. T.W. Allies, elected in 1833, spent his first three years on a tour of France and Italy; see Allies, *op. cit.*, 5; the 1850 Royal Commission was told that 11 out of 15 Fellows of Wadham were non-resident; see W.G. Brock, *Hist. of Univ.*, vi.

37. Jackson, *Recollections*, 104–5; Symons attempted to appeal to the Visitor against the admission of Nonconformists, but was not upheld; WA, Convention Book 2/4, 107, 114; and WA 7/23. Symons may be considered the victim of longevity and the lack of a statutory retiring age.

38. He did not consult the College about buying an estate (Hampton Gay) in 1862, though formally at least the proceedings seem to be in order; Jackson, *Recollections*, 104; WA 2/4, 97, 100. He was an active businessman on his own behalf (e.g. as Chairman of the Oxford Canal Company). Whether he actually embezzled the College property, as tradition has it, would not be easy to establish. Maurice Bowra's *Memories* (1966), 130, quotes Bursar Dixey's allegation that Symons embezzled £200,000. But, as T.C. Keeley remarked, 'Dixey liked to exaggerate and Bowra even more so'. Another dubious anti-Symons story told by Dixey relates to Symons, as a Curator of the Parks, having a tree felled during the absence of the other Curators for his own profit; see R.T. Gunther, *Oxford Gardens* (Oxford, 1912), 241.

39. See the controversy between J.P.D. Dunbabin and Arthur Engel in *Economic History Review*, ns, 28 and 31 (1975 and 1978), and Engel, *From Clergyman to Don* (Oxford, 1983), cap. v. Also comments by Wright-Henderson, WA 11/11 A, 8 ff. Some alleviation of the depressing picture was provided by trust funds, targeted largely on Scholarships, and a test for the ingenuity of Bursars.

40. Wells, *Wadham*, 172. Admissions even dropped, in the late 1870s, to 13–14 a year.

41. WA 11/11A, 1.

42. Amongst much else, Griffiths acquired the seventeenth-century copies of Raphael's cartoons, now in the Ashmolean; and a huge collection of prints and medals referring to the history of the College, now in the Library.

43. Wright-Henderson describes a man of 'singular dignity of manner and a certain preciseness and reserve … very accurate and business-like'; WA 11/11 A, 2–3; see also Wright-Henderson, *Glasgow and Balliol*, 69–71.

44. See *Gazette* (1980), 29–32. The Librarian H.P. Richards, one of the targets of student wrath, had, in 1871, as a young Fellow and secretary of the Oxford Republican Club, written to Karl Marx, enquiring about the International. The 'whole College sent down' story still appears in print; e.g. Hugh Casson, *Hugh Casson's Oxford*, (Oxford, 1988). The threat of wholesale expulsion seems to have been used by a number of colleges in an attempt to overcome student rowdiness in the 1870s; whether it was ever implemented is unclear; see Mark Curthoys's chapter on social life in *Hist. of Univ.*, vii.

45. WA 110/13. Crisall's father may have been a working boatbuilder, not the owner of a boatbuilding firm, to judge by his absence from *Kelly's Directory*.

46. Jackson, *Recollections*, 26, 43.

47. WA 11/11A, 15.

48. *Oxford Univ. Calendars*. For more details see *Tutorial Teaching at Wadham*.

49. *Gazette* (1899), 84. The evolution of the rules of football seems complicated and there were various attempts at codification in the 1860s; the Cambridge, Harrow and Sheffield rules jostled for position. Presumably the Wadham meeting was to settle an Oxford code, and had little effect nationally. See Geoffrey Green, *The History of the Football Association* (1953). Interestingly, 'football' to Wells in 1898 meant rugby; see Wells, *Wadham*, 205.

50. Wells, *Wadham*, 201 (barge). The cricket ground was at Cowley Marsh. Other games were played in the Parks until 1903, when the College acquired the previous Oriel ground at Cowley; *Gazette* (1903), 55, 75.
A sports ground at Marston was acquired and brought into use between 1908 and 1911, thanks largely to the efforts of J.B. Wells, and financed by an 'appeal', apparently the first of its kind for a significant purpose; *Gazette* (1907–11), *passim*.

51. F.W. Hirst, *In the Golden Days* (1947), 100.

52. Wells, *Wadham*, 206.

53. *Gazette* (1928), 356.

54. WA 11/11A, 13–14, 'desired by all except the boating men, who found the interval between their rowing practice and dinner long and exhausting'.

55. For analysis of Jackson's career, see William Whyte, *Oxford Jackson: Architecture, Education, Status and Style* (2006).

56. For all these see *OxDNB*. William Plomer (ed), *Kilvert's Diary*, 3 vols (new edn, 1969), iii, 21–4, 313.

CHAPTER FOUR
'A LIBERAL PLACE': 1900–1938

My thanks are due to the following people, who generously gave up time to talk to me and who made an invaluable contribution to this chapter: Henry Phelps Brown, Alan Bullock, Vere Ducker, Tom Griffiths, Bill Haden, Harold Harley, Mrs Howes (niece of Joseph Wells), George Forrest, Robert Wade-Gery, Charles Wenden; and Mark Curthoys and Mark Pottle of the History of the University of Oxford project.

1. J. Bardoux, *Souvenirs d'Oxford*, (Coulommiers, 1898),29–30. An English translation was published in 1899: *Memories of Oxford*, tr. W.R. Barker. Wells drew attention to the book in the *Gazette*, noting the 'strange mixture of interest, insight and inaccuracy', but quoting with pride the mention of Wadham. He omitted to mention the gloss on the superiority of Balliol. See *Gazette* (1899), 81.

2. See graphs kindly produced by Mark Pottle from the *History of the University of Oxford Database:* Wadham versus all men 1901–40; Balliol versus all men for the same period. The analysis is based on five-yearly samples, points being given for different classes gained (on the same principle as the later Norrington analysis of Schools results). Over the period as a whole, Balliol was consistently at least five percentage points above the average for all men; Wadham's results fluctuated, rising three percentage points above the average in 1910, dropping to the same

level below the average in 1915, coinciding with the average in 1920, dropping seven points below in 1925, and then gradually improving until they almost coincided with the average in 1935, and crept just above in 1940.

3. *Gazette* (1900), 167. In 1899, of 100 undergraduates, 41 were reading for Honours in Final Schools, 20 for Honours in Moderations, and 37 for a Pass degree, which represented a rising proportion of Honours men. *Gazette*, i, 82.

4. R. Kelf-Cohen, 'Wadham College Sixty Years Ago', *Gazette* (1975), 26–7, at 27.

5. Humbert Wolfe (1886–1940) read Greats. He became a civil servant concerned with issues of labour and employment; he was also a poet and literary figure. See *OxDNB*.

6. H. Wolfe, *The Upward Anguish* (1938), 38.

7. Wolfe cites the case of Victor Fox, the supreme Wadham dandy, who spent his

evenings with fellow Malvernians at Balliol, University or Magdalen. Fox, a godson of the Kaiser, was ironically to be one of the first Wadham men to be killed in the First World War. See *Gazette*, (1915), 331; cf. Humbert Wolfe's poem, 'V.D.F. Ave atque Vale', *Gazette*, (1916), 400.

8. Wolfe, *Upward Anguish*, 56–71.

9. WA 223: P.W. Whitcomb (1911), memoir.

10. *Gazette* (1900), 139.

11. *Ibid.* (1903), 59.

12. See Wolfe, *Upward Anguish*, 13–14: he cited a Univ. man saying 'Somebody said the other evening in Hall that one of the scouts, who dropped a plate, was a Scholar of Wadham'; cf. 75, quoting a wine merchant: 'Wadham … yes, that will be the 4s. 6d variety'.

13. *Isis*, 242 (10 May 1902); 498 (25 January 1913); 191 (10 March 1900); 461 (3 June 1911).

14. P.W. Whitcomb, memoir.

15. P.A. Wright-Henderson, 'Oxford, Past and Present. By the Warden of Wadham', *Blackwoods*, 185 (1909), 187–89, 335.

16. See *Gazette* (1906), 17.

17. *Ibid.* (1908), 168.

18. *Ibid.* (1906), 9.

19. In the period 1900–14 History was the largest school in the University (150–191 finalists p.a.), followed by Greats (126–156 p.a.). Theology was a small school, producing between 30 and 65 finalists in the University as a whole; Wadham seems to have continued to produce a higher proportion than the average in this subject – 4 p.a. in five of the years 1900–14. One Chemist from Wadham took schools in each of the academic years 1901–2, 1904–5, 1905–6, 1908–9, 1910–11 and 1912–13 (out of between 26 and 31 p.a. in the University as a whole); there was one English finalist in each of the years 1903–4 (out of 15 in the University, only four of whom were men), 1905–6, 1909–10, 1910–11, and three in 1911–12 (out of 42, 16 of whom were men); one Modern Languages candidate took Schools in 1909–10 (out of 23, 12 of whom were men), and there was a single candidate in all but one of the subsequent pre-war years (the school was first examined in 1905); there were Physiology finalists in 1904–5, 1905–6, 1907–8 and 1908–9 (out of between 11 and 22 p.a. in the University as a whole). There was one Wadham finalist in Geology in 1907–8 (out of 5 in the University), and Wadham provided the sole Geology finalist in the whole University in 1914–15; the subject remained a tiny one. Botany was represented in 1910–11, 1912–13 and 1913–14; in the last pre-war year, Wadham produced 2 out of the University total of 3. Wadham produced the only Oriental Studies candidate in the University in 1912–13 (there had been Wadham finalists also in 1906–7 and 1910–11); in the same year (1912–13) Wadham produced its only Engineering finalist in this period (the University total was 9 in 1912–13): there was not to be another Wadham finalist in this subject until 1933–4. From 1900–14 there were no Physics or Zoology candidates, and the only Mathematics and Physics candidate did Schools in 1915–16. Data kindly produced by Mark Pottle from the *History of the University of Oxford Database*. MPWAD4; MPWAD5.

20. *Gazette* (1912), 96–97. It is worth comparing this with a further survey which was done by Wells for the 144 men who completed a course at Wadham between January 1920 and December 1922. Thirty came from abroad; of the remaining 114, 21 went into teaching; 17 took Holy Orders; 15 went into business; 14 into the Civil Service; 12 to law. See cutting from *Evening News* 7 Jan. 1926 in WA, Wells Papers. Wells had written in response to a rather different complaint from Sir Robert Baden-Powell, that men were not pulling their weight in the service of the country.

21. Wolfe, *Upward Anguish*, 77.

22. See the moving obituary in *Gazette* (1931), 63–65.

23. L.A.G. Strong, *Green Memory* (1961), 169.

24. *Gazette* (1914), 266; 270–71; (1916), 393.

25. Strong, *Green Memory*, 190.

26. WA, Wells Papers, J. Wells, 'Oxford in the War', cutting from *Oxford Magazine*.

27. *Gazette* (1917), 49. E.A. Webster had arrived at Wadham as an undergraduate in 1898, and was elected to a Fellowship on graduation; he began his tutorial work in Philosophy in 1903, and was evidently a stimulating Tutor. Theodore Wade-Gery had been elected just before the war, but did not come into residence before joining up.

28. R. Graves, *Goodbye to all That* (1929), 304–6; 372.

29. *Gazette* (1916), 4; *ibid.* (1917), 31; S.H. Paton, 'Wadham College just after the First World War', *Gazette* (1975), 43–44, at 43.

30. *Ibid.* (1916), 418; *ibid.* (1917), 54.

31. *Ibid.* (1916), 4.

32. *Ibid.* (1917), 29–30.

33. WA, Letters to Wells.

34. *Gazette* (1919), 204.

35. Strong, *Green Memory*, 164. 36. Kelf-Cohen, 'Wadham College', 27.

37. WA, Debating Society, 113/1/8.

38. *Gazette* (1920), 302.

39. See B. Harrison, 'Undergraduate Life in the Interwar Period', *Hist. of Univ.*, viii.

40. Henry Phelps Brown (1924), personal communication. See *Tutorial Teaching at Wadham*, eds Davies and Garnett (2008) for more details.

41. C.M. Bowra, *Memories 1898–1939* (1966), 144–46.

42. F.A. Iremonger, 'Dr. Joseph Wells', in his *Men and Movements in the Church* (1928), 113–125, at 120.

43. See *Gazette* (1915), 355–6: an old member had left his estates in Somerset to the University to endow Scholarships in Biology. Wells expressed regret that he did not leave anything to his old College, and glossed a comment on the poverty and needs of the College: 'We have no endowment at all for Modern History, we have no Repairs Fund, we have little means of helping deserving men apart from examinations, we have still less for assisting our best scholars to continue their studies after their degree.' Wadham had suffered the largest drop in income of any college except Worcester over the period 1883–1911, according to L.R. Price's calculations – from £4,200 to £2,720. See *Gazette* (1913), 146–47.

44. *Gazette* (1909), 197. See also *ibid.* (1905), 243, on Barker's success in drawing record numbers of undergraduates to his lectures in Wadham.

45. See n. 32 above; cf. *Gazette* (1919), 207 (redecoration of the hall).

46. Henry Phelps Brown, personal communication. Sir Henry Phelps Brown

read History and then PPE. He was subsequently Fellow of New College (1930–47), and Professor of Economics of Labour at London University (1947–68). He wrote extensively on wages and prices, and British industrial relations. He died in 1994. See *OxDNB*.

47. W.D. Haden (1928), personal communication.

48. WA, C.A. Rivington (1921), memoir, 3.

49. S. Day-Lewis, *C. Day-Lewis: An English Literary Life* (London, 1980), 36–7. Cf. H. Phelps Brown, personal communication.

50. H. Phelps Brown, personal communication.

51. *Gazette* (1923),45. For similar sentiments held by an undergraduate up at Wadham in Wells's time, see Vere Ducker(1923), 'Rowing and Christian Life. A Sermon preached for the Henley Royal Regatta Service, 8 July 1990', *Gazette* (1991), 75–6.

52. Iremonger, 'Dr. Joseph Wells', 119–20.

53. See D. J. Wenden, 'Oxford Sport between the Wars', *Hist. of Univ.*, viii.

54. *Isis*, 739 (30 July 1927), 7 (A.F. Heppenstall, 1924); *ibid.*, 789 (22 Jan. 1930), 7 (P.D. Howard, 1928).

55. WA, Debating Society, 113/1/8.

56. H. Phelps Brown, personal communication; cf. WA 222/2, R.N. Turner (1931), 'From the Depths of my Memory' (1976), 32.

57. *Gazette* (1924), 134. Cf. *ibid.*(1927), 323; *ibid.* (1937), 351.

58. WA, C.A. Rivington, memoir, 13. For the rules of the Book Club, see Bodleian Library, Wadham College Scrap Book (G.A. Oxon. c. 289), 26; cf. J. Wells, 'The Annals of the College Book Club', *Cornhill Magazine*, ns 34 (1913), 802–10.

59. See 'Brasenose and the Strike', *The Brazen Nose*, 4 (1926), 154. See also Wenden, 'Oxford Sport'.

60. C. Day-Lewis, *The Buried Day* (1960), 171; Bowra, *Memories*, 179; H. Phelps Brown, personal communication. Phelps Brown

recalled the President of the Boat Club speaking of the Strike as an annoyance because it was interrupting Eights training.

61. *Isis*, 888 (7 Feb. 1934), 5.

62. *Ibid.*, 878 (18 Oct. 1933),7. Michael Foot arrived in Wadham in1931. George Devine (1929) was an actor and producer. He was Director of the Old Vic, 1946–51, and founder of the Young Vic; he was Director of the English Stage Company (Royal Court Theatre), 1955–65. See *OxDNB*.

63. In the inter-war period, History became by a large margin the biggest school in the University, producing around 250 finalists p.a. (over double the total for Greats). English and Law caught up with (and occasionally overtook) Greats, to be joined by PPE and Modern Languages from the early 1930s. The number of Wadham candidates was roughly proportionate: there were 2 Wadham PPE finalists (out of 41) in 1923–24, and an average of between 2 and 4 thereafter. Modern Languages also produced between 2 and 3 (5 in some years) through the 1920s and 1930s. But in the 1920s and 1930s there were usually 6 or 7 History finalists, more often between 4 and 6 in Greats, and between 5 and 6 in Law. Of the schools which were very small in the University, Wadham had one candidate in Engineering in 1933–4 (out of a University total of 9), and none in Geography; there were no Wadham Mathematics finalists until 1934–35 (the year 1936–37 produced the inter-war maximum for the University as a whole of 36); there was one finalist in Zoology in 1923–4 (out of 8), and subsequently one appeared in 1924–25 and again in 1934–35: the numbers in all these subjects remained relatively small. There were more Wadham Physicists, although this was also a small subject overall: Wadham produced one out of 4 in 1919–20; then none until 1927–28 when it produced 2 out of 10; thereafter one, occasionally 2 a year until 1937–38 and 1938–39, when there were 3 out of totals of 17 and 19 respectively. In Physiology

there were one or 2 Wadham finalists (3 in 1931–2) in nearly every inter-war year from 1921–2. After 1927 there were no Theology finalists in Wadham until 1935–36 (one) and 1936–37 (two). Data kindly produced by Mark Pottle from the *History of the University of Oxford Database*, MPWAD4; MPWAD5.

64. See C.S.L. Davies, 'Maurice Bowra Elected Fellow', *Gazette* (1984), 26–28.

65. *Ibid.* (1920), 273.

66. *Ibid.* (1921), 357.

67. WA, C.A. Rivington, memoir, 11.

68. *Ibid.*

69. WA, H.W. Parke, memoir; Cf.H. W. Parke, 'Wadham College in the Twenties', *Gazette* (1986), 58.

70. H. Phelps Brown, personal communication.

71. W.D. Haden and R. Wade-Gery, personal communications.

72. Iremonger, 'Dr.Joseph Wells', 121.

73. A. Bullock, personal communication. My thanks are due also to George Forrest for talking about Wade-Gery with me. See also A. Andrewes, 'Theodore Wade-Gery 1888–1972', *Proceedings of the British Academy*, 59 (1973), 419–26.

74. Parke, 'Wadham College', 57. He was also the lover of the novelist Naomi Mitchison.

75. W.D. Haden, personal communication.

76. R. Wade-Gery, personal communication.

77. G. Hogg, 'Wadham College Fifty-Five Years Ago', *Gazette* (1977), 31; cf. *ibid.*, 33 (reminiscence by R.B. du Boe).

78. A. Bullock, personal communication. Alan Bullock (1933) read Greats and then History. He was Fellow of New College (1945–52), Censor of St Catherine's Society, Oxford (1952–60), and founding Master of St Catherine's College (1960–80). He is the author of books on central aspects of twentieth-century history. Died 2004. See *OxDNB*.

79. R. Wade-Gery, personal communication.

80. Parke, 'Wadham College', 56.

81. WA, L. Wilson (1926), memoir, 4. Alan Bullock, notably, disliked the social atmosphere around Bowra, and was initially unhappy at Wadham.

82. H. Phelps Brown, personal communication.

83. W.D. Haden, personal communication.

84. T.C. Keeley, 'Reminiscences', *Gazette* (1975), 30. Cf. C.A.Rivington, memoir, 10, on Bowra's taking the office of Dean seriously.

85. C. Day-Lewis, *The Buried Day* (1960), 164.

86. See, as an early example, R. Lennard, 'Agricultural Labourers and a Minimum Wage', *Economic Review*, 22 (1912), 367–79.

87. This was to be a fully collegiate enterprise. In 1925, a provisional list of eight chapter titles was published in the *Gazette*, and Lennard asked readers to pass on any relevant references which they might come across in the literature of the period 1558–1760. See *Gazette* (1925), 190. The published version was rather shorter than originally intended, containing four essays. (The authors were Lennard himself, W.P. Baker, R.F. Bretherton, and R.N.K. Rees and Charles Fenby, who produced a joint contribution.)

88. *Gazette* (1931), 71; R. Lennard(ed.), *Englishmen at Rest and Play. Some Phases of English Leisure 1558–1714*, by members of *Wadham College, Oxford* (1931), 77–78.

89. WA, letter (25 Mar. 1929) from Lennard to Shaw on his election as the first George Calder McLeod Scholar of Wadham.

90. R.F. Bretherton, 'Reginald Lennard in Wadham between the Wars', *Gazette* (1979), 25–29; L. Wilson, memoir; Bowra, *Memories,* 132, 145; conversations with Harold Harley, Henry Phelps Brown, Alan Bullock, Charles Wenden. The last three were all examples of Lennard's good judgment in the selection of those who had not originally thought of applying to Wadham. Bowra, Wade-Gery and sometimes Brabant also took groups of undergraduates on reading parties – usually to Kent or Devon. For appreciation of Lennard's Lake District reading parties, see WA 222/2, R.N. Turner (1931), 'From the Depths of my Memory', 30; WA 223, Reminiscences, T. Griffiths (1921).On his death (in 1967) Lennard bequeathed money to the College to support reading parties. In 1971 Ray Ockenden began organizing a spring reading party in Cornwall, which has taken place nearly every year since.

91. H. Cranborne (ed.), *David Cecil: A Portrait by his Friends* (Wimborne, 1990), 39–40; *OxDNB.*

92. *Ibid.*, 53; E. Longford, *The Pebbled Shore* (1986), 64.

93. Keeley, 'Reminiscences (continued)', *Gazette* (1975), 39, 94. Bill Hart was the rival candidate for the Wardenship.

94. See above, n.2.

95. See above, n.2.

96. *Gazette* (1933), 151.

CHAPTER FIVE

THE BOWRA YEARS: 1938–1970

My main source for correcting the vivid memories of someone who has been a Fellow since 1947 has been the *Wadham College Gazette*, not always accurate but usually revealing. In addition, I have been greatly assisted by the many old members who have responded to my requests for recollections of the Bowra years in the *Gazette*, and look forward to receiving more. Meanwhile I must thank Gordon Philo and Geoffrey Smerdon for helping me with the wartime period, and Ray Dawson and Peter Placito for unearthing a few nuggets on the post-war years.

My chief debt, however, is to my friend Ian Crombie, who has produced a remarkable set of lengthy memoranda on aspects of life at Wadham since the 1930s. These I have used constantly to test my own capacity for recall. If I may borrow a phrase from my old tutor, A.J.P. Taylor, I have extracted from 'this inexhaustible quarry … countless fragments and hewn them into shapes which I fear' Ian

may not always recognize. For Bowra see now the excellent biography by Leslie Mitchell, *Maurice Bowra: a Life* (Oxford, 2009).

[*Editorial note*] Footnotes have been provided by the editors in order to explain allusions to later generations while retaining the air of personal memoir in the text. A.F. (always 'Pat') Thompson was Fellow and Tutor in History, 1947–87; he was also a major participant in the affairs of which he writes, as Domestic Bursar (1948–54), Senior Tutor twice (1954–7, 1962–4), Tutor for Graduates (1964–7) and Sub-Warden twice (1968–9, 1975–8). See P.J. Waller (ed.), *Politics and Social Change in Modern Britain: Essays Presented to A.F. Thompson* (1987). Ian Crombie was a long-serving Tutor in Philosophy (1947–83), as well as Librarian (1950–64), Senior Tutor (1964–7) and Sub-Warden (1972–5). Both became Emeritus Fellows. Pat Thompson died in 2009.

1. William Hart, born 1903, Law Fellow 1926–47, Bursar 1928–40; a wartime civil servant, subsequently general manager of Hemel Hempstead Development Corporation, Clerk to London County Council, and Director General of Greater London Council. Knighted 1961. Died 1977.

2. Stenning died in 1959.

3. The reference, somewhat anachronistic, is to the story, *ben trovato*, of Keeley, unable to find a dog-sitter, taking his dog Nicholas to *The Cruel Sea*. Asked whether the dog had enjoyed the film, Keeley replied, 'Yes, but not as much as the book'.

4. By some arrangement Keeley was able to use the secretaries provided for him as Administrator of the Clarendon Laboratory on Wadham business; 'day and night nurses' was a Bowra epithet for the morning and afternoon shifts.

5. With Lennard's retirement from his Fellowship in 1946 (although continuing as the University's Reader in Economic

History until 1951) and Bill Deakin's departure to be Warden of St Antony's in 1950, only Keeley and Jack Thompson (elected 1936) remained from pre-war Wadham among the Tutorial Fellows. Much of the *élan* of the 1950s was due to the unusual cohesion of a group of committed young Tutors, for the most part ex-servicemen.

6. R.J.P. Williams, born 1926, Chemistry Tutor 1955–74, Royal Society Research Professor 1974–91, Sub-Warden 1991–3. Emeritus Fellow.

7. Humphry House (1908–55) had been elected Fellow and Chaplain in 1931, being then in deacon's orders. He lost his faith before proceeding to the priesthood and resigned his Fellowship in 1932. After an academic career in India and at Cambridge, he was appointed University Lecturer at Oxford in 1948, and Senior Research Fellow of Wadham in 1950. The best known of some remarkable books is *The Dickens World* (1941). See *OxDNB*.

8. The *Gazette* (1993), 98, reporting John Currie's death, failed to spot that he was anything more than 'Director and Partner of Prompt Contract Cleaning Company'.

9. E.A. Milne, 1896–1950, Rouse Ball Professor and Fellow 1928–50; he had been FRS at the age of 30. See too Bowra, *Memories*, 350–1. Jack Westrup 1904–75, Heather Professor and Fellow 1947–71, knighted 1961. *DNB 1971–80* mentions his 'complete self control' and 'a presence which alarmed those who did not know him well'. For both see *OxDNB*.

10. F. A. Lindemann, 1886–1957, Dr Lee's Professor 1919–56; Lord Cherwell, 1941, member of the wartime government 1942–5, and Cabinet Minister 1951–3. *OxDNB*.

11. 1916–74, Rouse Ball Professor 1947–72, Professor of Theoretical Chemistry, 1972–4; Vice-President of the Methodist Conference and Chairman of Oxfam. *OxDNB*.

12. The Robbins Commission investigated higher education on a national level, 1961–4; the Franks Commission (1964–6) was established by Oxford to overhaul its own administration following criticism and implicit threats in Robbins.

13. J.H.C. Thompson, Estates Bursar, 1945–65; P. B. Carter, 1965–77; For Jack Thompson, see below. Peter Carter, born 1921, was Law Tutor, 1949–88, then Emeritus Fellow. He died in 2004.

14. H.B. (Ben) Arber, Scholar of the College and oarsman, 1924–7, served in the Sudan Civil Service, eventually as Governor of Northern Province; Domestic Bursar 1958–72, Fellow 1967–72, died 1986.

15. Graduate students are supervised on a University rather than College basis. The campaign to make their presence felt in College has been vigorously fought by successive Tutors for Graduates (a role created by Pat Thompson) and by the officers of the MCR.

16. Retired as Warden in 1970, died 4 July 1971.

17. Keeley retired in 1963, thereafter devoting himself to the affairs of the Wadham Society (founded 1963). He kept his rooms in College under an arrangement not repeated, and died peacefully in his armchair on Christmas Day 1988, at the age of 94, having retained his faculties to the last; see the obituaries in *Gazette* (1990), 14–21.

18. J.H.C. (Jack) Thompson, Mathematics Tutor 1936–75, Estates Bursar 1945–65, prominent too in University affairs, running the Finance Committee of the Press. Died 17 June 1975.

CHAPTER SIX

SINCE 1970

1. *Gazette* (1994), 63.

2. *Franks Report* i.132, cited in K. Thomas, 'College Life, 1944–1970', *History of the Univ*, viii, 215.

3. Cf J.M. Crook, *Brasenose: The Biography of an Oxford College* (Oxford, 2008), pp. 413–14.

4. See Jason Leech, 'First of the Last; Wadham College and the Decision for Co-Residence to 1974', B.A. thesis, 2004, in WCA 2B.

5. Maurice Bowra's reply to a letter from Mary Bennett, Principal of St Hilda's, WCA 2B.

6. Personal communication, 2009.

7. *History of the Univ*, viii, 213.

8. In WCA 2B.

9. For details see chapter 9.

10. *Gazette* (1994), 68.

11. *Dorothy's Lip* (1993).

12. *Gazette* (1975), 7.

13. *Gazette* (1986), 39.

14. See Peter Wright, *Spycatcher* (1987).

CHAPTER EIGHT

THE GARDENS

1. Beyond Jackson's *Wadham*, the Convention Books and College Papers, including the annual reports of the Keeper of the Gardens held in the Archives, and reminiscences by T.C. Keeley and others in the *Gazette*, sources for this chapter are: R.T. Gunther, *Oxford Gardens* (Oxford, 1912); E.S. Rohde, *Oxford's College Gardens* (1932); David Sturdy, *Twelve Oxford Gardens* (privately printed, n.d., c. 1989); Mavis Batey, *Oxford Gardens*, (1982); Ronald D. Gray and Ernst Frankl, *Oxford Gardens* (Cambridge, 1987).

2. Quoted in Jackson, *Wadham*, 210.

3. Evelyn, *Diary*, iii, 110.

4. *Ibid.*, iii, 110.

5. Robert Plot, *Natural History of Oxfordshire* (Oxford, 1705; repr., Chicheley, Bucks, 1974), 240.

6. Jackson, *Wadham*, 215.

7. Gunther, *Oxford Gardens*, 234.

8. *Ibid.*, 234.

CHAPTER NINE
THE BUILDINGS

1. The original building was described at length, with extensive and expert use of the building accounts, in Jackson, *Wadham;* and of course has been frequently described and analysed since; most notably by the Royal Commission on Historical Monuments, *The City of Oxford* (1939), and in Nikolaus Pevsner's *Oxfordshire* (1974) in his Buildings of England series. For that reason this chapter has concentrated rather more on the more recent buildings than does the normal guide-book account. Dorothy Wadham's brother, Lord Petre, objected to the original plan as 'too spacious and sumptuous'; Nancy Briggs, 'Foundation', *Oxoniensia* 21 (1956), 72.

2. For Arnold, see the entry in Howard Colvin, *Biographical Dictionary of British Architects* (4th edn. 2008). Arnold was far from being a mere provincial craftsman; indeed there was a danger that he might be enticed away from Wadham by Lord Salisbury; Briggs, 'Foundation', 67.

3. Its original mechanism, allegedly designed by Wren, is now on loan to the Museum of the History of Science in Oxford.

4. Jackson, *Wadham*, 176.

5. See Pauline Croft, 'The Religion of Robert Cecil', *Historical Journal*, 34 (1991), 773–96.

6. Jackson, *Wadham*, 161.

7. Croft, 'Robert Cecil', 787 n.43.

8. Jackson, *Wadham*, 158–62.

9. Strangways is commemorated by a large portrait in Hall. For the van Ling window see Jackson, *Wadham*, 163–70, and Michael Archer, Sarah Crewe, and Peter Cormack, *English Heritage in Stained Glass: Oxford* (Oxford and New York, 1988), 24–6.

10. Jackson, *Wadham*, 174–5.

11. Gardiner, *Registers*, i, 67–8. He was third baronet, having held the title less than 10 months since the death of his elder brother. For the Portman family, see M.J. Hawkins, 'Wardship, Royalist Delinquency and Too Many Children: the Portmans in the Seventeenth Century,' *Southern History*, 4 (1982), 55–89.

12. See Ch.4 above, n. 93.

13. The balls are on loan to the Oxford County Museum, Woodstock.

14. Its master mason was 'Master Peisley'; i.e. Bartholomew Peisley, *c*.1654–1715, of a dynasty of Oxford masons. Colvin, *British Architects* (2008), 795. Wren was, of course, very grand by 1693. The building had been altered a good deal over time and was very successfully restored to its original condition by Robert Potter in 1968.

15. Eprime Eshag, Economics fellow 1962–86, himself an Iranian, was largely instrumental in bringing this about.

16. See J.H. Mee, *The Oldest Music Room in Europe* (1911).

17. W.F. Oakeshott (ed.), *Oxford Stone Restored* (Oxford, 1975); and conversations with Bert Archer.

18. 'Tender Townscape', in *Architectural Review* (Oct. 1971), 210–16.

Index

Locations for illustrations are in **bold**

APPENDIX V

List of Subscribers

This book has been made possible through the generosity of the following:

Mark Abrahamson	2003	Arnd Bauerkamper	1982	Tymon Broadhead	1985	Nick Clarke	1995
Mark Addley	1998	Prebendary Roger Bauld	1955	Edward Broadhead	1938	Richard Clarke	1982
Stephen Agar	1980	Perry Bayliss	1978	David Christopher Brown	1976	Tom Clayton	1954
Mark Aitman	1982	Dr M. Dominic Beer	1975	D.A. Brown	1972	Patrick Clerkin	2002
Toby C.R. Allen	1996	Lenon Beeson	1944	Christopher Bryan	1954	Dr Mike Clugston	1969
Austin Allison	1965	Nick Benbow	1973	Tim Brydges	1966	James A. Cochrane	1938
Roger Almond	1953	Revd D. Paul Beresford-Hill		Bruce T.H. Burke	1971	Jim Cocke	1947
Emefa Juliet Afi			1990	Edward Burn	1941	Terry Cole	1965
Amoako (née Takyi)	1999	Sir Frank Berman	1961	Piers Burton-Page	1966	Dr Paul Collier	1995
Julian Anderson	1957	Christopher D. Bertram	1968	Rob Butler	1977	John Collins	1957
Kara Cox Anderson	2004	D.S. Betts	1955	Phil Butlin	1976	Andrea Connell	1986
Matthew Andrew	2008	Anna Izabela Bisewska		Derek Button		Kenneth W. Cook	1943
John Andrews	1953	(now Dickson)	1974	Dr Duncan Bythell	1959	Mr and Mrs Ian Cox 1983, 1987	
Professor John Andrews CBE		Michael Bishopp	1968	D.H. Calam	1956	Dr Richard Cranage	1968
	1953	Debashish Biswas	2001	Alexander M.G. Campbell	1991	Peter Craven	1957
David Andrews-Jones	1942	Major J.T.L Blackler ERD	1941	Colin John Campbell	1951	Penelope Cream	1984
Dr Alan Armitage	1949	Richard Blackmore	1949	Dugal Campbell	1952	Wayne Crumb	
Tobias Arnold	1994	W. Seymour Blake	1938	Anthony and Rosemary		Dr Neil Cuddy	1976
Dr Peter Arrowsmith	1975	Catherine Blanshard		Cantwell	1966	Darron Anthony Cullen	2002
Ms Susan Arthur	1977	(née Bellamy)	1999	Charles Cantwell	1966	John Patrick Cullinane	1973
Bryan Ashenheim	1964	Joost Blom	1970	Francis Carpenter	1961	Professor Anthony Cullis	1964
Peter Atley	1962	John C. Bonnycastle	1958	The Revd C.F. Carter	1956	Terence Curran	2007
Anna Austin	1998	Polly Botsford	1990	Suzy Carter (née Roessler)	1978	James Currey	1955
Iradj Bagherzade	1962	Roderick Boucher	1968	David Cashdan	1946	Robert Currie	
Julian Thompson Baird	1960	E.G. Boulton	1943	Frances Cassidy	1980	Julie Curtis	1974
John A. Baker	1943	Elizabeth Boulton	1983	David J. Cast	1961	Emily and Tom Daniel	1984
Paul Baker	1978	Ulick Bourke	1958	Ian Castello-Cortes	1981	David Dare	1961
John Howard Bamforth OBE		Dr R.G. Bowers CMB OBE	1960	Sally Caswell	2006	Mark Darian-Smith	1984
	1943	Gareth Boyd	1988	Leona M.T. Chan	1990	Patrick Daunt	1946
Nicholas Barber	1959	Patrick Boylan	1991	Neil Cheshire	1954	Revd W.W. Davidson	1946
Hon. Daniel A. Barker	1977	Jeremy P. Bradshaw	1971	J.K.W. Cheung	1987	Professor J.K. Davies FBA	1955
Charles Barnard	1950	Emily Bratt	2001	King Yan Cheung	2006	Lynne Davies	1987
John Barnard	1956	Tony Brennan	1985	David Chivers	1983	Richard C. Davies MA DPhil	
Samuel Barnes	2003	Tom Breslin	1984	Michael Clapham	1959		1956
Dick Barton	1956	J.R. Bretherton	1962	Andrew Clark	1984	Jonathan Davis	1999
Revd Wendy Baskett	1979	David S. Brett	1970	Gerard Clarke	1981	Ian G. Dawson	1957
Catherine Bateman	1978	Denis H. Bridges	1943	Laurence and Catherine Clarke		Rogier de Kok	1994
Edward Bateman	2001	Nick Britton	2000		1998	John De Nordwall	1949

Miss K.A.G. Tania De Silva	1988	David Garvie	1988	David Hodgson	1951	Krogh Lars-Jacob	
Dean & Associates		Dr William J. Gatens	1973	Nick Hodgson	1977	Tony Lawdham	1957
Andrew Dean	1968	A.W. Gates	1946	Benn Hogg	2001	Dr D.A. Lea	1959
Stephen Dell	1965	Alan A. Gaves	1948	Terry Hole	1988	S.J. Ledsham	1978
Roger Devlin	1975	Neil Gerrard	1960	Peter Hole	1956	Carol F. Lee	1976
B. Gale Dick	1950	Richard and Ursula Gibbons		Marc Holland	1993	Dr Norman Lee	1981
Clive Dickinson	1972		1977	B.R. Holland	1973	Jason Leech	2001
Brian Dimmock	1953	Revd Derek V. Gibling	1953	V.P. Holloway MBE	1951	Christine Leigh	2005
Joanna Dixon	1989	Ian Kenneth Gibson	2008	Frank Holroyde	1942	Professor Jörn Leonhard	
Peter Dixon	1973	Sydney Giffard	1945	Michael Hopmeier	1970	Jonathan and Diana Lewis	1975
Michael Dixon	1955	David Gilliuer	1967	R.C.O. Howard	1965	Gareth Lewis	1992
Barrie Dobson	1951	Roger Gillott	1990	Laura C.H. Hoyano		P.R. Li Morgan	1945
Ian Dodds	1962	Dr Keith Gilroy		Dr Norman J. Hoyle	1970	Wendy Light (née Climie)	1986
Tony Drake	1967	Michael Goldman	1949	Jonathan Huddleston	1997	Lionel Lightman	1946
Canon Mervyn Drewett	1946	Peter Goodford	1951	Dr Sarah Huline-Dickens	1987	Jonathan Lipkin	1989
G.G. Dron	1964	Miss Jessica C.B. Goodman	2008	J.M. Hunt	1957	Andrew Littlejones	1961
Brendan Drummond	1961	Guy S. Goodwin-Gill	1965	Manar Hussain	1990	Dr Dave R. Livingstone	1967
Colin Drummond	1969	Harumi Goto-Shibata	1987	Frank Hytch	1946	Danica Lo	2000
Hugh Drummond	2000	Haydn Gott	1963	Chika Ikeda	1994	Patrick Locke CBE	1954
Daphne Dumont	1974	Humphrey Graham	1961	G.R.H. Isard	1971	Marcus J. Lofting	1960
Ian Duncalf	1968	Paul Gravett	1994	Nicholas Jackson	1972	Richard Lowndes	1952
Catherine Dunford	2000	Dr R.W. Gray	1962	Hannah Jackson	2000	John Luetchford	1965
M. Dunworth	1957	Alan Green	1948	Robert Jackson	1962	Caroline Lunzer	1976
Professor Keith Dyke		Mrs J. Greenshields and		Sidney R. James	1940	J.L. Lunzer	1946
Warren and Amanda East		Dr C. Greenshields	1988	Raymond Jeffers	1975	Antony Lydon	1956
	1980, 1981	Graham Philip Greenwood	2005	Angela Jefferson, Staff	1988	Canon John D. Lytle	1946
The Revd Dr David A. Edwards		John Gregson	1962	Graham Jenkin	1965	Gordon Mabb	1954
	1944	J.H. Grey	1971	Robert Jenkinson	1962	Kirsty MacDonald	
Rear Admiral J.P. Edwards		W. Robert Griffiths	1949	Helen Jewell	1995	A.D. Macro	1957
CB LVO		Mathew Gullick	1995	Michael Jewell	1995	Samir Maha	1995
John Edwards and Sally Edwards		Daniel Hacking	1991	Miss Kathryn Johnson	2001	Ben Maling	2005
(née Strahan)	1975, 1976	J. Hackney	1959	Katy Johnson	1996	Dr John Manners	1953
Pearl Eliadis	1985	Cordelia Mary Hall	1976	Pat Jolly	1940	Jessica Mannix	
Mathew Elson	1984	Tony Halmos	1969	Carole-Ann Jones		W.D. Manville	1966
Dr Heike S. Urich-Erber, MJur		Robert Ham QC	1968	(née Tuer)	1988	John Margetts	1955
	2003	Richard Ham	1975	Ralph H.C. Jones	1968	Robert Margolis	1983
Linda Eshag		Garry Hambleton	1958	A.K. Joy	1977	Paul Marsden	1973
Robin Esser	1952	Alexandra N.J. Hamburger	2008	Richard B. Kapnick	1980	John Marsh	1969
David Evans	1982	Matthew Handley	1996	S.C.K. Keels	1951	P.P. Marshall	1954
David H. Evans QC	1968	Sigurdur Hannesson	2003	Richard Kendall	1980	P.J. Marshall	1954
Dr Hywel Wyndham Evans	1988	Gerald E. Hare	1956	Geoffrey Alexander Kennedy		Blythe Marston	1981
Dr Keith Evans	1968	Martin J. Harris	1985		1956	Glenn Martin	1967
Simon T. Evans	1978	C.C. Harris	1955	Michael Kerin	1973	R.P. Martineau	1962
John Eyles	1966	R.I. Harris	1977	Mohsin Khan	2005	E. Walter Mason	1953
William H.D. Facey	1967	Khalid Hasan	1948	Barry Kidson	1961	Karen Masters	1997
Alan Farquharson	1956	Frode Ernst Haverkamp	1972	P.M. Kilty	1965	Caroline Mawson	
Jerome Farrell	1976	John Hawes	1956	John Kiteley	1952	Peter J. Maybury	1963
Dr Clive D. Field OBE	1968	Revd Dr Anthony Haws	1965	Morgan Spencer Knight	1932	Christine Mayou	1994
Nick Finn	1967	Nick Hay	1979	Jane Knowles	1974	Harry Mayou	1994
Michael Fleming	1956	Michael Heartsong	1966	Richard Koch	1968	John E.G. McCarthy	1974
Jean Flemming		The Revd Duncan Heddle	1953	Hugh H. Kolb	1963	James Angus McDonald	1943
James W. Flint	1952	Thomas G. Heinersdorff	1971	Andrzej Korzeniowski	2002	Alec McGivan	1972
Sir Roderick Floud	1961	Ian Henderson	1951	Professor Nick Kuenssberg OBE		Iain McKendrick	1981
M.A. Floyer	1974	Keiran Hendrick	1992		1961	Dr Brian M. McKenna	1987
A.J. Forey	1951	Katharine Henson	1985	Martin Kukla and Alison Kukla		Paul McKeown	1950
David M. Foster	1954	Kathryn Hesketh	2002		1978	Peter Meanley	1956
Dr Eric L. Foster	1952	John Hewitt	1964	Peter Kwan	1994	Keith Medford	1958
Jim Fowler	1988	J. Richard S. Higham	1956	Wilson Wai Shun Kwok	1992	Louise Felicity Meltzer	1976
Richard Alan Fox	1966	John Higham	1962	Matthew James Lacey	1992	Mark Menhenney	1975
Walter Frank	1949	Roger N. Higton	1987	Professor James Lahore	1953	Euan Menzies	1986
Tim Franks	1986	Susan Hitch	1975	Tony Lambert	1956	Anthony Merifield	1954
Colin Gamage	1953	Michael Hobkirk	1942	Professor David Lanham	1962	Henry K. Miller	1998
Roy Garthwaite	1947	Richard N. Hobson	1972	Frank Larkins	1966	Ian Miller	1963

Peter Milliken	1968	Juliet C. Pickering	1987	D.G.J. Shipley	1974	Roger Undy	1969
David K. Mills	1956	Christopher Pierpoint	1956	Bryan Short	1952	Ian Vellins	1957
David S.R. Mills	1956	Michael Pinkerton	1969	Jo Sidhu	1984	Matthew Vernon	2008
Alison Milner	1989	O.J. Pointer	1976	Brian Simpson	1965	Gianni Vesuviano	2005
Yeap Miranda	1989	Nigel R. Pond	1979	H. and M. Skoda	1999	A.L. Vincent	1955
Andrew Mitchell	1998	Charles A. Pope	1967	Professor William J.L. Sladen		Emma Wahlen (née Sims)	1993
Christopher M. Mitchell	1974	Victoria Porter	1995		1955	Sam Walden	1995
Julian Mitchell	1955	Ian C. Porter	1970	Antony Smith		Professor Geoffrey Walford	
Stephen Monsell	1966	T. Peter R. Pound	1999	Sir David Smith FRS FRSE		Carmichael J.A. Wallace	1968
Jeremy Montagu		Anthony Preston	1974	Revd Heather Noel Smith	1979	Philip Waller	1964
Denis Montgomery	1947	A.C. Preston	1974	Julian Smith	1992	Mike Warne	1974
Steve Moon	1979	Dr P.C. Price		Dr Martin J. Smith	2000	Dr Antony Warner	1951
Roger Moore	1955	Peter E. Quint	1964	Simon Smith	1976	Dr Richard Warner	1979
Leonora Moore	2002	Mark Radford	1979	Stephen Smith	1987	Dr Thomas Warner	1981
Lucy Moore	2003	Samantha L Randall	2003	Bob Smyth	1962	Edward Warrington	1991
E.A.L.L Morgan	1952	Melvyn Randle	1969	Jonathan Snary	1989	Chris Wathen	1964
Leigh Morris	1992	Professor Dr R. Ratnalingham		Dr Robert Solomon	1955	J. Watson	
James Morrison	1944		1966	Professor Tom Solomon	1984	John W. Watson	1973
P.L. Morson	1937	Martin Read	1956	Jenny Sonderlind	2002	Edward J. Wawrzynczak	1976
Bruce C. Mortimer DFC FM		Colin Ready	1980	William Sooby	1974	Timothy Weakley	1953
Jamie Mortimer	1966	N.W. Rees	1981	I.P.G. Southward	1964	Neil and Joanne Welch	1985
David Moskowitz	1960	Martin S.B. Reid	1969	J.A. (Tony) Spencer	1943	Richard Welch	1964
Charles Edward Muir		Dr Aribert Reimann		Stephen R. Stacey	1974	Francis Weston	1949
Gregory Mullaly	1976	James Rennard	1994	Ian and Richard Standen		Josephine Whitaker	2005
Dr Gordon Mungeam	1950	John Rhodes	1967		1961, 1988	S.H. White	1970
Murayama Junko PhD	1991	John A. Rhodes	1950	Rosie J. Staniforth	1990	Holly E.A. Whitlock	1987
Peter Murray	1976	J.F. Richardson	1953	Alan Stanton	1967	Roland Wilcock OBE	1946
Henry Mutkin	1954	Steven Ridgeon	1977	Revd Dick Staunton	1943	Miss Julia Wilcox	2003
Namenicola Muir	1997	Frank Riess	1962	W.A. Stephen	1949	Colonel Eric Albert Delaney	
Heather V. Naylor	1976	Stevan Riley	1995	Sian Stickings	1976	Wilde OBE MC	1940
Kwong Luk Ng	2000	Chris Riley	1964	A.J. Stirling		Hon. Daryl Williams AM QC	
Helen Mary Nicholson	1996	Fred Ris	1968	Dr Bianca Stroll	1997		1965
Dr F.A. Nizami	1979	Mark Roach	1983	Patrick Strong	1950	David E.A. Williams	1980
Gerald Normie	1950	Ilona and Gareth Roberts	1997	Dr K. Ronald Sujithan	1994	Dr M.R.W. Williams	1985
Ray Ockenden	1974	Sir Denys Roberts	1948	Neil Sullivan	1963	Timothy O. Williams	1980
P.W. Ockleston	1953	Mark Roberts	1999	Professor Brian J. Sutton	1972	David Wills	1973
Orla O'Connor	1991	Michael Roberts	1965	Michael Swan	1989	Graham Wilson	1963
Katsumi Onaka	1996	Martin Robinson	1960	Chris Swinson	1967	R.J.A. Wilson	1967
Henry Onions	1981	Jonathan Roe	1974	Clive Syddall	1967	Dr J A Winder	1965
David Onley	1953	Daniel Rolfe	1993	John Tait	1964	Edward Windham-Bellord	1965
Roger Orcutt	1945	Brian Rolfes	1989	P.J. Tansley	1968	Dr Ruth Windscheffel	1991
Bernadette O'Reilly (née Dorr)		The Rt Hon. Sir		David Tatham	1957	Peter Winter	1969
	1976	Christopher Rose	1957	Ashley David Tathan	1983	Athena and Anthony Wong	1992
Len Osborn	1954	Hohn-Arne Rottingen	1999	Andrew Taylor	2006	Maj. Gen. David M. Woodford	
Jane Osborne	1996	Peter G. Rowland	1943	Annabella Taylor			1948
Joanna Otterburn	2004	Joshua Rozenberg	1968	David C.L. Taylor	1953	N.D. Worswick	1959
N.A. Otton-Jones	1951	Kevin Ryall	1977	Professor David Taylor	1965	Anthony Wray	1949
Robert Padgett	1962	Andy Ryde	1983	Mrs Sarah Taylor	1976	Emma Lianne Wright	
Julian C. Pallett	1977	David Rymill	1987	Adam John Temple	2000	(née Sturtivant)	2004
Philip Palmer	1999	John Sabapathy	1994	David Thomas	1983	Malcolm C. Wright	1955
Jeffrey Papps	1988	Dr Konstantinos Samaras	1996	Ewan Thompson	2000	Wendy Wu	1979
James Parker	1996	Neil Sanders	1961	P.C. Thompson	1966	Robert M. Yalden	1984
Skylar Paulich	2002	Christopher Saunders OBE	1963	Dr Richard Thwaites	1960	Rex Yan-Kit Liu	1993
Lauren Peacock	2001	Randal Scott	1968	Anna Tobias	2004	Jamie Young	1998
Joanna Pearson	1981	Dr Alexander Sedlmaier		Anya Leonie Todd	2006	Young-Min Kwon FRCS FRACS	
Dr V.A.H. Pearson and family		Nicholas Serck	1953	Robert Tomlinson	1965		2007
	1978	David Shamash	1959	Philip Tranter	1978	Dr Rob Young	1981
Arthur Percival	1952	Chris Shapland	1995	Jonathan Trouncer	1969	Wendy Yung Wen Yee	1981
N.J. Perkins	1977	John Edward Sharp	1953	Professor Brian Trowell		Noga Zivan	1999
Sarah Perman	1987	Nick Sharp	1966	Elina Tsalicoglou	1999		
Peter Phillips (né Peter Pfeffer)		Malcolm Shaw	1971	Henry Tsz-King Wong	1981		
	1953	Michael Shearer	1974	Bradley Tucker	2007		
Richard John Phillips	1983	Clive Sheppey	1952	Paul Turnock	1997		

APPENDIX VI

Acknowledgements

THE CONTRIBUTORS

All the contributors are members of the College. Robin Robbins was Tutor in English 1981–2005, and is now Emeritus Fellow. Allan Chapman is a notable historian of science, and a member of the College since being a graduate student. Cliff Davies was Tutor in History 1963–2001, now Emeritus Fellow and Keeper of the Archives. Jane Garnett has been Tutor in History since 1987, and is currently Sub-Warden. A.F. (Pat) Thompson was Tutor in History 1948–87, then Emeritus Fellow. He died in 2009. Oliver Pointer was a History student as undergraduate and graduate, has been a bookseller and librarian, now teaches; he catalogued and rearranged the historic collection in the Library. David Mabberley was Tutor in Plant Sciences and Keeper of the Gardens, 1976–96, and is now Keeper of the Herbarium at Kew. Matthew Kempshall has been Tutor in History since 2001, and Keeper of the Gardens since 2007. Andrew Little has been Head Gardener since 1984, and Michael O'Day Assistant Gardener since 1963. Patrick Martineau was Junior Research Fellow 1968–72, then Tutor in Mathematics 1972–2002, and Estates Bursar 1988–2004; he is now Emeritus Fellow.

PICTURE ACKNOWLEDGEMENTS

The College is grateful to the following for providing pictures for the book. All other pictures come from the College Archive or Library; photographs of this material were provided by Keith Barnes, Jane Garnett, Gervase Rosser and Bi Scott. Unless separately acknowledged, all the photographs of the College portraits were taken by Thomas Photography, Headington, Oxford. **Chris Andrews**, p.148 (left); **Bodleian Library**, University of Oxford, pp.43, 44 (top left), 45 (bottom three images), 47: *Shrimpton's Oxford Caricatures* – G.A. Oxon. 4° 415, f.668; G.A. Oxon. 4° 412, f.28; G.A. Oxon. 4° 414, ff.581–3; G.A. Oxon. 4° 413, f.248; p.65: *Isis*, Oct. 18, 1933 – Per. G.A. Oxon. 4° 145, no. 878, p.7; p.119 (left): 'The Scene of Matthew Arnold's Leap at Wadham College, Oxford Where he Cleared the Railings Shown', from W.C.P. Ford, 'Some Famous Fancy Leaps', *Strand Magazine*, 51 (1916), 481 – Per. 2705 d.272; **Geoffrey Brooker**, pp.116, 128 (top); **Cornelia Carson**, pp.78, 124, 146 (left), 151 (bottom left); **Dr Hugh Cecil**, p.69; **Peter Derow**, pp.9, 76, 86 (left), 93 (bottom), 132 (top left and bottom); **Richard Einzig** /**arcaid.co.uk**, p.151 (top); **John Freeman**, pp.16 (right and left), 19, 22, 39 (right), 41, 73, 110 (right), 114, 118 (right), 121 (bottom), 123, 125 (right), 126 (top), 127 (left), 129 (left), 133, 134, 138, 139 (right), 141 (all pictures), 142 (right), 145 (top right), 147; **Jane Garnett**, pp.128 (bottom), 129 (right), 132 (top right); **Hulton Deutsch Collection**, p.75, 'Oxford's War Time Guests', *Picture Post*, 23 August, 1941; **Rob Judges**, p.111 (top); **Caroline Mawson**, p.94 (left); **Jill McCleery**, p.93 (top); *Oxford Mail and Times*, p.85; **Oxford University, Museum of the History of Science**, p.34; **Oxfordshire Photographic Archive**, p.121 (top); **Norman Parkinson**, reproduced courtesy of *Vogue* © The Condé Nast Publications Ltd, p.79; **Tom Phillips** 1993, all rights reserved DACS, p.100; **Jake Polonsky**, pp.6, 91, 96 (all pictures); **Reading Museum Service (Reading Borough Council)**, © all rights reserved, p.13 (top); **Patrick Rigby**, p.95 (right); **Gervase Rosser**, p.136; **Bi Scott**, pp.2, 8, 15, 17, 20 (left and right), 23, 35 (top and bottom), 53, 87, 92, 94 (middle and right), 97 (all pictures), 98 (left and right), 99 (left and right), 101 (top and bottom), 102 (left and right), 103, 104, 106 (all pictures), 109 (left and right), 111 (bottom), 125 (left), 126 (bottom), 127 (right), 130, 131, 135 (top and bottom), 140 (left and right), 143, 145 (left and right), 146 (right), 148 (right), 149 (top), 150, 151 (bottom right), 152, 153; **Georgina Thomson**, p.95 (left).

D. Loggan delin. et Sculp. cum Privil. S.R.M.